PRINCESS MERLE

ALSO BY CHARLES HIGHAM

The Films of Orson Welles
Bette: The Life of Bette Davis
Errol Flynn: The Untold Story
Kate: The Life of Katharine Hepburn
Marlene: The Life of Marlene Dietrich
The Art of the American Film

ALSO BY ROY MOSELEY

My Stars and Other Friends

Princess Merle

The Romantic Life of Merle Oberon

CHARLES HIGHAM
ROY MOSELEY

Coward-McCann, Inc.
New York

The authors gratefully acknowledge permission from the following to reprint photographs in this book:

Mrs. Gerald Brockhurst; Mrs. Janet de Cordova; Culver Pictures, Inc.; the Samuel
Goldwyn Company; Mr. J. Lee Morgan; Ms. Patricia Morison; Captain Harry Selby,
I.N. (Retd.); United Press International, Inc.; Wide World Photos, Inc.; Mr. Robert
Wolders; *Women's Wear Daily*, a Fairchild Publication.

The text of this book has been set in Janson.

Library of Congress Cataloging in Publication Data

Higham, Charles, date.
   Princess Merle: the romantic life of Merle Oberon.

   1. Oberon, Merle, 1911–1979   2. Moving-picture actors and actresses—United
States—Biography.
I. Moseley, Roy.   II. Title.
PN2287.018H54   1983   791.43′028′0924 [B]   82–18201
ISBN 0-698-11231-8

Printed in the United States of America

FIRST EDITION

for Thomas Ward Miller
                    —Charles Higham

for my mother and father, with love
                    —Roy Moseley

I the sapidity of waters, O son of Kunti,
I the radiance in moon and sun; the Word
of Power in all the Vedas, sound in ether . . .
The pure fragrance of earth and the brilliance
of fire am I . . .

From the Bhagavad Gita

She was one of the magic presences of the twentieth century. The rich black hair, the high, noble forehead, the smoky, opalescent eyes, now hazel, now seeming to be green, the sensual lips, the exquisite neck and shoulders and the full, generous, voluptuous body all remain fascinating and desirable in photographs and in films. At her best, as in *Wuthering Heights*, the movie for which she is most often remembered, she was an actress of striking gifts. But she was a woman before she was an actress—a woman of rare strength, daring, independence and style, who was also a true romantic, in love with the sea, sunsets, flowers, trees, physical beauty in people, fine painting and sculpture, the lovely transience of all living things. She was mystical also—her friend the designer Luis Estevez has called her a true child of God— who believed in survival after death, who in spirit walked among the stars; who was in love with everything that was transcendent. She could have been a poet; her life was filled with intimations of immortality. Her beauty was not only on the surface: it shone from within.

And yet this mysterious, radiant and joyous figure, exuding womanly wisdom and honesty and kindness, was ironically forced to live her life as a lie, a lie caused by the racism and snobbery of the era in which she was raised. Because no woman of "colored" blood could become a star of the screen in those days, because the idea of suggested miscegenation was repellent to the powerful women's clubs and religious groups that controlled the audience, she had to pretend, on studio instructions, to be white. And because a poverty-stricken origin was considered disgraceful, she had to pose as a woman born to money and position, under the protection of the titled. And, having lived that lie during her screen career, she felt compelled to continue it after she had emerged as the leader of the international social set. She had to deceive her nearest and dearest: her husbands, her adopted children, her intimate friends. There is no question that this deception caused her, with her high standards of honesty and truthfulness, untold private agony.

She rose from depressing circumstances in India to become a guest of Buckingham Palace and a close friend of the entire royal family. Her life was one that most women envied. In only a few years she emerged from the job of hostess in a London nightclub to marry first one of the greatest producers of the day, and later one of the richest men in Latin America. Finally, she discovered happiness with a man a quarter of a century her junior, who really loved her. She had a legendary collection of jewels, and four great houses at the same time, one of which, the fabulous Ghalal in Acapulco, she created as a fairytale retreat. She was a multimillionairess whose clothes were personally designed for her, and she enjoyed the friendship of many heads of state. During World War II, she was a heroine, the first star to tour for the troops under bombardment, and one of the select few actresses earning Winston Churchill's lifelong admiration and gratitude.

Yet she deserves compassion: she had to deny her birthright; she could never in the completest sense be herself.

To determine the truth of her life was no easy task. Biographers of great figures of the screen are always being edged toward a repetition of earlier mythologies; to disclose the truth is often considered undesirable. But truth disclosed with compassion is surely the essence of a decent account of any life.

She always said she was born in Tasmania, the island state south of the Australian mainland where Errol Flynn was born. I met her first in 1965, when she was in Australia on an inaugural flight from Mexico City. She talked to me and to other reporters of having been born in Hobart, Tasmania's capital, by an accident of geography; her parents, she said, happened to have been passing through that area by ship on a long Pacific voyage. The story did not jibe with previous accounts she had given over the years, of being born to a distinguished army man connected to the Tasmanian government who had died in a hunting accident, or from pneumonia, before she was born. I began to wonder what the truth might be, but I did not actively pursue the matter. I did notice that when I asked her about the invitation of the then Lord Mayor of Hobart to appear at a civic reception in that city she became tense and uneasy. In the next hours, as more pressure was put upon her to visit her alleged birthplace, she became increasingly ill and told me on the second day that she was returning to Mexico at once.

I realized that there was some disturbing reason that she had become sick. Even after eighteen hours of a grueling flight in one of the old Boeing 707s she had been fresh, lovely; she had exuded perfect health. What had happened?

I scarcely thought of the matter for the next fifteen years. Then, when I was asked to write the present book, I began thinking again. I determined that there were no birth records for her in the meticulously maintained municipal files of Hobart. Clearly, I would have to go farther afield. But where?

There is no worse problem for a biographer than not knowing where his subject was born. I placed a letter in many Australian newspapers asking for information. I did not disclose my knowledge of the fact that she was not a native of Australia. When I wrote my life of Errol Flynn, I had received a large number of letters. This time I received only a handful. Two of them proved to be of interest. One was from an old tin miner in northwest Tasmania, who said that Merle was the scion of a mining clan named the Chintocks, who were quarter-caste Chinese. Much later, I received a communication from a niece of that family who for a lifetime had sincerely believed that Merle was her long-lost aunt, the illegitimate child of a Chintock girl and a hotel keeper. But investigation by telephone and letter in Tasmania produced a barren result.

The other letter proved to be more significant. A Mrs. Frieda Syer, living on an island off the coast of Queensland, wrote to me saying that if I believed Merle Oberon was born in Australia there was no further point in correspondence. If I did not believe it there would be some point in our being in touch. Intrigued, I called Mrs. Syer on her island. I caught her in the middle of her lunch. She told me she knew for a fact that Merle Oberon had been born in India. I asked her how she knew. She said she had been a neighbor for several years of Merle Oberon's half-sister, in an apartment building in Bombay.

I pressed her for more information. No mention of a half-sister had ever appeared in print. I felt the same sense of discovery that I had when I found out the existence of Errol Flynn's equally unknown associate and friend, Dr. Hermann Erben. Once again I was struck by the capacity of the motion picture publicity machine to suppress facts that the public in a more naive era were not supposed to know.

Mrs. Syer told me that Merle's half-sister, Constance Joyce Selby, had died a year earlier. She gave me the address of the dead woman's son, Captain Harry Selby, a retired naval man who was working for an important Indian company as a representative in the glassware division. He traveled frequently to and from Bagdad.

I wrote to Captain Selby at once. He replied promptly. Months of telephone conversations to and from Bombay went by, which were not only drastically expensive but extraordinarily difficult to conduct. The circuits were busy day and night. Satellite technology appeared not yet to have reached India. When the frustrated caller finally got through, the voice at the other end would often sound like a mouse caught in the storm drain. Sometimes the conversation would be cut off without warning at a crucial moment, and it would take hours to restore the connection. When Captain Selby would call me, a shrill female voice would interrupt every few minutes with piercing instructions to "speak up! speak up!" and there would follow a reminder, delivered with a schoolteacher's peremptoriness, that time was moving along, a fact of which neither Captain Selby nor I needed to be reminded.

It finally became obvious that Harry Selby must quickly be brought to Los Angeles. The question of documentation on Merle's birth arose. If I were to confront her loving family with the truth, I had to have concrete evidence.

Captain Selby did not have any documentation. Nor did he have a clear picture of how it might be obtained. I called the Indian Embassy in Washington; I determined that birth records and baptismal certificates could be found in churches in India. There were dozens of churches in Bombay, however, and the Selby family had no idea in which district Merle was born. With great enterprise, Harry Selby went from church to church until at last he located the records in almost the final one on his list: a tiny, obscure place of worship on the border of two suburbs: Khetwadi and Girgaum. It was a moving experience for him to see the font in which his aunt had been baptized.

He flew to Los Angeles in June 1982. He proved to be a charming man, a delightful companion and a fountain of information on every aspect of Merle's early life. Through his eyes it was possible for me clearly to see the pattern of Merle's early development and the tragedy of the crippled half-sister whom she perhaps never knew was her own flesh and blood.

I grew to understand the Indian background of those long-ago years of the Raj, when Anglo-Indians were caught in the middle between Indian nationalism and British imperialism, when blood was everything and shame overcame those who were not of pure racial origin. Anglo-Indians are an amusing, delightful, inventive, energetic, religious and forward-looking group, but they never really belonged anywhere; despite their clinging to British ways they could never escape the misery of being looked down upon, not only by the

British, whose ways they so carefully emulated, but by the Indians whose blood ran in their veins and whose rich heritage they could not in their deepest hearts accept.

The anguish of the Anglo-Indian was heightened in Merle, not only because of her extreme sensitivity, concealed behind a mask of composure and elegance, but because of her need to have a career. Her early compulsion toward success, money and fame later evolved into a Hinduist rejection of the importance of material possessions, tempered by her powerful Anglo-Indian's need to be accepted at the top of white society.

Hence the many lies that grew up about her: the lies that she was a streetwalker in Calcutta and London; or, most colorful of all, that she was sold into the brothel cages of Bombay as a child. Hence the many jealous comments that had her using Sir Alexander Korda or the millionaire Bruno Pagliai for her ambitious purposes. She was not a saint—her extraordinary line of romantic affairs testifies to that—and in her younger days she could be willful and explosive and temperamental. Some people found her cold and haughty, not understanding that she was a woman with a secret. But it was against her romantic nature to include money in her motives for loving a man; she was drawn sometimes to great intellect and power, as with Korda and Pagliai, sometimes to physical beauty, as with the young and delicate Leslie Howard or the more robustly handsome David Niven, Robert Ryan, Rod Taylor, and Robert Wolders, but never to money as such. She was a bold woman, liberated before her time, who wanted men to be neither subservient nor dominated, but to be her equal, her partner and friend as well as her physical lovers. For all her worldliness, she was innocent, and she disliked any perverse or obscure variations of sex; she was passionate and intense in her love relationships, but she knew nothing of kinkiness.

It would be a mistake to regard her life as a succession of romances. Much of it was spent not only working in films, to which she lent her unique presence, but in creating things of beauty. Perhaps her masterpieces were her houses: the homes in Los Angeles that she redesigned with extraordinary elegance, originality and taste in a city that, to say the least, is not noted for its good taste, and the homes in Mexico that she altered to remove the vulgarity that often erupts in the houses of the Latin American rich. Most particularly, she created the shimmering white palace in Acapulco that still stands, though it has been severely changed by its present owners. In the arches, cool recesses and intricately wrought structures of that exquisite retreat, Merle Oberon at last found the physical mirror of her spirit.

Those who loved Merle remember her above all for her childlike purity and laughter, laughter that covered up sorrow, but happy laughter just the same. In her final illness, in the bravery with which she and her husband, Robert Wolders, bore the decimation of her beautiful body, she achieved greatness.

Charles Higham, Los Angeles

In the apartment in Bombay, overlooking the sweep of the harbor, in the monotonous drumming of the monsoons and the long steamy dry seasons, the old woman never seemed to be content. Her family struggled to give her the best of comfort, but she would fret and rave and fret again, brooding over the contents of her rolltop desk, a desk that was always locked against intruders, and that none of her children or grandchildren could ever penetrate. One day, a letter came, and she managed to tear it open with her one good hand; it was a letter from America, the expensively delicate blue-gray envelope addressed in a distinctive, aristocratic, bold style with a touch of the ancient Indian script in the formation of certain letters. She locked her door and read the letter and when she had finished it she began to cry. She tore the letter to shreds, keeping only the top fragment with the sender's name, large, bold, and in imposing print, as a last link to the past. Finally, the woman, already paralyzed in her left arm and leg, was possessed by a strange malady. She began to bleed in her armpits; she felt she was going to die.

At last she rallied, just sufficiently to pour out, in a period of less than a week, a series of poems, filled with anguish, with reaching out to the famous actress and social beauty who had sent that letter. They were the poems of a sister, calling to her own kin; to that half-sister, she had been merely a nuisance, the unwanted offspring of a mother who had died forty-three years before; a tiresome, irritating, querulous creature who had written again and again over the years, in savage demanding letters that screamed for money, that gave a picture of poverty and starvation and misery in page after page after page, written in a scrawling, mission-school script. Now the old woman wanted, with every bone of her eighty-year-old being, to tell the truth, that her own mother had cast her out, to hide the shame of birth at the age of fourteen years and nine months. In the Indian community, such a birth would have meant nothing, and in the Christian community before 1929 it was at the least technically legal; but in the strictly religious, fastidious community of Anglo-Indians it was unheard of, outside the scheme of things. And having lied from the beginning to cover up this ancient scandal, the woman could no longer turn around and unravel the skein of lies that had grown more complex with the years.

Not long afterward, the old woman, very feeble now, began to destroy the mementos of a lifetime: letters, diaries, photographs, almost everything that could remind her of the past. Nobody must find anything after she was gone. She must eliminate eighty years as completely as dry leaves burned on an autumn evening. Most of her precious, private things were in the rolltop part of the desk, but some few stragglers remained in drawers that were heavy, made in the days when craftsmen were craftsmen: too heavy for her weak hands to pull out. In the burdensome drawers were letters from London, from that same half-sister, and from her mother; letters from her mother's nurse-companion;

financial receipts, or transaction notes showing pathetic amounts paid by film companies or business managers over almost half a century, and a tiny brown notebook that contained family records of births, a list of all the jewelry she had once owned that had been plucked from her fingers, neck, and ears by her ferocious sisters-in-law; and at the very bottom of the largest of the drawers, the most precious possession of all: two minute earrings, scarcely larger than a child's fingernail, made of the cheapest metal, wrapped in a shred of lined notebook paper, on which the woman had written long ago, in her feeble hand, Merle's earrings at the age of three.

If she were to call her family and have them open the drawer, the truth she had fought so hard to hide would be disclosed. At last, she gave up the unequal struggle and her spirit died in her. Her heart burned out as she sank back into her chair. Now all that was left for her was to wait for the end.

Chapter One

Travel back over eighty years, across the Indian Ocean, through waves shining like fire opals in the moon, and dolphin, flying fish, and water snakes gamboling under the sun, to the port of Colombo on the island of Ceylon, on September 11, 1897. The atmosphere is heavy with the scent of cinnamon, musk, oil, and tar; the water of the harbor is flat, amber, rippling like polished silk. Enormous clouds like spun sugar drift against a sapphire sky. Flying foxes gossip in the rain trees that hold their moisture through the profound tropical night; green-winged butterflies, almost as large as hummingbirds, flutter in thousands over the mauve-and-scarlet bougainvillea. Against the wide streets of the Fort, or European quarter, with its fine parade of ladies and gentlemen at four in the afternoon, can be set Black Town, the native quarter, with its straggling maze of mud, bamboo and palm-leaf huts, its streets alive with women cooking fish over braziers, gamblers squatting and chittering in the gutters, pariah dogs prowling in nervous packs, and pet parrots squawking from cages in the windows. And everywhere the breadfruit, banana, and mango trees rustled by the southwest wind.

At evening, a sudden gust of rain comes, ahead of the imminent monsoon, thudding on the bullock carts and their irritable drivers, on the tin roofs, with a loud persistent hammering and sighing; on the copper statues that bleed green. As darkness sets in, gas jets and penny candles flicker in glass globes, barely making themselves felt, and now the rain is heavier, blotting out the moon.

In a ward of the women's hospital, the heat barely relieved by Tamil servants exhaustedly waving palm-leaf fans, a Eurasian girl of fourteen years and nine months is writhing in the agony of labor. Her name is Charlotte Constance Selby. She is small, lovely and dark,

17

with black hair parted in the middle, liquid brown eyes, and exquisite firm, high breasts, inheritances from a part-Maori background.

She had been living with a tea planter's Irish foreman out of wedlock, a common Eurasian practice in those days. Now her pregnancy has ruined all chance of her future well-being. Her lover, Henry Alfred Selby, has been forced to marry her in a magistrate's office and to seek an immediate dissolution. Marriage to a girl of that age had to be kept secret, and on no account could be solemnized in a church.

Charlotte hates the child in her, blames her for wrecking everything she had planned for, and the delivery is agonizing, her mind fighting her body. Even when the baby is born, prettier than her mother, with curly dark hair and huge liquid eyes, a lighter skin, and the hint of a sensuous mouth, Charlotte looks at her with as much disdain as she might accord a spider.

Much as she hated the baby, Charlotte had to have her baptized: any other prospect to a God-fearing Christian girl was unthinkable as well as unlawful. She found an obscure church that no one would think of investigating, and named the baby Constance Joyce. Then she scraped together her meager savings, pressed her husband's family for more, and set sail as soon as she could, encouraged by the Selbys.

She had had some experience as a nurse's assistant. She was uncertified, like most Eurasian girls of the time, but highly valued because of her rigid discipline and firmness with young children. There was much recruiting of nurses in Bombay, which had been stricken with plague just one year before. Excessive rainfall and insufferable heat, along with a high level of sewage, greatly increased humidity and masses of wet grain stored in dark granaries had bred armies of rats in Bombay, whose fleas carried the contagion through the city and into the hinterland. When Charlotte arrived with her daughter, in October 1897, Bombay was in the grip of terror. A strange yellowish haze and the stench of thousands of dead bodies hung over the legendary port. Charlotte disembarked in a city that was almost deserted. Scores of thousands had fled to the hills, and many of those left behind were cloistered behind locked doors, their houses marked with bloody crimson crosses and circles indicating that death lurked in there. There were riots in the streets as the healthy population tried to drive the stragglers out of town. Sanitary workers had fled their jobs and left the gutters running with excrement to scavengers who eked out their lives selling garbage rights to custodians of the plague regions. At the time Charlotte and her baby Constance arrived, 2,250 people were dying each week.

A nurse's work was emotionally devastating and exhausting. The hospitals were crammed to overflowing, with the dead and dying heaped in the corridors and spilling out into the street itself. There was no way to relieve the heat or stem the tide of anguish. Even Charlotte, so indifferent to her baby, had sufficient maternal feeling not to want Constance to grow up in such a place. She had to get her into a mission school out of town, where she would be relatively safe from disease—and could also be conveniently forgotten. She settled upon the military garrison of Poona, high in the hills 110 miles southeast of the city, protected from the worst of the plague by the strength of the British Army's sanitary precautions, a place much prized as a refuge and long since used as the summer capital of the presidency. On the journey to Poona, which mother and daughter undertook early in 1902, inspectors stopped the train, seemingly every few minutes, to examine its human cargo, looking for symptoms of disease and insisting upon seeing certificates of health. Evil-looking winged cockroaches flew through the windows, but Charlotte followed the Sinhalese rule of never killing an insect, and she did not attempt to destroy these unpleasant intruders. When the train stopped at a station, its carriages abrim with dust and cinders from the engine, tea and coffee sellers poked their heads through the windows, offering refreshment. The wooden seats burned like hot coals on the back; the air had the intensity found in a fever swamp. Only in the first-class section could ice be found, wrapped in silk cloths and pressed to the foreheads of wilting British passengers, but Charlotte and her daughter were traveling third class. Outside, the views began to compensate for the torment of the journey. The drooping palms and heat-drenched shrubs and palm groves and jungle and mangrove swamps and glimpses of ocean began to fall away in favor of red earth, hillocks, rich green grass, oxen grazing, bubbling streams, and a touch of breeze for which the miserable travelers gave blissful thanks.

Poona was a corkscrew journey upland, and the ride took ten hours, due to the torpid laziness of the engineers and the constant stops for inspections. Poona was a pompous and self-important town. Centuries before, it had been the capital of the Mahrattas, who had broken the power of the Moguls. Far cooler than Bombay, the garrison bristled with barracks and military hospitals; there were wooden bungalows with jalousies and shady verandas where the middle class lived, the military officers and their wives and children, superficially proper and correct, attending church every Sunday; these dwellings were hives of gossip and promiscuity and surreptitious adulterous affairs conducted to alleviate frustration and boredom.

Everywhere were graveyards to remind the inhabitants of the

constant danger of the northwest frontier, with touchingly brief lives recorded in simple dates on the headstones. Those who were saddened by the memory of so many vigorous young Englishmen struck down in the flower of their youth could obtain consolation by riding out into the foothills of the glorious mountain range known as the Western Ghats, where ancient forts could be seen, and picnics could be enjoyed in lush green forests filled with mysterious and exotic plants and flowers that bloomed red and yellow and mauve. There was the inviting hill station of Mahabaleshwar, with its cool trees and dappled shade. Everywhere in Mahabaleshwar there were flowers: roses and dahlias and chrysanthemums and marigolds; and there were parks alive with shrubs and trees. Life in Poona had a military rhythm and monotony; the sound of the bugle and the loud command of moustachioed, red-faced sergeants often clashed with the soft whir of pigeons and the ever-busy cawing crows.

Charlotte obtained a position in the Sassoon Hospital, the only hospital in Poona that took in nonresident nurses, where every sign of plague was watched for and eliminated. The job was poorly paid, but at least she could now afford a bungalow and meet army men and at night she could forget the drudgery of long hours on her feet with bedpans and swabs and offer her voluptuous body to the lean brown Englishmen who desired her. The chief problem was Constance. It would alienate men if they found that she had a little girl of five when she herself was so young, barely nineteen; and something had to be done about the unhappy, angry child she had mothered, and who hated her, knowing she was not wanted. Charlotte took Constance to the American Methodist school known as Bishop Taylor. It was run strictly and grimly by mission teachers for the offspring of mothers with little or no money. Charlotte killed two birds with one stone: she was rid of Constance, and she had assured her a decent education without the necessity to foot large bills.

But she still had to do something about Constance during the school holidays. She had nursed a distinguished family of Parsis, the Kabrajis, one of whose members, K. N. Kabraji, was editor of a Bombay newspaper. The Kabrajis offered to take care of Constance. They brought the child into their home as one of their own, a most uncommon practice for such a strict sect. Constance moved from the endless Bible lessons of the Bishop Taylor to a handsome home where ancient rituals were practiced. Prayers were uttered five times a day, liquor was offered to the sacred fire that burned constantly in a large brazier, and elaborate celebrations of birth or death took place. When a family member died, the body was washed with the urine of a young bull, circled by white paint or chalk in the presence of a dog that would drive out evil, and at last carried to the Towers of Silence overlooking the harbor of Bombay to be picked clean by the vultures.

It was a strange upbringing for a child. Although Constance loved the Kabrajis, who were well educated and intelligent, she hated the mission school and resented her mother's abandonment of her. Meanwhile, Charlotte was enjoying the company of many more military officers. No doubt, she hoped to snare one in marriage and make her way to England, but she was very dark, and there was no way she could pass for white. She suffered from the curse of the Eurasian: she did not belong to the pure-blooded British and she was out of place with the Indians. She often spoke of her two brothers in Ceylon, who were white-skinned and fair—a not uncommon phenomenon in families of mixed blood—whom she envied. But no one ever really knew if those brothers existed.

One of her lovers was a mechanical engineer on the railways, without the scarlet uniform that distinguished most of Charlotte's companions of the night. His name was Arthur Terrence O'Brien Thompson. He came from Darlington in the county of Durham, a city of smokestacks and black skies and mean streets and clanging trams and pinched, gray, semidetached houses in row after row. At home, he would have been running a machine shop or working in a minor managerial job in a factory, living in a depressing small flat; but out here in the hill country of India he could afford a pretty bungalow and he could have his pick of Eurasian girls. He was a belligerent, aggressive young man with the strong lusts of youth, who was much fascinated by Constance on her rare visits to the house. She was prettier than her mother, and at fourteen she was already a young beauty. Constance hated Thompson with a savage bitterness, almost as much as she hated her mother; he was always seizing odd moments when Charlotte was out of the room to put her on his knee and fondle her in places that made her blush with embarrassment.

Even when Charlotte married Arthur, probably under pressure because she was pregnant, he kept up his unwelcome attentions to Constance. This created great strain on the family relationship and encouraged Charlotte to leave Constance in Poona when Charlotte moved with Arthur to Bombay in October 1910. Arthur was transferred to a job in the railway depot of Bombay, the huge, rambling, exotically Gothic structure called Victoria Station. The plague in Bombay was over, carried by travelers into the heart of India, and the city was crowded once more: enormous, complex, and labyrinthine. The Thompsons had very little money, and once again Charlotte turned to her Parsi friends for help. The district known as Khetwadi was dominated by Parsis. Charlotte had friends there and knew people who had worked for the Kabrajis in Poona. Khetwadi was a sleazy district of dancing girls, petty criminals, opium dens, and shabby, low-caste people living on the edge of poverty. Khetwadi was only a step from the horrifying red light district of Kamathipura, where young girls, dredged up from the sewers of the Indian Ocean, were sold in brothels with locked bamboo doors, known as the cages. At night, Khetwadi was a rabbit warren of ill-lit streets, where nobody asked questions; even the police hesitated to go there after the huge orange sun of Bombay sank in the sea.

Arthur and Charlotte arrived at Victoria Station in Bombay in the first week of October 1910. The monsoon had just ended, and the train was crowded with the returning people of Poona; the stench and steam and noise of the depot were overpowering. The couple had to fight their way through crowds before emerging into sticky sunlight to hail one of many horse-drawn victorias with drivers half sleeping on their perches. For a mere two annas, or less than a penny, they were able to ride to their destination, a three-quarter-hour journey at the time. They saw a picturesque spectacle as they ground along on creaking wooden wheels. The buildings were mostly built in three or four stories, with washing hung over the balconies and people swarming as many as three families to one room. Nobody seemed to have heard of paint or lye wash, and the feeble stucco on the jerry-built structures cracked and fell in the sun. Thousands of birds flapped about: kites, hovering silently over the slow-moving bullock carts, their feverish eyes looking for food; crows, flitting from overhead wire to wire or clustering thick as black leaves on the rooftops; vultures, their serrated wings like tattered flags, swooping with unerring aim on the Parsi dead heaped up in the Towers of Silence above the Bay.

The streets that Arthur and Charlotte saw were a blaze of variety and color: the Parsis with their black umbrellas and their wreaths of tuberoses and oleanders to give to their friends; the spidery coolies; the Muslims, always on the verge of attacking the hated Hindus. There were Arabs, Burmese, Sinhalese, Lascars, Hindus, Jews, Chinese, Japanese, and Turks. An unrivaled variety of turbans made the streets a dazzling display. The garish Indian dyes were subdued by time, sunshine, and rain, so that harsh reds, yellows, and greens were rendered soft, pastel, and pale.

People squatted on the pavements, chins propped on their knees as they jabbered at the passersby. Many carried animal skins, fat with water, on their backs; others unwound their loincloths and, naked, washed the thin cotton in the gutters. Conjurers were everywhere, accompanied by bag, basket, and small boy. Crowds of people sat in half-moons around the performers. The conjurers offered a mongoose, a goat, two small snakes, and a cobra. They packed a man in a basket, stabbing the basket with a sword, and then produced the man unharmed. They palmed coins, plucking them from noses or ears of the onlookers; they made a goat stand on an iron bar only two inches wide. They made cobras rise in their baskets and weave their heads around and even kissed them without injury. Nearby, snake charmers used bent pipes, swollen at one end into a bulb, and waved the pipe with its eerie, thin music in circles over the snake. The cobras then raised a third of their length above the muscular coil of the body, distended their thin broad cheeks, and waved to and fro, watching with their flat sinister stare and striking with terrifying swiftness.

The variety and color of the environment were overpowering. So crowded were the streets that the *jehu*, the victoria driver, had to scream and shout to clear a path through the swarming mass of humanity. At last husband and wife reached Khetwadi, where they fought the inevitable fight with the *jehu*, who overcharged outrageously just for clearing the way there. There was a buyers' market in flats in those days; building after building with their sagging balconies and cracked, peeling facades carried notices in English, Arabic, and Hindi announcing rooms for let.

The Thompsons found the Parsi building they were looking for at 344 Khetwadi Grant Road. It had a traditional living room with bedrooms opening off it, and a small kitchen. The flat was unfurnished, and Charlotte went out and bought cheap plywood furniture with varnish and a kitchen table with tacked-down linoleum on it, and rattan matting for the floor. She contacted a laundryman and a cheap *ayah*, or nurse.

Charlotte had to work until very late in pregnancy, at various hospitals that were engaging private nurses to supplement their overworked staffs. She would make her way on the tram through streets twisting like earthworms, past open-fronted shops with brasses, cottons, silks, embroideries, and jewelry; gutters used as public latrines, haunted by children, dogs, cows, bulls, and sheep; and people shouting out wares of fried fish, rice cakes, curry, and sticky sweetmeats. Meanwhile, the unhappy, irritable Constance had to stay in Poona, utterly abandoned.

Charlotte had many contacts in the hospitals because of her work. She had special connections through nurse friends at St. George's Hospital, the newest and most highly regarded medical institution in Bombay. She selected St. George's as the place where she would give birth; it had the advantage of being next door to Victoria Station, where Arthur worked on the railways; and it would be easy for him to come for an hour or so on his lunch break. Yet another consideration was that it was a government hospital and government employees on the railways were given free care.

Like all of the other hospitals in Bombay, St. George's was seriously overcrowded. Conditions there were so difficult that the nursing sisters who had previously run the hospital had abandoned their impossible task eight years earlier and surrendered the running of the wards to a motley collection of untrained and unregistered nurses, many of them drawn from the lowest levels of society. So clumsy was Charlotte's delivery on February 19 that the little girl who was born developed a heart defect that left her with a murmur for the rest of her life. Her name was Estelle Merle O'Brien Thompson.

The first sound she heard was the clanging and shunting of the freight cars next door where her father worked, and the blasting of the dock construction of the new Ballard pier that suggested travel to better climes. Ballard was to be a name significant in her life many years later. The patients complained day and night of the noise; and the talk surrounding the baby was that the hospital might very well have to be moved.

Estelle Merle's birth registration was signed by the Assistant Surgeon, E. H. J. Hendricks, who delivered her; apparently Charlotte herself witnessed his signature. When Charlotte was released from the hospital, she and Arthur took the baby back to the noisome quarter of Khetwadi, a most unsuitable place for a young child to grow up in, but the best they could afford. They carried little Merle on foot to the tiny, dark, obscure Protestant church of St. Emmanuel's, located in a lane flanked by shade trees on the border of Khetwadi and the neighboring suburb of Girgaum. There, the minister, the Reverend Thomas W. Sharpley, performed the ceremony of baptism on March 16. The birth certificate does not contain the names of any godparents.

Despite her miserable circumstances and the constant din at night of hawkers and girls banging their tambourines and inviting men to join them in their rooms, Charlotte managed to create an attractive and scrupulously clean environment for her child to live in. She hung framed photographs of Indian scenes, scrubbed the wooden floor to a polish, and constantly dusted the plywood furniture and the rolltop desk that was an inevitable feature of Anglo-Indian homes. The Anglo-Indian community was Christian, correct, and upright, loosening up only at Saturday night socials. Most Anglo-Indians were amusing, skittish, flirtatious, and full of fun, and loved music and dancing. They aped British airs and if they were fair enough tried to pass for English. They were very conscious of the King and Queen and talked of the United Kingdom as "home." All dreamed of saving enough money to pay their fares to Britain on the slow-moving and suffocating Peninsula and Orient Line steamers.

Most Anglo-Indians worked in the railways, as nurses, or as office clerks or telephonists. They were despised by all Indians except Parsis and condescended to by the British, who regarded beautiful Eurasian girls as fair game. The girls were famous teasers, looking for marriage before sex; but few Britishers were prepared to marry them, since marriage to a "chee-chee" was considered a mistake in British middle-class society. Relationships between Eurasian girls and young British officers or clerks in the big merchant companies tended to be on the level of light, meaningless flirtations in those innocent days.

Merle was known as a most sweetly dispositioned child, who benefited from her mother's devoted and loving care. Whereas Constance, rejected, lonely, and miserable in her Dickensian school in Poona, had never known love from Charlotte and was thus filled with bitter hatred and sorrow for the rest of her life, Merle seldom cried, and neighborhood women were captivated by her sweet little face, heart-stoppingly beautiful even at the age of three, her fair hair (which darkened later), unusually high forehead, intense hazel eyes, and surprisingly light complexion.

In 1911 King George V and Queen Mary went to India to attend the Durbar in New Delhi, and all Bombay was *en fête* for this last sunset burst of empire. Many children were called Queenie in honor of the female monarch. Merle was given Queenie as a nickname, and it stuck to her for several years; another reason for the name was that Merle greatly amused the people in her building with her imperious airs and habit of dressing up in fancy clothes and twirling around admiring herself in mirrors. She was adorable; she had an infectious giggle no one could resist, a daintiness and elegance that resembled an expensive doll. She had a collection of dolls, including a pair of Chinese dolls that were twins, and she acted out little scenes with them, as though directing a play.

In 1914, when war broke out between Germany and England, young men of military age, especially those who had mechanical skills, volunteered to serve at the western front. Arthur Thompson, strong and virile and eager to serve his country, wasted no time in answering the call to arms. He sailed for England and France in 1914, and went as a "sapper," or noncommissioned engineer, to the front. In the Battle of the Somme, drenching rains, infestations of rats, and rotting corpses caused disease to sweep through the trenches. Thompson, who no doubt had visions of dying a hero's death from a bullet, was swept away by pneumonia. The news was shattering to Charlotte and she did not have the courage to tell little Merle the truth. Instead, she said that Father was a ship's engineer who was permanently away at sea; later, she changed the story to his being an army major who had died of pneumonia on a hunting trip before Merle was born. Merle always said in later years that liars needed to have perfect memories; Charlotte had a very poor memory and kept changing her story of Merle's parentage to the confusion of everyone.

After Arthur's death, Charlotte worked desperately hard to improve her circumstances. In 1915, she moved to the more respectable neighborhood of Ripon Road, again on the edge of the poverty line but inhabited by a better class of people. She found a flat in a nondescript apartment building. It had been pretentiously named Imperial Mansion on the occasion of the royal visit. The flat was on the ground floor and looked directly out into the busy street. It was noisy, with open trams clanging by and the constant din of hawkers and passersby; it was stifling when the windows were shut against the noise, and the chics, or bamboo blinds, were let fall. But little Merle seemed to sleep through everything; her calm and strength amazed her grandmother and everyone who visited her.

Charlotte found work easily. She graduated from hospital nurse to the better paid job of lady nurse in families. Many of these were military families, and she was very popular because of her strictness and sternness; she not only worked as a nanny to children but took care of the elderly, the sick, and the dying.

Imperial Mansion was an Anglo-Indian building. Charlotte's affinity for Parsis had not decreased. Three floors up lived a doctor's family who meant as much to Charlotte as the Kabrajis had. The daughter, now eighty-two, then a pretty fourteen-year-old girl, still remembers to this day looking after Merle when Charlotte was working.

As time went on, as the fourteen-year-old neighbor's girl curled Merle's hair and made sure she was given lively birthday parties, Merle's character began to emerge. Sometimes the child echoed the real mother's temper fits: when Charlotte promised her a balloon and gave her a doll instead, she tore the doll to pieces.

But her most dominant characteristics were a dreamy, self-enclosed romanticism, a fondness for fairy tales, a loving attention to animals, other children, and dolls, a fascination with anything beautiful, a strong-willed independence of spirit, a refusal to kill insects or harm anything living, a love of life, and an overpowering desire for her own private, enclosed world within the larger world. Even as a little girl, she radiated an amazing, yet innocent, sexuality. Everyone knew she would be a beauty one day; but everyone also felt, wrongly, that her self-effacement, her modesty, her detachment would prevent her from emerging as anything.

While Charlotte raised Merle with tender loving care, the rejected, bitter Constance succeeded in obtaining a good education at the Taylor School in Poona, and, by 1916, when Merle was five and she was eighteen, Constance went to Bombay and obtained a job as a secretary in Thacker's Bookstore. Whatever secretarial skills she lacked were made up for by her charm toward male customers and staff alike. She began looking for a husband who could ease her loneliness and suffering. However, she lacked a pleasant disposition, and when men grew tired of her rages and fits of tears, they would reject her coldly. She was at once too available and too difficult; she was her own worst enemy.

One day in 1917, Constance was riding on the tram to work at Thacker's when she ran into a pretty Goanese woman, Antoinette Soares. Antoinette told her that she lived in a handsome house not far away in the fashionable Mazagon district. Antoinette said she had a brother, Alick, short for Alexander, a well-to-do importer of toys, chocolates, and automobiles, who was thirty-four years old and recently bereaved by the death of his wife from consumption. Antoinette felt that Constance would be perfect for Alick and she invited her home to tea that weekend.

Constance was excited. Admittedly, her chief goal was to marry an Englishman and go to England, but at least Alick had money and social position. She was very impressed when she arrived at the house, a large building with stables at the bottom and a grand staircase going up to bedrooms and an elegant dining room, a huge kitchen, and separate servants' quarters. Alick was slim, correct, precise, with a clean-cut, bony face, a pencil moustache, and pince-nez balanced on his well-chiseled nose. He was faultlessly tailored, haughty, chilly, aloof, and had perfect manners. He had a household of five servants, as well as a butler, chef, coachman, and *ayahs*. The great rooms of the house, airy and cool and swept by newfangled electric ceiling fans, were separated by a spacious yard and a gate from the hubbub and heat of Bombay.

It took little time for the attractive Constance to get Alick into bed and not much more to bring him to the altar. But from the first, she ran up against his six overpowering sisters, who disapproved of her violently and knew she came of a degraded pedigree. They accused her of fortune-hunting (that had a hint of truth in it) and made her life a misery. But the effect of their hatred stimulated Alick still further. He *would* marry Constance, come hell or high water.

There was no question of Constance's inviting either Charlotte or Merle to her wedding; she still hated one and envied the other. Luckily, by 1917 mother and daughter were already on their way to Calcutta where there was better work with European families.

The elaborate nuptials took place in November 1917. Determined to remove any possible link to her mother, Constance changed her mother's name to Charlotte Elizabeth when entering it on the marriage certificate.

Charlotte and Merle found Calcutta more modern and pretentious than Bombay. Admittedly, it had a climate as steamy and suffocating, and the Hugli River, a tributary of the Ganges, was darker than the Thames at London Bridge and filled with rubbish. But Dalhousie Square, with its statues of English kings and political leaders, could take their minds off the vultures that hovered over the riverbanks and the scores of thousands who lived under canvas or cardboard in the open streets.

Calcutta was a bloody and violent city, with constant clashes between Muslim and Hindu that made the gutters run with blood. It offered a pretentious top dressing of quasi-American movie theaters that glittered seedily at night with huge posters of the stars, and European legitimate theaters and flashy restaurants. Calcutta offered an allure: an insistent suggestion of what could be obtained by a smart, flirtatious, young, pretty Eurasian girl on her way up.

One school for girls that was considered a prize was La Martinière, a grim, stern institution behind gray stone walls. Yet it offered a good education, including French, Hindustani, and history, mathematics, needlework, and science. The children who went there were usually of well-to-do families, but La Martinière did accept the occasional "foundation" pupil, who would be admitted free of charge if the father had died in action in the war. Charlotte went to the school and pleaded her case for Merle; Miss Daisy Coutts, the stern British headmistress, looked at the almost black and very humble woman in front of her and hesitated. But Charlotte succeeded in melting her heart, and when pretty little Merle asked for help, only granite could have resisted.

Because of the prestige, entering La Martinière excited most children, despite the fact that it offered a cheerless environment. But

Merle was unhappy from the beginning. Foundation children suffered from being "different" and Merle was ashamed of her dark mother, who used to come, dressed all in black, and fuss over her hair and face in front of the other people, to her acute discomfort. Vicious girls in the school spread rumors that Merle was illegitimate and had been abandoned. When, many years later, Merle appeared in the film *These Three*, about a monstrous lying schoolgirl, the experience awakened memories of La Martinière.

A fellow pupil of Merle's recalls:

The impression I have carried with me all these years is that Queenie Thompson was a lost soul. All you knew about her was that she was *there*. No one took any interest in her, nor was she interested in anyone. She was silent and resentful; anxious to keep her family life much to herself.

Her mother, whom I remember very well and felt sorry for, used to come to see her on Saturdays: visiting days. As the parents arrived, a slate was carried by a bearer to the mistress on duty with the name of the girl the father or mother wanted to see. The mistress would tinkle a bell to get the attention of the girls and then call out the girl's name. When she called "Queenie Thompson" we would see her mother in the distance. What a pathetic figure she was! Shabbily dressed in black, a black hat half way down her forehead, shading her eyes, she was unsure, timid, unwanted. She had a sort of smile—but so unsure!

For a couple of years we slept in the same dormitory. Queenie came and went and nobody took notice. She would never join in the fun and frolic of boarding school life. She would sit silent and alone, dreaming. She endured the discipline along with the rest of us. It was almost military. Five meals a day, exactly on the dot. A shower at 6 A.M., cheese, biscuits and tea with milk at 7; cereal, fruit, bread and butter for breakfast at 9 A.M. 12 noon lunch, consisting of thick soup and bread and butter; meat, vegetables and pudding at 3 P.M.; soup and fried potatoes at 7 P.M., lights out at 8. We had to sit straight, elbows off the table, grace before and after meals. The food was totally inedible but we had to eat every bite before we left the table. Not even pepper was allowed. Our uniforms were white sacks. Not even dresses. Prayers were every morning and every night, taken by the Lady Principal, Miss Daisy Coutts. Every Sunday we went to St. Paul's Cathedral and every Sunday afternoon we had to memorize the Collect of the day and recite it to the Mistress on duty before we could have the afternoon to ourselves. Through all this Queenie was silent, angry, and lonely. It was the biggest surprise years later when I found out she was world-famous.

In time, the powers of invention of Alexander Korda's publicity man, John Myers, would present a totally different picture. Merle was obliged to repeat a fantasy in fan magazine reviews for much of her life, even to her children: that she was the most mischievous girl in school, the ringleader in every prank, that she teased her Dutch schoolteacher over a parrotlike, or "Pollypocker," nose. She was supposed to have been caught passing a note about the nose, and the whole school had to stay in until she confessed. In fact, there was no Dutch teacher in the school, and Merle, though inattentive in class and reprimanded for dreaming, was incapable of mischief.

Depressed by her orphan status, her "Singhalese" mother, her terrible loneliness, and her sense of inferiority as a foundationer, Merle was clearly not going to be able to pass her Junior Cambridge examination, which was obligatory for all students. It was a custom in those days not to enter foundation students for the Junior Cambridge if they were not brilliant, since failure would bring disgrace to the school. Merle was let out at the age of eleven—probably with some relief. She remained at home, taking lessons from her mother and from various friends. She started to prepare for business school to become a clerk, and was allowed to enter business school at the age of fifteen, then worked as a typist in a department store.

She appeared in junior plays of the Calcutta Amateur Dramatic Society. In photographs of her at the time she is dressed as a moth, or as a sailor performing a hornpipe. Released from the drudgery of La Martinière, she was starting to find herself. Photographs show her having a high time posing on a friend's horse or in a friend's car, or fooling around with two girlfriends on a small rivercraft on the Hugli or posing exotically as a vamp on a chaise longue. With Anglo-Indian chutzpah, she found her way through to the daughters of well-to-do people; pictures in her albums show her, already attractive, sexy, and full of fun, enjoying herself away from her gloomy apartment and her embarrassing though loving mother.

Meanwhile, Constance, star-crossed as always, was running into trouble in Bombay. Alick's many sisters, all of them imposing and imperious and haughty, hated her. They spoke Portuguese with each other and to Alick in order to infuriate her and make her feel out of things. They accused her of using Alick in order to reach her position and they undoubtedly suspected her background.

Constance was extravagant, or at least so the many sisters alleged. She liked fine jewelry and loved to gamble at the Bombay races, and all of her clothes were of the finest quality; these expenses began draining her husband's budget. Moreover, he, who had inherited his fortune from a family that went back to the flourishing of Mazagon in the nineteenth century, had little business acumen and was so besotted by his wife that he seemed scarcely to know what he was doing. The ill luck that dogged Constance seemed to fall like a shadow on her husband. In the late 1920s, he was importing a large consignment of Chevrolet automobiles from Europe when they were severely damaged in a storm. He had been cheated by the agent; there was no insurance. And Alick was faced with the danger of ruin.

During this period Charlotte moved several times, to Dacres Lane, opposite Government House, and to 5 Hospital Street, and then, in 1927, to the best address of all: Lindsay Mansions, at 15A Lindsay Street; Merle got a job with a telephone company as a switchboard operator.

Merle moved into Lindsay Mansions with Charlotte. The flat was so expensive that only a rich protector of Charlotte could have made it possible. It was large and spacious and in a good part of town. Moreover, it offered the glittering allure of movies, whose huge stills shone in the lobbies of half a dozen nearby cinemas. Lindsay Mansions was in the heart of the movie district: only a step away from the Lighthouse, the Tiger Cine, and the New Empire. A large electric light sign announcing the latest releases from Hollywood flashed on and off from the New Empire which directly faced the Lindsay Mansions windows. And not far away was Firpo's, the most popular and glamorous night spot in Calcutta.

As Merle discovered motion pictures and nightclubs and fun in her teens, the unhappy Constance ran into even worse trouble in Bombay. Despite the railing and screaming of the Soares sisters, Alick plunged into ruin and the sisters moved in, took possession of his house, stripped Constance of her jewelry and expensive clothes, sold or pawned them to meet their brother's debts, and literally threw Constance into the street. Constance and her children were reduced to poverty. They were split up from Alick and moved into one room, where Constance fretted over her lost gems and made a miserable living by sewing and making teapot covers. Partly because of her misery and shock and partly because she inherited high blood pressure from Charlotte, Constance was brought down by a near-fatal stroke at the age of thirty, and lost the use of her left arm and leg. So dark and negative was her nature, so perverse her desire for pity in her crippled state, that she never took a single remedial exercise to recover the use of her limbs. All she seemed to want to do was grumble and moan so that her children would gather around her and express their sorrow at her wretched condition.

Meanwhile, Merle had a marvelous time. Pampered by Charlotte, she was, in 1928, a stunning beauty. At the age of seventeen, an extrovert now, ambitious and sexy, she loved music and dancing and studied at a dance school until she could perform classical and modern ballet like an expert. Her dusky hair, smoky eyes, glorious full lips, and ravishing figure surpassed Charlotte's beauty at her best. And she was so sweet and adorable a charmer that no boy could resist her. Although she was often accused of being a prostitute because of her seemingly loose ways, there was nothing in her of the user. Instead, she was giddy, excitable, in love with the idea of love. She would fall in and out of love in a day or two, she was thrilled by the idea of romance, she devoured romantic novels and movies, and she had an acute awareness, never admitted by girls in those days, of the male body. Her favorite place to go, where she loved to dance, and indeed danced with grace and elegance, was Firpo's, not far from Charlotte's apartment at the time. There she would swing lightly to the music of a jazz band, tight in the embrace of her handsome regular beaux Jimmy James, David Hammersley, Oswald Maitland, and other blades around town from the brokers' offices, like Gordon MacDonell, who later became the author of a story from which Alfred Hitchcock made the film *Shadow of a Doubt*.

MacDonell remembers:

> Queenie, as we all knew her, was certainly very attractive. There were stories that she slept around, which certainly were intriguing. I don't know whether they were true. I remember her as being a marvelous dancer, always in a backless dress, with white makeup to eliminate the color in her skin. She had a very high-pitched Anglo-Indian voice which rather shocked you when she opened her mouth. You expected it to be soft and sultry. It's amazing what she did with it, later on. She was very popular with the various blades who worked for the stockbrokers and racetrack owners of the time.

The world Merle lived in was marked by violence. It was dangerous for a young Anglo-Indian girl to stay out late at night in case she was mistaken for a Hindu. But Merle was carefree and disregarded Charlotte's urgent instructions to her to stay at home after dark.

She began to develop characteristics reminiscent of Constance, who was fussy about her bed; so was Merle. Throughout her life, Constance's mattress had to be turned every night and her sheets taken out and washed. She would keep her own accounts down to the last cent, and she knew to a fraction how much money was in her purse if one of her children asked permission to raid it. Constance would never let anyone touch her hair; only she must brush it. She was diet- and vitamin-conscious. Constance's patron saint, like Merle's, was St. Jude, the saint of the impossible, and she had many medals of St. Jude in her possession. Her favorite dish—and Merle's—was oxtail stew; she was very severe with children in her care if their grades were not good enough: she became furious and sent them to their rooms if they had more than one bad grade. And she drank only very small sips of white wine. Amazingly, even though Merle never knew this side of her half-sister, all these characteristics emerged in her in later life.

Merle met many businessmen at Firpo's. It was the only place in Calcutta where young Eurasian women could make romantic dates with men. One of those she dated there was the merchant prince Sir Victor Sassoon; another was Mark Hanna, head of Paramount Pictures in India, who gave her the old line that she should be in pictures. Although in later years she was to claim that she had been picture-mad since childhood, her family in India states that this is totally untrue. It was Hanna, no doubt on the make just as she was, who inflamed her senses with thoughts of movie stardom.

One night at dinner in Hanna's comfortable apartment, he introduced Merle to Colonel Ben Finney, a former motion picture actor whom he had known when he represented Paramount in Shanghai. Finney, a well set up, clean-cut, strapping, twenty-eight-year-old big game hunter, was the heir to a Virginia fortune and a prize catch for Merle. Moreover, he could, she felt as he talked on about starring in pictures, pave her way to the movies as Hanna had indicated.

Finney was supposed to leave Calcutta in the spring of 1929 for a tiger hunt in the jungles of Bengal, but he was held up by some trouble over his guns, and while Mark Hanna helped him sort out the problem, he dated Merle every night for a week. They would go to the Great Eastern Hotel as well as Firpo's to dance, and as always Merle caught all eyes as she swayed across the floor in the popular tangos and fox-trots of the time. Although Merle worked hard at flirting with Finney—he says she would have done anything to get ahead—he proved rather cool because of fear of a dark child and simply took her primly and properly home by cab to Lindsay Mansions every night. One late evening he noticed that the light was out on the staircase of the building and he insisted on accompanying her to her door. She grew tense, not wanting him to meet Charlotte. Posing as white, she knew that Charlotte's presence might unsettle Finney. No doubt she hoped Charlotte was asleep, but to her dismay just as she and Finney reached the top step the light went on, the door opened, and Charlotte, looking very black, appeared in a robe. Finney was horrified. Although Merle dissembled, it was obvious that Charlotte was not a mere maid. Finney decided on the spot that the relationship was already over, but in order to ease Merle out of it as gently as possible, he promised her the next day that if she came to see him at Antibes in the south of France where he intended to spend the summer, he would introduce her to his friend, the director Rex Ingram who was making films in nearby Nice.

Finney left for his tiger hunt and Europe, silently praying that Merle would never raise the fare to come to France. But Merle was inflamed by the opportunity Finney offered. She had no idea who Rex Ingram was and thought all films were made in Hollywood or England—apart from the garish movies India produced—but she certainly wouldn't pass up a chance like that.

How was she going to raise the fare—or rather two fares—since Charlotte would undoubtedly want to come with her? The money, Captain Selby is convinced, came from Sir Victor Sassoon, Merle's lover.

The news that Charlotte would be leaving India greatly provoked Constance, who, in her crippled condition, took two of her children to Calcutta by train. There was an angry confrontation. Charlotte brutally ill-treated Constance's children and shunted Merle out of the apartment so that she wouldn't know what was going on.

On one occasion, Merle rushed home to change. Constance walked into her room unexpectedly. Merle was naked, turning and turning before the mirror, admiring her beautiful young eighteen-year-old body. Charlotte caught her and was furious. She said to Merle, "What if the sweeper should come in?" Merle said, "Lucky sweeper!"

Ruthlessly, Charlotte decided to send Constance back to Bombay. Years later, Constance wrote in a poem that Charlotte had begged her with tears streaming down her cheeks to abandon her children and accompany her and Merle to Europe. But this is obviously absurd, Constance's way of pitying herself and looking for pity. In fact, she had been cut out of Charlotte's life as though she were a boil.

Marseilles, the port of call for Antibes and Nice, burned in

Merle's brain that summer after Constance returned to Bombay and eight more years of living in one room. It was in late July that Merle set out at last with Charlotte, aboard the Italian Lloyd Triestino freighter *Aquileia*, which plied between India and France.

Before they sailed, mother and daughter stopped off briefly in Bombay, staying at the Majestic Hotel, an expensive hostelry paid for, like the fare to England, perhaps by Sir Victor Sassoon. They visited with Constance, who was now living in a nunnery; and they visited her sister-in-law Priscilla and Constance's husband Alick. Whether or not Merle knew, then or later, that Constance was her half-sister, is open to question. Merle's nephew Harry Selby states categorically that she did know and so does her second husband, Lucien Ballard; her third and fourth husbands, Bruno Pagliai and Robert Wolders, do not accept the story.

Mother and daughter set sail in 1929. The day they left Bombay, Mark Hanna sent a cable to Finney, who was enjoying the fleshpots of the elegant Hôtel du Cap at Antibes. It read: MERLE SAILED TODAY FOR MARSEILLES—AND YOU.

✳ ✳

Chapter Two

✳ ✳

In Antibes, mixing with the social set, Finney began to panic. He realized what might happen if he met and entertained an obscure Anglo-Indian girl whose dark limbs would stand out against the white littoral of Eden Roc, the famous bathing pool at the end of the hotel garden. He told the switchboard operator that if a Miss Queenie Thompson called, he had left the day before for Paris. He made a mental note that as soon as the operator alerted him to Merle's presence, he would disappear through the back door. He had the decency to call Rex Ingram in Nice and say that a young hopeful from India would be coming soon and to be sure to give her an audition.

Merle and Charlotte arrived in Marseilles at the beginning of August 1929; Charlotte continued to London. Merle telephoned Finney's hotel from Marseilles; the obedient operator said that Finney had left town. But Merle refused to believe the story and went straight to the hotel to find that Finney had fled. She was filled with fury and disappointment. The Hôtel du Cap was far beyond her purse, so she proceeded to Nice.

It was an exciting trip along the Riviera. In 1929, the south of France was at the height of its luxury, social *réclame*, and subtropical splendor, far removed from the ugly, quasi-American collection of coastal suburbs that it has become today. Here the rich and beautiful people of the Roaring Twenties giddily pursued a circuit of excitement and pleasures, swirling through Cannes, Antibes, and Nice to Monte Carlo—the hub of society, complete with the most popular gambling casino in Europe. The coast was ravishingly beautiful and still virtually unspoiled. Palm, lemon, and orange trees flanked the winding roads of the Corniche; the traffic was bumper-to-bumper, with screaming, laughing drivers calling out to each other and klaxons sounding above the glittering azure sea. Merle saw the construction of new wedding-cake hotels, and new villas to house the wealthy immigrants from England and Germany. It was a spectacle that Merle never forgot; at every opportunity she would return and make the Hôtel du Cap or the Hôtel de Paris in Monte Carlo her home.

The first sight of Ingram's famous Victorine Studios in 1929 was breathtaking. Paintings by Ingram's widow, the beautiful actress Alice Terry, still perfectly evoke its appearance at the time. Like a white stucco Moorish palace, the studio rose from the waving palms and mimosa bushes, the scarlet and purple jacaranda trees, high up on a hill overlooking the multifaceted surface of the sea.

Ingram! The very name was magic in those days. His impact on Merle at their first meeting cannot have been anything less than electric. Everything about the great director was romantic, colorful, and irresistible. He was as handsome as any movie star, with carved, strong features, piercing eyes, broad shoulders, a powerful chest, and a narrow waist. He was a striking combination of athlete and artist. He swam far out in the Baie des Anges, he boxed with a punching bag while extra girls admired his muscles, he performed calisthenics, and was known to have stood on his head while directing a scene. He was surrounded by an entourage of African traders in turbans; giants, midgets, and dwarves; and Moslem women in veils. He spoke with the musical lilt of his Irish ancestors. Although women chased him relentlessly, he was devoted to his wife, and dedicated all of his art to decorating her talent.

He was thirty-six years old. He had immigrated to the United States at the age of nineteen, after a period as a pilot in Britain's Royal Flying Corps. At thirty-two he had become world famous, launching the career of Rudolph Valentino in *The Four Horsemen of the Apocalypse*. In Nice, he created his own magic world of movies, making his exotic, picturesque films in a complex of four studios, a four-hundred-seat restaurant, laboratories, projection rooms, and photographic services. At the heart of the complex stood his famous house, the Villa Rex, a focus of parties the whole year round. The rich flocked to him. George Bernard Shaw was a frequent guest; Shaw, the soprano Grace Moore, the opera star Mary Garden, and others appeared as extras in some of his films.

Merle entered a paradise at the Victorine. Ingram, with his fondness for the Oriental and the exotic, took one look at her and hired her on the spot. Merle obtained her first extra role in a picture Ingram was just completing. He added her hastily to a party scene. The movie was *The Three Passions*, a society story typical of the period. The Three

Passions were money, religion, and love; the story dealt with the conflict of labor and management in the Jazz Age.

Merle learned much from Rex Ingram. He was a director of great sensitivity who understood the lack of experience and frailty that existed along with Merle's resolution and ambition. She made only brief appearances in the film, but he made sure that they were telling and apt. He decorated her beauty with his usual refinement of camera and lighting; she would forever be grateful to him that he had given her her start.

With whatever money she had made from the picture, Merle sailed to London at the end of the summer of 1929. Charlotte had found them a reasonably pleasant residential area to live in; they settled on Nottingham Place, near Baker Street. They moved into two unfurnished rooms and found that they needed furniture immediately, but had almost no money left.

Advertisements in the local paper told them that the Times Furnishing Company stores were the best places in London to obtain cheap but decent furniture on time payments. Merle walked to the local branch to save the bus fare. Dressed up in her best clothes, she strolled with seeming casualness into the store and, brushing aside a clerk, coolly stated that she would consider being served only by the top man. The clerk was so impressed by the manner of this beautiful and exotic young Anglo-Indian girl that he called up the owner, known as Uncle Jacobs. Uncle Jacobs came down the stairs and was totally smitten. She told him that she would like to speak to him privately. Looking him in the eye with startling boldness, she said she had no money for the down payment on the furniture, and would he please help her? Dazzled, he agreed without even thinking. She then asked him whether he would agree to her buying the furniture on deferred and greatly reduced terms without a down payment. Again, he was so intoxicated with her he said, "Yes, at once." He even bustled about picking the best possible furniture for her and insisted on moving it in and arranging it. His brothers, who owned the chain of Times shops, were not amused. They thought he had gone mad.

But Merle captivated them all by paying off the debt in full as soon as she could. Over thirty years later, David Jacobs, the famous London lawyer and nephew of Uncle Jacobs, stayed with Merle in her white marble palace in Acapulco and they exchanged memories of that marvelous story of that humble beginning. Surrounded by priceless antiques, Merle said to David, "Quite honestly, Uncle Jacobs saved my life."

Once she was set up in her modest digs, Merle began to look for work. She discovered that work was available at the well-known Hammersmith Palais de Dance, which had a good, twelve-piece band, and where young people could get jobs as hostesses or male dancing partners. She took the bus there, a red double-decker with a curved outdoor metal stairway, on a Saturday night when the young clerks and secretaries and shopgirls and errand boys arrived in pairs for a jolly good time. Members of the upper classes arrived also, in Daimlers and Rollses on slumming sprees, to start off an evening doing the rounds of the night spots. Chauffeurs parked automobiles nearby and the flaming youth emerged in tuxedoes and white ties and evening gowns and jewels.

Given her looks and stunning figure, Merle had no problem getting work as a dance hostess. She was paid sixpence a dance and usually got free drinks; wealthy men and working-class boys alike enjoyed her flawless dancing, her pleasantly giggly, happy company, and her elegant, graceful good manners. Soon she was able to save enough to buy herself an inexpensive but attractive evening gown in a bargain sale.

Inevitably, she acquired beaux. She was whisked off to the heady pleasures of London's West End, where she whirled around such "in" night spots as the underground Café de Paris on Coventry Street, the Café Anglais in Leicester Square, and the Embassy Club in Bond Street. It was a glittering world. Customers enjoyed fine wine, excellent food, and matchless orchestras and cabaret performers. The center of the social set was a man whom Merle saw only across the room but who would later become a close and lifelong friend: the handsome, charming young Prince of Wales, later the Duke of Windsor, eldest son of the King and man-about-town. Always with a bevy of beautiful girls surrounding him, always laughing, smoking through a holder, drinking, he was the focus of the Smart Set wherever he went. Merle was fascinated by him, as every woman was.

Now totally movie mad, Merle went to see pictures whenever she could, in the afternoons or on her nights off, gazing at the stars and longing to be one of them. She used to travel on many days on a double-decker bus to Wardour Street just off Shaftesbury Avenue, the headquarters of the film exchanges and distributors. The magic names of Paramount, MGM, Warners, Universal, and Columbia beckoned to her. The offices of Film Casting, the central casting office, were on that street. They were a magnet for beginners.

Merle, dressed cheaply but with studied elegance that gave an impression of money, walked in one morning and gave her credentials to the secretary at the front desk. The secretary filled out a card and filed it along with her photograph and type, described as "exotic."

After a long wait, she at last received a call summoning her to an audition for a walk-on in a Fox film, which was held at the same Café de Paris that she frequently visited at night with the fashionable crowd. The applicants had to walk down the curved left-hand staircase framing the dance floor for an interview by the casting director, who watched them carefully for grace, movement, and style as they descended. The casting director was seated at a table in the middle of the floor; he interviewed Merle, asking her conventional questions while astutely sizing her up. Those he approved stood nearby waiting while those he ruled out walked as cheerfully as they could in the circumstances up the right-hand stairs.

Despite her natural ease of manner and the polished way she descended the stairs, Merle received a shock when she reached the table. The casting director told her she could go up along with the other rejects. She asked him why. He told her brutally that she had a cast in her left eye. There was an almost imperceptible misalignment there, but not a cast; she protested uselessly. Whereas other applicants reacted with a shrug, Merle was so consumed by ambition that she might as well have received a blow to the face.

She reached the top of the right-hand staircase and was surprised to bump into the well-known entertainment manager of the club, Leonard Urry. She recognized him immediately from her visits there as a social butterfly and seeing him added to her embarrassment. She started to cry. Leaning against him, much to his surprise, she said, through sobs, "They won't have me!" She mentioned the cruel slight about her eye. She went on, "It's my last chance! I promised Mummy that I would go home to India if I didn't get this job!"

Urry was touched by her naïveté, the childlike response of this exquisite girl to a setback. He took her down and had a conference with the casting director, who told her that the real problem wasn't the slight flaw in her eye, but the fact that she was too short, whereas the other girls were tall; she was also too "specialized" in her looks to fit in. He tried to soften the blow by saying that the pay was nothing anyway: just two pounds (then ten dollars) a day. This certainly rubbed salt in Merle's wound: ten dollars a day was a fortune for an eighteen-year-old beginner who would be lucky to earn that much in a week in a store or office. Urry asked her more about her background. She lied that her tickets were booked home and if she didn't get a job within a week, she'd have to sail. The tale worked like a charm. Urry took pity on her and said he could offer her a compensation prize for not appearing in the movie. She could be a hostess at the nightclub instead.

To be a hostess at the Café de Paris was a great distinction at the time. It carried a considerable cachet and ensured entrée to the highest social circles. The Café de Paris hostesses were noted for their glamour and attraction. They could marry into the aristocracy as easily as Ziegfeld or Cochran girls. Operating by a rule book of conventlike strictness, they had to report at precisely 9:00 P.M. each night in evening gowns bought from their salaries. They were not permitted to eat with the customers but had a special table of their own on the balcony. They must never be known to spend a night with a client nor must they enter into any sexual situation with one. They were required to supply light conversation, relaxation, and female company for prominent single men; they were forbidden to sit with married men—a careful check was run on all male customers. They had to restrict their drinking severely and smoking was not encouraged. So exclusive was their circle that usually a maximum of five hostesses operated at one time in the rather cramped club. One of these was to become the famous socialite millionairess and owner of a gold Daimler, Lady Nora Docker.

Merle had a problem. She had no proper evening clothes; her dresses were not of the required standard. So Leonard Urry issued her an advance before she worked a single day; like Uncle Jacobs, he was unable to refuse Merle anything. She quickly became the most popular hostess in the café. She was part of a charmed circle that included the famous maître d', Poulson; the bandleader, spritely Jack Harris; the managing director, Robin Humphreys; and above all, the famous manager, Charles. Night after night, the stars glittered in the club. The atmosphere was charged, airless, filled with perfume and tobacco smoke under the pink ceiling lights as the black comedy team of Layton and Johnstone, Rudy Vallee with reedy voice and megaphone, Gertrude Niesen throatily rendering "Life Is Just a Bowl of Cherries," the red-hot mama Sophie Tucker, and the red-fezed magician Gully-Gully captivated the customers.

In the daytime, Merle at last obtained work in pictures at Elstree Studios near London, where a young man named Reginald Truscott-Jones, later known as Ray Milland, noticed her—more than noticed her—in the commissary. He says today, "She was the most exotically beautiful creature I had ever seen. I didn't take my eyes off her for the next nine months." Friends recall that Merle worked part-time in a flower shop that year, next to the famous male club known as Buck's. There, undoubtedly, she met many prosperous men who could help her.

The actor Edward Ashley says, recalling Merle's ambition at the time:

I was visiting my wife of that time, Nora Swinburne, on the set of a film when I suddenly saw this beautiful young dark girl standing next to me. She introduced herself as Merle O'Brien. She noticed an assistant director standing across the sound stage. She asked me if I knew him. I said I did. She then said to me, "Will you make a test with me if he can arrange it?" I was quite well known and I was rather startled by her directness, but I weakly said yes. She then, without a word, went over to the assistant and said that I had agreed to make a test with her and would he let her make one? He crumbled at once and said that was fine. So she went ahead with me into the test. It was done for Irving Asher, who was boss at Warners in England then. As soon as she started the scene, she got nervous, forgot all her lines, and started to cry. It went on all day and I felt so sorry for her I got her through it somehow. Irving sent the test to Jack Warner who replied by telegram: IF YOU WANT TO SLEEP WITH WOMEN GO AHEAD. BUT DON'T WASTE MY MONEY TESTING THEM.

Aided by her hard-working agent, Alfred Zeitlin, who also handled Jessie Matthews, Merle got a job with Ideal Films. A company that was part of Gaumont-British, with Michael Balcon as chief executive producer, Ideal was preparing a picture entitled *A Warm Corner*, based on a popular farce by the French dramatist Georges Feydeau. The director of the film, the forceful thirty-one-year-old Victor Saville, offered her the part of an extra in the picture under her own name of Estelle Thompson. Saville remembered years later:

My brother Alec met Merle at the Café de Paris. He was so enchanted with her that he arranged a double date: her and Alec and my wife and myself. I met her and shared Alec's enchantment. I decided on the spot that this very young, very beautiful girl should be given a break. I engaged her on the spot.

At last Merle was in pictures as more than one in the crowd. She could be seen in a few sequences. When not required to work, she stayed back to watch the star, Leslie Henson, a legendary comedian who had co-starred with Fred and Adele Astaire, counterpointing their inspired dancing with his witty comic routines. Merle also watched, even more carefully, the women in the cast, studying every nuance and gesture in order to master the secrets of screen acting.

With the aid of Richard Beville, Merle moved on to another comedy, *Alf's Button*, and minutely studied the actress Polly Ward, a pretty ingenue from the West End stage, who to this day remembers the "outstanding Eurasian girl" who stood out like a gold coin from the humdrum lines of extras; she spoke just one line—in Hindustani.

Merle wanted to see the tricks actresses used, the movements that emphasized their sexual allure, the timing of dialogue, in that age of the infancy of talkies, the way in which they measured their steps and acted with or against their leading men. Given little natural talent as an actress, but great beauty and presence, she learned from studying leading ladies how she might advance herself best. She was single-minded to the extent of fanaticism. Anyone who could help her she would dazzle, wheedle, and impress. She could draw blood from stones.

She early was romantically interested in the distinguished, lean, moustachioed, and military-looking actor-director Miles Mander, a member of the upper middle class who perfectly personified the British gentleman. He began dating her regularly; it is probable she became his mistress. He cast her, as she had hoped, in a bit role in his film *Fascination*. Reginald Denham, playwright and production boss of Paramount–British, remembered later:

> One day Miles brought a young girl onto the set at Elstree whose beauty electrified the whole studio. Stagehands in platoons whom I had never seen before appeared miraculously from behind scenery to stare, electricians clambered down from their bridges, and clerks and secretaries sneaked out of their cells.

Mr. Denham mistook the reason for this turnout. New to the studio, he didn't realize that she was already one of the most familiar beauties around the lot. The attention clearly was caused by the fact that Mander had found a new light of love; she had risen in the hierarchy so fast and with such remarkable skill.

While she was at the Café de Paris in 1930, Merle took another major stride up the social ladder. Her romance with Miles over, she became involved in a romantic liaison with the legendary "Hutch," Leslie A. Hutchinson, the rage of London society and, because of his popular and always jam-packed appearances on tour, the rest of England. Hutch was black.

A Jamaican about thirty-five, a man of remarkable good looks and powerful physique, he was reputed to have the body of a black Adonis and a beautiful singing and speaking voice. He would sit at his large, highly polished Steinway grand piano with the lid up, in white tie and tails, a large white silk handkerchief tucked up his sleeve which he would frequently draw out in a carefully calculated gesture and use to mop his sweat-beaded forehead after each number. He always sipped champagne from a glass on the piano. He sang Cole Porter, Youmans, and Coward to perfection, and his signature tunes, "These Foolish Things" and "Begin the Beguine," made him a fortune in records. He was a legendary stud. Society women flung themselves at him in order to be able to tell their eager friends that they had succeeded in the ultimate thrill: going to bed with a Negro. It was a time when blacks were regarded as badges of honor for the titled and sexually voracious. Several of his lovers were duchesses and countesses, including one member of the Mountbatten family, yet he was married with children and had a humdrum domestic household; his black wife was never seen, even out shopping, by society.

Having an all-out romantic affair with Hutch greatly elevated Merle's status. She was now, at least in one sense, a cousin to female aristocrats. Through Hutch, she reached into the top levels of society. Undoubtedly, this is how she met the many aristocrats who later became her friends, as well as several prominent figures of the movie world.

The most outstanding of these film leaders was to be a major influence in her life. The great producer-director Alexander Korda had arrived in Britain after an ill-fated brush with Hollywood and an equally unsuccessful sojourn in France. Born, like Merle, in poverty, he was, also like her, irresistibly attracted to glamour, to the opulent, extravagant, and exotic. This princely figure was compelled by ruthless ambition. Warm and genial, with sharp eyes flashing knowingly through horn-rimmed spectacles and a captivating smile, he was a striking combination of supersalesman and colossal dreamer, and a producer and director of extraordinary gifts, with the romantic tale-spinning ability of Scheherazade. Passionate, creative, intermittently inspired, he was endlessly planning dozens of pictures at the same time, most of which were in the public domain and didn't require the buying of rights. Also, by throwing out lists of projects, most of which never got made, and by promising the allure of glamorous women and possible trips to Hollywood, he could captivate the bored, dull, and stodgy heads of business enterprises into investing in his pipe dreams. A major victim was the staid but looking-for-thrills Sir Connop Guthrie, head of Prudential Life Insurance, who plunged several fortunes into Korda—and lived to regret it.

Returning in 1931, Korda swallowed up England. But he gave much back: he brought, along with his con-man's skills, genuine excitement, color, and fantasy to a half-dead, enervated industry; he turned the British studios into a kind of Hollywood. He showed that Britain could make pictures that were luxury goods like Dunhill lighters or Crown Derby plates. And he provided propaganda for the British royal family, with whom he conducted a lifelong love affair, exploiting rich veins of patriotism for the export market. Floating the colored balloons of imaginary projects, using the press with inspired flamboyance, he lived to the hilt in the middle of the Depression.

John Myers, Alexander Korda's sharp-witted publicist, decided with Korda's approval to create an elaborate fantasy version of Merle's life. This fairy tale would disguise her Anglo-Indian origins, disclosure of which would have been fatal to her career if discovered by the still-racist public and press. Myers made her memorize certain "facts," which she would have to regurgitate in interviews for the rest of her life. He made it clear to her that those who wanted to be stars had to be given fictitious backgrounds in order to make them more interesting and, more important, to cover up any inconveniences. Much as she hated lies, Merle realized that she had no alternative but to lie, at least to the press, if she wanted to be a star, so she went along with Myers' absurdities.

After fifty years, the actor Maurice Bredell, who was to appear with Merle in the film *Men of Tomorrow*, still recalls how Myers roared with laughter as he fabricated Merle's origins. Myers pretended that Merle was born in Tasmania, an island state of Australia so remote that most people had not the slightest idea where it was. He elevated her father's rank from sapper to major and changed his death from pneumonia in the trenches to Charlotte's story that he had died of pneumonia on a hunt before Merle was born, and then to Charlotte's other version—that he had been killed on that hunt.

As Myers' imagination worked overtime, the story grew more and more elaborate. He had Merle's mother reduced to less affluent circumstances by "Major" Thompson's sudden death. When the child was seven, her mother accepted the invitation of Lady Monteith, Merle's godmother, to visit her at her lovely residence in Bombay, where Lord Monteith was an important official.

Merle flourished, in Myers' version of her life, under the wing of the Monteiths until they left India, and her mother invested her savings in an American automobile agency. But the man who had pushed and promoted the agency turned out to be a crook and ran off with the money. Penniless, Merle and her mother moved to Calcutta to live with an imaginary uncle who "accepted his new dependents with kindness and generosity." In Calcutta, in a colony of army officers and government officials, Merle grew to be a local beauty, and she was told by many people she ought to be in movies. Later, her "uncle" went to Europe with her where she studied in Paris and London and then returned to finish her schooling in Darjeeling.

This romantic daydream, suggesting gentility and graciousness in unfortunate circumstances, appeared in magazines and newspapers for over forty years. It even turned up in editions of *Who's Who* in Britain and America and in the allegedly accurate annual *Current Biography*, entries in which are traditionally sent to the subjects for checking, in 1941.

Like a silkworm spinning a fine substance from its innards, Johnny Myers wove this fantasy out of the existing facts. The name Monteith was drawn from the name of the acting governor of Bombay in 1905, Sir James Monteath. By the alteration of one letter, the author of the fantasy avoided the legal dangers of a false claim. The American automobile story was clearly based upon the disaster that helped ruin Alick Soares. In later years, Merle added the tale that her uncle was a Major General Sir George Bartley. Needless to say, no such person existed; the name was probably a combination of Sir Bartle Frere, another former governor of Bombay whose name appeared in many public documents, and Ernest Hartley, father of Vivien Leigh, who was the boss of the Piggott company in Calcutta, and the chairman for whom Merle's former beaux Jimmy James and Gordon MacDonell had worked.

Chapter Three

Merle's first real break came in a Korda picture called *Wedding Rehearsal*. Life imitated cliché when one of those accidents that is supposed to happen only on stage or in the movies actually took place. The star, the cool, blond actress Ann Todd, who was cast as a mousy secretary transformed into a beauty by love, smashed her car and Merle, without warning, was rushed in to replace her. She scarcely knew what she was doing: she had no comedy talent to speak of and the part called for it, and in addition she was irritated by the horn-rimmed glasses she had to wear. To cast her as a mouse bordered on insanity. She was more convincing in the later scenes, but on the whole made little impression.

She was slightly stronger in the next Korda picture, *Men of Tomorrow*. Shot partly among the dreaming spires of Oxford, it was a lighthearted comedy about undergraduates, during the shooting of which she, Emlyn Williams, and Joan Gardner, who later married Alex's brother Zoltan Korda, had fun sending up the Korda brothers. Merle called Alex Con Korda, Williams called Zoltan Dis Korda, and Joan called the art director, Vincent, Misery Korda. One day they were playing this silly, childish game when Alex jumped up behind them. They giggled helplessly as she said, "Have you forgotten the Lost Korda?" They were barely able to work the rest of the day.

Merle was very fond of her leading man in the picture, Maurice Bredell, today a picture restorer in New York. But she hated the director, the formidable Leontine Sagan, one of the few women directors in the world who had had an enormous success with her first film, *Mädchen in Uniform*, a study of life in a severe German girls' school that had created an uproar because of a lesbian theme. Mannish, strident, and aggressive, Leontine Sagan hated Merle and Merle hated

49

her. Bredell recalls that Sagan constantly said to Merle with snarling emphasis, "What's the matter, why do you spend so much time fiddling with your eyelashes? Try to spend more time studying your part. You're a lousy actress!" Sagan spoke with an extremely thick German accent and seemingly tried to hypnotize the cast with her enormous eyes. She told everyone they were so British that they talked like typewriters, and that they should all watch a film of the Polish actress Elisabeth Bergner who, like Sagan, came from the Max Reinhardt school of drama.

The cast decided to get their revenge for having to sit through Bergner's dreary film *Ariane*. One day, Sagan came into the studio cafeteria and everyone turned and greeted her, very sweetly, in a highly mannered and affected Bergner manner, *in German*. She turned in fury and walked out. Whereas Merle was unable to relate to Sagan, she was amused by Sagan's husband, a tiny man with a crippled leg encased in an enormous surgical boot. He spoke only one word of English. He would sit on the set and when anyone spoke to him he would reply, "Oosbend."

In addition to Hutch and Miles Mander, Merle had a fling with the famous golfer-tycoon Charles Sweeney. He was with her when she concocted her screen name. He never forgot her jotting down possible names on a sheet of paper. She began with Merle O'Brien, then O'Brian, then Auberon* (but that was the name of a firm in Bond Street), then Overell, then Avril Oberon, then Merle Oberon. In her characteristic, very Oriental handwriting, she boldly wrote *Oberon* at the foot of the list—which still exists today.

Oddly, it was Alex's jealous wife, Maria Corda, who noticed Merle in the commissary, ravishing in a green dress, and drew her to his particular attention. Seeing the dark hair, the oblique eyes, the lovely figure, she said, "What a striking girl!" Korda had noticed Merle, of course; but it took Maria to single her out. Maria was, paradoxically, trying to win Alex back at the time, but by drawing his attention to Merle, she sealed the death warrant of her marriage.

Korda fell in love with Merle, but there could be no question of an affair yet. First of all, given his Hungarian virility and appetite, he had his pick of women. Secondly, he did not want to become involved seriously with her; he knew instinctively how ambitious she was. He could not afford to have a relationship with an obscure actress. Instead, he must find a way to build her up, to make her into a star so that he could become involved with an equal.

---

*She had worked, as Estelle O'Brien, as a model for cheap beauty-product advertisements in movie fan weeklies.

In February 1932, he formed London Films, famous for the trademark of a loudly chiming Big Ben against a black-and-white or mulberry-colored background. He set out to put British films in ascendance. Cash flow was bad: the company operated on credit; again and again, Merle and the other players were forced to take salary cuts. Korda, as usual, spent everybody else's money and sailed piratically through every problem. Summoned before an angry group of bankers at a board meeting, he lured them out of the stuffy boardroom to his more lavish offices for an expensive lunch brought in from the Ritz. The leading banker, though softened by wine and food, had to say, "Mr. Korda, we are used to making allowances for the artistic temperament, but we must—" Before he had a chance to say "stop any further credit," Korda broke in with, "Gentlemen, the only temperament I have ever experienced has been from bankers!" The group dissolved in laughter, brandy and Havana cigars were enjoyed by all, and a further loan was provided.

It was this kind of marvelous boldness, of a big man among big men, that ensured Korda his stunning career with London Films. He surrounded himself with a motley collection of Hungarians, including his favorite writer, a Budapest hack and former statesman in Hungary named Lajos Biró, and even a baroness, Moura Budberg, who was his reader and chose his subjects. He drove in a chauffeured Rolls-Royce, even when he was most broke. Characteristically, he went for the top almost immediately: he hired Charles Laughton, then the most famous actor in England and already a Hollywood star, to appear as Henry VIII in a garbled account of the monarch's private life. He decided to direct the picture himself.

With his writers, Korda settled on making the picture a mixture of the comic and the dramatic, with the emphasis on the former. Virtually the whole crew was foreign. In many ways the movie was an echo of an earlier Hungarian picture, a version Korda had made of Mark Twain's *The Prince and the Pauper*, in which Henry VIII had appeared as a character. The movie had much the same bounce, wicked good cheer, and cheese-pared budget that led many people to assume, probably correctly, that the bulk of Prudential's investment disappeared into Korda's pocket.

During the production, Merle fell ill. She had noticed pain during intercourse with various men she dated and now she was shocked to discover bleeding. She went to see a gynecologist who told her that she had tumors. He decided to operate at once. She took the news with amazing strength and resolution for a girl of barely twenty-one, and simply said that he should do whatever was necessary. He promised her that in this case the chances of recovery were good: the cancer was a rare form, located in her fallopian tubes.

The results of the operation were distressing. Not only did Merle become partly conscious during it, but in fact both tubes were cancerous and had to be removed. The doctor did not tell her; he knew that the shock of knowing she could never bear a child would be devastating. Furthermore, peritonitis set in and flooded her body with poison. These were the days before antibiotics and nothing could be done except hope.

Merle went into a coma. She was declared medically dead. In her suspended state, she felt herself floating free of her body and could see her corpse on the hospital bed surrounded by doctors and nurses trying to resuscitate her. She saw the faces of staff she hadn't seen before and memorized their conversations.

She felt herself float up through the ceiling into a funnel of light that led into a strange, dark region from which she knew she could not return. But something, perhaps a voice, told her to go back. She found herself imprisoned in her body again, feeling heavy and restricted, and came to, amazing the doctors and nurses by describing what they had said. There was no way, in her state of death or near-death, that she could have known the gist of their discussions. Nor could she have described them so accurately. It was to be almost fifty years before similar out-of-body visions became extensively authenticated by Elisabeth Kübler-Ross and others; Merle was to have a similar experience in 1969, when she almost died from an allergic reaction to antihistamines in Mexico.

Merle recovered with great resolution. She took off to Margate, an oceanside resort where, the actress Joan Gardner recalls, "Even in her weakened state, Merle got into a romantic situation. Korda's accountant, a mousy little man, came to see her to bring her financial aid, and she took that mousy little man to bed! I'm sure it was the best time he ever had! It was quite the talk of the hotel!"

Then Merle had a stroke of luck.

When he was about to wrap up *Henry VIII*, Korda had an inspiration. He decided to add an early sequence in which the tragic second wife of Henry, Anne Boleyn, would be executed for adultery on Tower Hill. On a typical impulse, he decided to give Merle the chance of her life and offered her the part. She became very excited— but when the script arrived at Margate there were only three pages devoted to her, or less than three minutes on the screen. In interviews later, over the years, she stated that she was so furious at this treatment that she burst into Korda's office and unsuccessfully demanded an improvement in the size of her part.

She failed to change his mind. Resigned—and always a good

sport—she went in her weakened state to the National Portrait Gallery in London to look at pictures of Anne Boleyn. She bought books on the ill-fated queen and borrowed others from the library. Francis Hackett's biography of Henry VIII was a hit in London that year, and she devoured it at a sitting. She bought prints of Anne Boleyn and hung them in her new, modest flat on Crawford Street, near Baker Street. She splurged on her promised earnings in order to fix up her flat with yellow and beige furnishings—and several mirrors.

The character of Anne Boleyn was perfect for her. The queen was ambitious, eager, attractive, and she loved beauty. She had immense courage, style, grace, and charm, and was sexually impossible to resist. Even her features, high cheekbones, and mysterious, opalescent eyes, were not far removed from Merle's. Alex knew what he was doing when casting her. He chose her with instinctive understanding and love.

The scene was shot in two days. Merle looked wonderful in the period costume and the tight-fitting cap. She concentrated all her carefully acquired knowledge of acting into an impressive miniature, precise, calculated, and with genuine feeling. The scene of preparation and execution was handled by Korda with an intensity absent from the rest of the movie. The headsman whistles cheerfully as he tests the fine edge of his sword; ladies-in-waiting feel the royal bed as they test it for its inevitable new occupant Jane Seymour, and when Anne enters, strong, calm, fighting fear, a lady asks a woman in front of her to remove her hat so she can see the execution better. Anne remarks with a tiny, wry smile that was to become Merle's trademark, "I shall be known as 'Anne *sans tête*,'" and touches herself, saying, "Mine is such a *little* neck," before she kneels for the death blow.

On November 15, 1936, Merle told the *London Observer:* "When I found they had given me exactly two [sic] minutes on the screen, that made me mad, and I thought to myself I'll make them remember those two minutes whatever else they forget. If I don't, they may get rid of me in a subtitle the way they got rid of Catherine of Aragon. It wasn't difficult, really; the lines were so lovely and simple—'Mine is such a little neck'—I remember crying afterwards and saying to Alex, 'What in the world is the matter with me?' and he said, 'Don't worry, that's acting, Merle!'"

Korda was thrilled by the scene. It was everything he had hoped for and more. Word spread around London, then New York and Hollywood, that Merle had wiped the other wives off the screen. They never forgave her. A new star had been born, and later the reviews were to confirm it.

As part of a publicity campaign, she attended the world premiere of *Henry VIII* in London, with all the other wives, including Binnie Barnes and Elsa Lanchester, and with Charles Laughton. Then—thrill of thrills!—she traveled to Paris and Berlin for the European premieres. Audiences spontaneously applauded—a rarity in those days—her poignant, disturbing portrayal; it was so haunting that many who saw it never forgot it.

Merle began keeping a scrapbook of quotations, passages of favorite verse or prose that illustrated her dreamy, mystical, romantic nature. Many of the poems in the book, which still exists, bound in sturdy Morocco leather, celebrate the importance of love; authors popular at the time, including Elizabeth Barrett Browning, James Elroy Flecker, Keats, Walter Pater, and Oscar Wilde are heavily represented. Ernest Dowson's famous *Cynara* was also there; and perhaps the most significant passage in the book illustrating her romantic nature came from the poet Sa'di:

> If of thy worldly goods
> Thou art bereft
> And of thy mortal store
> Two loaves alone are left
> Sell one, and with the dole
> Buy hyacinths to feed thy soul.

Armed with money and new success, Merle moved from Crawford Street to a better address, 61 Gloucester Place; Charlotte lived in a flat two floors up. Merle took out the ugly grate and replaced it with a stepped fireplace with antique wrought-iron dogs. She lined one wall with bookshelves, changed the color of the walls and ceiling to parchment tones that caught highlights when the room was lit up at night, and she used motifs of gold; she had glass curtains of deep cream silk net and a beige pile carpet; she herself designed the strip lights in opalescent glass with golden tips, and she painted the woodwork deep cream. She had elephants everywhere—of amethyst, ebony, or ivory, all with their trunks up, pointing toward the door for luck, and a unique record player given her by Korda that played twenty-four records and turned over the disks. It was a modest start of a lifetime of exquisitely redesigning her various homes.

Merle waited restlessly at Gloucester Place to be cast in a new Korda picture. The ever-inventive producer began dreaming up a number of prospects, including the life of a ballerina based on Pavlova, and the part of Natasha in *War and Peace*. Merle was excited and anxious over these opportunities. She began reading lives of the great Russian dancer, and the Tolstoy novel, with her usual intensity, diligence and driving ambition. But she was quickly disillusioned. It was obvious to her after several weeks of talk and meetings at the Korda offices that all this discussion was just a lot of hot air. She was becoming wise to the ways of Korda and the film industry as a whole: constant self-puffery and self-exploitation, pipe dreams and schemes and a total lack of conscience in involving other people in them.

She was dismayed when Korda, signing her to a long-term contract, used his wiles to prevent her from seizing an opportunity to go to Hollywood. She was offered a starring part in *The Count of Monte Cristo*, to be made with John Barrymore (it would star Robert Donat). Shocked to think she would even be talking to American producer Edward Small, Korda called her in his office, and shamed her cunningly by saying, "If my own brother did this to me I couldn't do any worse." Many actresses would have slapped his face for less; Merle, hypersensitive and bitterly disappointed, broke into tears.

Korda threw her the sop of a chance to go to France on loan-out to another Hungarian charmer, the director Nicholas Farkas, to whom he owed a favor. Ironically, after she had gone to such extraordinary lengths to conceal her racial origins, Merle was to be cast as an Asian. She was to play the Marquise Yorisaka, wife of a Japanese naval commander (Charles Boyer) in the Russian-Japanese War of 1904, who throws herself at the British naval attaché in order to obtain strategic secrets; the naval commander commits hara-kiri at the end.

She traveled to Paris. Nicholas Farkas was a robust *bon vivant* who made his home in the heart of the city. He was surrounded by Hungarian exiles and White Russians who had icons nailed to the walls of their apartments and sang Russian gypsy songs far into the night. Merle was whisked off on a giddy round of Hungarian restaurants and Russian nightclubs, feeling somewhat alienated; she liked neither to eat heavily nor to drink more than an occasional glass of wine. The portly, cheery men in the Farkas entourage stuffed and tippled relentlessly while she did her best with grim good humor to put up with it all. She had to go into long hours of difficult makeup sessions as the Japanese heroine, and she had to learn from a Japanese exile the correct forms of behavior. She felt uncomfortable in the complicated Japanese costumes and irritable with the endless difficult matching shots involving back projections of the war at sea. She also had to stand or sit on decks mounted on cantilevers, which swayed so heavily she got miserably seasick. Some shots were matched off the coast of Normandy and she got drenched with spray; fragile as ever, she developed a chest condition and influenza that slowed up production.

The only consolations in this dreary experience were that some scenes took her back to Nice and Antibes, and that she had to work only on alternate days. The French star Annabella, who later married Tyrone Power, was appearing in the French version of the film, which was shot alternately with the English version, so in Paris Merle had every other day off, when she was well enough to shop. She also became fascinated with art, particularly the Dutch and Flemish schools. She loved the precise surfaces of Northern medieval paintings, with their tiny, scrupulously rendered details, painted with a single hair of a brush stiffened with wax. In one painting of which she was particularly fond, at the National Gallery in London, Jan van Eyck's "Arnolfini and His Wife," the artist had limned the Twelve Stations of the Cross in the twelve knobs of a convex mirror, each knob no more than two inches wide.

Merle had a great capacity for learning, far beyond that of most stars, who were self-centered and lacking in intellect. Her passion for beauty made Paris one of her favorite cities. Years later, she was to own a personal memento of the city's greatness: a necklace of fine emeralds and diamonds given by Napoleon III to the Baroness Haussmann, wife of the genius who redesigned much of the French capital.

Back in London, Merle threw herself into intensive voice training; she was aware that she still had a hint of the odd, almost Welsh lilt of Anglo-Indian speech, and that she needed to have perfect elocution for the future. Once again she tried desperately to work against her racial origin and suppress her "exotic" character. She always looked for the best, and the finest voice coach in London was Margaret Yarde, an elderly actress of the Delsarte School, which influenced most of the silent performers. Ms. Yarde used very stylized gestures. With the advent of talkies, she had turned herself into an expert in elocution. Margaret Yarde was a driving, overbearing perfectionist who demanded total obedience and attention from her pupils. The exercises were daunting, involving various techniques of recitation of verse and prose, in combination with theatrical movements. The problem was that Margaret Yarde produced actresses who spoke with an irritatingly plummy over-enunciation. Merle drove everyone mad by walking around talking with flawlessly rounded vowels and clipped consonants. It took her years to shake off this baleful influence.

Meanwhile, her very peculiar relationship with her mother, Charlotte, continued. Charlotte was introduced to some people as *ayah*, the Indian term for a chaperone for young, well-brought-up white women, or as her "mammy," or her "nanny," or even as her maid. Charlotte would dress up in a frilly cap and apron and serve tea. Only a very few met Charlotte in her proper role as her mother. Diana Napier says, "One afternoon, I was having tea with Merle at her flat near Baker Street when for the first time I saw this little, plump Indian woman come into the room dressed in a sari. She stood nervously, hesitantly, as though waiting for orders. Merle was extremely embarrassed. She spoke to her mother in Hindustani. The lady hardly said anything at all. She was very, very quiet."

Lee Anderson, another friend of Merle's who later became Mrs. Vincente Minnelli, says, "I used to drive Merle out to the studio because she couldn't drive. One day she wasn't waiting at the foot of the steps as usual and I went up and knocked on the door. This little Indian woman opened it."

At the same time, letters kept arriving from Constance, who was still living in the one room in Bombay with three children. She called herself Joyce, and she gazetted the name Selby in order to divorce herself from any connection to the Soares family. Merle wrote mechanically to her; until the early 1970s she sent her small amounts of money, always grudgingly and irritably, wondering why she was supposed to be responsible for this obscure maddening woman who would rush out long letters filled with self-pity, bitter recriminations, and complaints. Constance was her own worst enemy in this matter, as in most things. If only she had written sweetly to Merle, congratulating her on her successes and saying how she wished she had known her better in India, perhaps Merle would have asked her to England in private and wanted to know more. But the aggression and hatred in Constance's letters along with the depressing stationery and the ugly uncultivated handwriting put Merle off completely.

Merle had to get out of all she had left behind. There was always the numbing fear that the past would reach up and drag her down with a strangler's hands.

Merle worked busily, restlessly redecorating her small apartment in Gloucester Place; the living room now had pale primrose walls, autumn-brown chair covers, and pale gold curtains and cushions. One entire wall was filled with books that reflected the amazing single-mindedness of Merle's ambition; almost without exception, the scores of volumes dredged up from practically every secondhand bookstore in London dealt with filmmaking, acting, techniques of singing and dancing, makeup, beauty care, plastic surgery, and histories of costumes and art. Her consuming ambition, as her possession of a dozen books on the subject and a script of her own authorship attested, was to expand the part of Anne Boleyn into a full-scale feature under

Korda's direction. She told a reporter, with great keenness, her mysterious slanting eyes flashing with excitement, "No one but a woman in love could have done what Anne did. Men can never understand that when a woman loves, she will do anything if she thinks it will help the man she loves. Anne was *really* in love with Henry, and was never untrue to him in her heart. Those who have written about her have mostly been dry old professors who do not understand women. One day perhaps I may write a book about Anne myself."

But Korda had other plans. He was busy preparing a successor to *Henry VIII: The Private Life of Don Juan*, as a vehicle for Douglas Fairbanks, Sr., in which Merle would play one of Don Juan's Spanish lights of love.

Merle was already part of the vivid circle that surrounded the elder Fairbanks and his son. Although past his prime as a great star, Doug, Sr., was still a name to conjure with in movie circles. He retained his powerful athletic figure and his clean-cut, handsome features. Although no longer the young, slim swordsman of such silent classics as *The Three Musketeers* and *Robin Hood*, he retained his grace, sparkle, and charm. His son, in those days not highly regarded as an actor, was one of the great male beauties of London. He had a bewitching wit and style, crinkly eyes and a flashing smile, and a love of pretty women, night life, and every kind of sport.

Father and son had gone further than any other stars in penetrating the inner circles of aristocracy and royalty. The Prince of Wales, his youngest brother the Duke of Kent, and the Duchess Marina adored the two Dougs, who had entrée to palaces, castles, and hunting lodges, where their unfailing good manners, expertise in athletics, and worldly wisdom were joyously received. Merle saw in them a direct passage to the top of society.

Prominent in the Fairbanks set were Lord and Lady Plunket and their adorable children. Terry and Dorothé Plunket were a wonderful pair: he was handsome, dashing, and a good sportsman; she, dark-haired and ravishingly pretty, rather like the actress Maureen O'Sullivan, was sweetness itself.

Merle's closest friend, almost a mother figure, was the attractive and fascinating Lady Morvyth Benson, married to the prominent London banker Constantine Benson. Doug, Jr., Merle, and a gang of bright young people used to junket down to Lady Benson's house, Shawford Park, between Winchester and Eastleigh, in Hampshire. Lady Benson's daughter, Lady Gillian Tomkins, recalls, "Merle was a family-minded person in the way she attached herself to us. She loved us as small children and followed us through, right up to our grown-up stages. She played an intimate part in all of our lives and we all adored her. I can remember going to a marvelous party in London when I was just out of childhood. Merle brushed my hair and made my face up and told me what clothes to wear just before I went. She was like a second mother to me in that sense. She was terribly romantic and in love with the idea of love."

In the giddy round of parties with the Dougs, the Plunkets, and the Bensons, Merle had a major setback on the verge of making *The Private Life of Don Juan*. She suffered, despite all her efforts, from a recurring skin problem that had plagued her in India, probably caused by her use of the highly toxic heavy makeup that was designed to whiten her face. It was a bitter irony that her perfect face began to break out severely in rashes, particularly around the mouth, where the problem became so obvious that at times she locked herself in her apartment and covered the mirrors. A doctor told her to concentrate on blood circulation. Lady Tomkins says, "I remember Merle telling me that you had to hang your head down to have your blood circulating and your skin glowing and it made your hair gleam. She was marvelous in following this kind of discipline and teaching it to a child."

Merle began to work on *The Private Life of Don Juan*. Her part as a Spanish beauty was not as prominent as she would have liked—it was a meaningless role which only allowed her a chance to show off her striking looks—but she threw herself into it with romantic passion and dedication. Most actresses would have played the part off the tops of their heads, since the film was not much more than a farcical story of adventure and love made for an uncritical audience, but she talked to Spaniards, went to see Spanish dancers, and even took Spanish lessons. The result was a convincing impersonation of Latin movements, speech patterns, and temperament that showed up the amateurishness of many of the rest of the cast. Of course, this was as she had intended.

Unfortunately, her efforts were ill-fated: the film failed to capture the vivid effectiveness of *Henry VIII*. It was embarrassingly obvious to critics and public alike that Doug was no longer capable of playing the youthful and virile Don Juan. The semicomic attempt to show an aging cavalier simply drew attention to his years and comparatively cramped movements. The picture went down the drain, seriously endangering Korda's always precarious relationship with his backers. But the devotion of his friend, the movie-struck Sir Connop Guthrie of the Prudential, saved him from disaster.

Korda began to scheme for Hollywood alliances. He was determined to enter into a partnership with the hard-driving Hollywood mogul Joe Schenck, who was on his way to London at the time. Korda decided that if he was going to hook Schenck, he had better encourage him by dangling before him the attractions of Merle Oberon. Deviously, cunningly, this charming Hungarian began plotting to throw Merle at Schenck's head.

Chapter Four

Joseph Schenck was not a handsome man. He was square, stocky, with heavy jowls and thinning hair, and he was running to fat. But he was a power in Hollywood; he was associated on the board of United Artists with Doug, Sr. Like Louis B. Mayer, he and his brother Nicholas, chairman of MGM, had come to the United States as penniless immigrants, rising rapidly from amusement park management to the fledgling film industry, where they rapidly made their mark. Joe Schenck was believed to have underworld connections that aided him in his rise to power and influence. In April 1933, this tough, aggressive man joined up with the impetuous, buck-toothed young Darryl F. Zanuck to form Twentieth-Century Pictures, releasing through United Artists. They reached an agreement by taking out Zanuck's Warner Brothers contract, cutting out the clauses they liked best, and pasting them up.

Beginning with the rough-and-tumble Wallace Beery vehicle *The Bowery*, and with George Arliss in the pompous *The House of Rothschild*, Schenck and Zanuck used tough, hard-selling methods to thrust the young company into an early and exciting success. Leaving the production activities to Zanuck, Schenck devoted himself to whipping up money from wealthy contacts to ensure a constant influx of money. He needed a new bride for social reasons: a bride who combined beauty with breeding and style and could help entertain the rich and powerful. His wife, the silent star Norma Talmadge, had had an affair six years earlier with the dashing Latin lover Gilbert Roland.

Now, in 1934, after a stormy few years, Schenck was finally losing Norma to a much less romantic figure: the comedian George Jessel; in April, Schenck heard that Norma and George had married, following a quickie divorce in March in Mexico.

61

In June Schenck sailed to England to find a British bride. English girls were supposed to bring distinction and "class" to the marriage bed. For men like Schenck, born in the gutter, men who made their way with their fists, an English rose would be the ultimate badge of distinction. He had his pick of women because of his great power, position, and financial resources. But he unhesitatingly used them as they used him, callously discarding them when he grew tired of them. When he was weary of young actresses, he would bar them from the lot so completely that they could not even collect their clothes from the dressing room. What he wanted now was a woman who could be his equal, not some extra or struggling bit-part actress, but someone of reputation and authority.

Schenck went to stay at Doug, Sr.'s, elegant town house in the West End of London. Merle's friendship with Fairbanks and son flowered platonically; she was a constant guest of Doug, Sr., and of his mistress, the former chorus girl Lady Sylvia Ashley. It was at one of the Fairbanks dinner parties in June that Schenck met Merle. He was instantly and electrically attracted, as Alex Korda had hoped. Merle's careful mask of good breeding, her over-elocuted voice, and her exquisite, scrupulously acquired taste in clothes effectively concealed her sensual, driving, and ambitious nature. Unaware of her racial and social origins, he saw her only as an upper-class British beauty.

Though reported as joyous and glamorous in the press, the Fairbanks dinner parties that summer, at which Merle met Joe again and again, were actually charged with tension. Lady Ashley was jealous of the fact that Doug was still unable emotionally to shake off his wife, Mary Pickford, and was secretly writing to Mary, begging her for a reconciliation, which Lady Ashley easily managed to determine. Moreover, Doug was locked in long conferences with Schenck on a problem from which the women were excluded: the Socialist muckraking author Upton Sinclair was running for governor of California. Schenck and Fairbanks were obsessed, infuriated, by the thought of Sinclair winning the election. They were convinced, with good cause, that Sinclair would cripple the industry by taxing it heavily, eliminating its corruptions, destroying its monopolistic strangleholds, increasing the power of the unions, and eliminating its brutal treatment of labor. While Lady Ashley and Merle sat visibly bored, Schenck and Fairbanks wrangled over the problem. They decided they must go back to the United States as soon as possible, fly to Mexico and Florida to see the local authorities, and arrange for the wholesale removal of the picture industry to one of these locations in the horrendous event that Sinclair should be elected.

Schenck began to take Merle out; but he was scarcely an exciting romantic companion. His worry over Sinclair brought on an ulcer: digestive attacks, sudden stabs of stomach pain, vomiting. Merle put up with everything, including Schenck's violent temper and rough manners, because Korda had told her to. Also, Schenck offered the allure of a Hollywood career, which she had dreamed of from the beginning, and which she apparently was convinced that Korda at this stage of his career could not satisfy. When Schenck dangled the promise of a major part in a very ambitious musical, *Folies Bergère*, which his partner Zanuck was about to produce with Maurice Chevalier, her eyes shone like jewels.

He gave her diamonds, furs—all the necessary gifts required in those days to ensure a woman's interest. She must have been in a state of extreme anxiety that he would come home to her simple flat and meet Charlotte, complete with sari; it is unlikely that she ever told Schenck about her mother. Instead, she somehow dissembled about her residence and spent nights at his hotel, the Savoy. The relationship ran along more or less satisfactorily until late July.

One evening Douglas Fairbanks, Jr., dropped in unexpectedly on one of his father's innumerable get-togethers for Sylvia Ashley, Joe, and Merle. Typically madcap, he suggested that the whole gang should hop on the next available plane and fly to the south of France for a quick vacation. What thoughts must have flashed through Merle's mind when she received the invitation! Her arrival at Marseilles, finding Ben Finney gone, the lonely journey to the Victorine Studios, the tiny part in *Three Passions*, the trip to London!

The four threw their clothes into suitcases and took off giddily for Cannes, Nice, and Monte Carlo, tooling along the Grande Corniche in a rented Citroën. For old times' sake, Merle insisted on spending a night at the Hôtel du Cap at Antibes. The local press was in a hubbub over the two pairs of famous lovers; Merle and Joe, Doug and Sylvia had great fun dodging behind palm trees or rushing up and down the companionways of millionaire yachts to avoid the endlessly snapping camera bulbs.

The dizzy quartet continued their journey on a surf of cocktails and laughter all the way to Monte Carlo. On August 4, 1934, Schenck threw an elaborate party at the Sports Club, with fireworks, a jazz combo, and the rich and glamorous of the Riviera in white ties and tails and stunning evening gowns, dancing on the balcony under the full moon. The waves lapped the shore; the palm trees stirred in a slight breeze. Merle, in a ravishing white Molyneux creation, swayed close to Schenck in a tango. Some of the guests ran headlong into the sea; it was a wildly extravagant occasion, typical of the period that also saw breadlines and Hoovervilles. At the height of the revels, Schenck called for the band to stop and cheerfully announced through the microphone that he and Merle were engaged. He presented her with an expensive diamond ring. She flung her arms around him, everyone laughed, and the band broke into a fox-trot.

The columnists had a field day with this glamorous event. The engagement of a Hollywood potentate and an up-and-coming exotic British star was something for the headlines. But there was really nothing in it. A few nights earlier, Doug, Jr., had suggested jokingly to Joe and Merle that since the world was talking about their romance they might as well announce their engagement. It would create a lot of attention for Merle and would be good for Schenck's reputation in macho circles. But why was Schenck not seriously interested in marrying Merle?

The reason was that he was now talking about her giving up her career, after the bauble of *Folies Bergère*, in order to devote her life to being a hostess for him. That was certainly not what Merle had in mind.

No sooner was the engagement announced than Schenck learned that Upton Sinclair was drawing ahead in the gubernatorial race in California. Schenck called up everybody to find out the quickest way to get to New York other than flying, which was uncommon in those days. He determined that an Italian ship was sailing from Villefranche three days later. He and Merle and Doug and Sylvia took off to Villefranche posthaste, and Schenck succeeded in buying out a couple of passengers by offering them three times the fare. While Merle, Doug, Sr., and Sylvia stood waving on the wharf, Schenck's ship drew out into the brilliant summer sea.

Merle had not done badly in the arrangement. She already had her contract to do *Folies Bergère*, and it was clear that her engagement, only three days long, would not commit her to a man of whom she was already growing tired. The fact that the papers were crammed with her and Schenck's pictures could only be of advantage to her, placing her more firmly in the hierarchy of the movie industry.

What was Schenck's motive in arranging this extravagant gesture of an engagement, then running out on his exquisite Oriental fiancée? The only possible interpretation is that not having found the ideal bride he wanted, he could now boast about a major conquest to his male friends in Hollywood and New York. In those days, movie executives were judged not merely on box office power, the capacity to select young unknowns and elevate them to stardom, to pick the right properties to entrance the bamboozled Depression masses, but on sexual conquests as well. In their brandy-and-cigars, white-starched-shirtfront world, in the atmosphere of ceaseless dirty talk and four-letter words and badinage, women were often tokens, to be chalked up on a scoreboard that would prove cocksmanship. Sexual performance was always compared over the brandy and cigars, and the fact that Schenck had succeeded in proving himself in bed with a sensual and desirable, much-slept-with exotic beauty would undoubtedly put him in the top category of lovers and ahead of his own brother, who was sedately married. He could keep Merle in suspense until he, the mighty Schenck, chose to return to make her his bride.

In those weeks on the Riviera, Merle snatched odd hours to read the Robert Sherwood script Korda had sent her for an important new film, *The Scarlet Pimpernel*, in which she was to play the tormented heroine Lady Blakeney, who is forced to act as a spy to protect her younger brother from the guillotine during the French Revolution. It was a sympathetic, cleverly written part which would use her narrow but convincing range as an actress to great advantage. She was very excited by the prospect of playing the part, and by the fact that the distinguished Oliver Messel would design her costumes, exquisite color sketches of which were awaiting her in London. Another great pleasure was that she would appear with Leslie Howard. He would play the Pimpernel, a daring British agent and master of disguise who led a double life as the foppish Sir Percy Blakeney.

Merle arrived in London at the beginning of September. She was rushed into a series of fittings with Messel, whom she instantly adored. Dazzlingly low-cut, one of them virtually exposing her flawless breasts, the costumes were fanciful, fairytale versions of Regency styles, infinitely flattering and captivating. Joe Schenck already half-forgotten, Merle met Howard, who was born in London of Hungarian parents, when he dropped by her dressing room; she was instantly attracted to him. He had scarcely noticed her before, except as a pretty girl in the commissary and on the set, but now he was riveted by her beauty.

In 1934, Leslie Howard was at his peak as a star. *Gone With the Wind*, a picture he despised, would in five years make him immortal, but already he was a power in the industry. His dreamy, pale, slightly equine face, romantically hollow cheeks and finely chiseled bones, delicately slender physique, absentminded, fastidious air, and habit of wearing turned-down hats that half-hid his face, belted raincoats that swallowed up his frail body, and umbrellas carried on the slightest provocation, gave him a look of a somewhat eccentric British poet.

His wry half-smile and his voice with its well-bred, carefully enunci-
ated diction and exquisite timing captivated everyone. He did not
exude powerful masculinity in the slightest degree, yet this seemingly
sexless creature of stage and screen was a stud in private beside whom
the screen's legendary lovers—Clark Gable, John Gilbert, and John
Barrymore—were mere Peter Pans. His list of conquests was legendary, and his performance in bed mythic. Women flung themselves at
him, not only because he was a matinee idol and movie star of surpassing fame but because they wanted to experience his rare capacity
between the sheets.

Howard was married to a fat homebody, Ruth, who was long-
suffering of his peccadilloes. His son Ronald and daughter Leslie
adored him and put up with everything because they knew that
Howard in the last analysis was the kind of man who would creep
home and put his head in his wife's lap like a child. Don Juan though
he was, he wanted everything: the comfort of a home to return to and
the consolation of a family. He was a difficult man: fussy, persnickety, easily bored, constantly fighting with his fiery fellow-pro-
ducer Gilbert Miller and with a Hollywood he hated. But he was an
actor of delicate refinement and skill, and appearing with him was a
mark of great distinction.

Merle's romantic affair with him began at once. Their attraction
was explosive. So intense was Merle's desire for him and his for her
that they could not always wait to go to a hotel to satisfy their lust.
One day they were making love in Leslie's elaborate star dressing
room when Ruth Howard walked in. She asked Leslie, not knowing
what else to say, "What are you doing?" He, very much engaged in
the task at hand, said, "Rehearsing!" She replied sharply, "Rehearsing
for what?" before turning on her heel and walking out of the room.

Shooting began on *Pimpernel* on September 7, 1934. The director, Rowland Brown, who had specialized in gangster pictures, had
been hired by Korda to direct the film but he was fired after three days
and replaced with the innocuous and obscure Harold Young. It was
obvious that Korda was really directing the picture. He was on the set
every day and night chewing away at a very expensive cigar, pouring
into the picture his patriotic feeling for England, his passion for
movies, his instinctive pictorial sense. It must have been painful for
him, in view of his growing love for Merle, to see the relationship with
Leslie Howard blossom before his eyes. But he had not yet exercised
his seigneurial rights over Merle and could scarcely afford himself the
luxury of being jealous.

Raymond Massey, one of the last surviving members of the cast, recalls that Leslie and Merle amused and intrigued the company by sitting behind a screen in the commissary while all the others sat out at tables. Hidden in this manner, the couple could hold hands in the blissful illusion—not long sustained—that not a soul knew of their romance. Ruth Howard stayed home, patiently enduring the gossip. But whereas she had shrugged off Leslie's other affairs, which had never seemed unduly serious, she couldn't shrug off this one. It became painfully clear to her that Leslie was in love with Merle, and that Merle was equally carried away.

The shooting was leisurely and relaxed in the British manner, with none of the pressures of Hollywood. Many scenes were shot in the countryside, and when the sun broke through and the correct shots had been achieved, Korda would cancel the rest of the day's work so that everyone could go swimming, picnicking, or playing golf or tennis. Often there were pleasant teas for the cast and crew, served with crumpets and cakes and cucumber sandwiches. Leslie was captivated by this casual schedule, telling reporters, as he told Merle, that Korda made a blissful contrast with Hollywood producers who thought only of time and money. He expressed his admiration to Korda in their native Hungarian. Merle was delighted; at night, she and Leslie and Alex watched the rushes together, making criticisms, and if there was a scene they didn't like, they could—luxury of luxuries—reshoot it the following day.

On weekends, Leslie took Merle to the polo stables at Hurlingham and Roehampton, where she fed lump sugar to the horses and talked cheerfully with his trainer. At night she would hear of Leslie's many conversations with leading figures of the government; even at that stage he was connected to British Intelligence and was discussing the threat of Nazi Germany with his peers.

As filming went on, *Pimpernel* became more and more patriotic. Korda, with Leslie's enthusiastic concurrence, even had Leslie recite John O' Gaunt's famous "This England" speech from Shakespeare's *Henry V*. The picture became a veiled comment on Nazi Germany, with the French Revolutionary rabble standing in for the Nazis. This was extremely valuable propaganda at a time when so many of the British aristocracy were leaning in Hitler's direction. Merle and Leslie shared not only an intense personal attraction but a deeply patriotic love of England as well.

Absence—and word of the affair with Howard—made Joe Schenck's heart grow fonder as he went from meeting to meeting raising funds and inciting enthusiasm to bring about an electoral victory in California. He even broke off his campaign in a surprising attempt to win Merle back and whisk her off into marriage as soon as *Pimpernel* stopped shooting. He sailed to England on the *Majestic*, arriving on October 18. When he got to Southampton four days later, Merle was not there to greet him; she was on set that day. Instead, Korda was there, saying that Merle was losing interest. Schenck drove headlong to London, checked into the Savoy, and called her, insisting that they be married at once. She refused to consider the idea; when reporters asked him about the possible break-off of the engagement he said, "There's still time. After all, we're both young." He was then fifty-four years old.

They met at the hotel on a Sunday. Schenck suggested they marry immediately, that she forget about *Folies Bergère* and give up her career. They would leave for Hollywood at once and she could help him in the campaign against Sinclair. So extreme was his vanity that he apparently actually thought Merle would accept this offer. But she turned to steel. She held him to his contract for *Folies Bergère*. She was forced to take off his superb diamond engagement ring with great reluctance, considering its fabulous nature, and hand it back to him.

Schenck was defeated but still practical. That same evening, he sold the ring at a profit to Douglas Fairbanks, who immediately put it on Lady Sylvia Ashley's finger. Schenck sailed back to Hollywood, to the consolation prize of seeing the hated Upton Sinclair defeated.

Chapter Five

Reluctantly, Korda gave Merle special leave to make *Folies Bergère* in Hollywood. Ironically, she was to play, under the direction of Roy del Ruth, a Eurasian society beauty, a straight part in a semimusical; the real pleasure of the opportunity was that she could co-star with the roguish Maurice Chevalier, whom she deeply admired. Just before she left, realizing she had lost Schenck for good, she resumed her affair with Leslie Howard. In order to make sure he would come to America, she encouraged him to accept, after much hesitation on his part, the leading role in *The Petrified Forest*, the script Robert Sherwood had brought to him on the set of *The Scarlet Pimpernel*. It was the story of a gangster, played by young Humphrey Bogart, who holds up an Arizona wayside café, in which Leslie would play an unhappy intellectual in love with a waitress-poet.

Merle set off for New York on the S.S. *Paris* in November 1934. On board, she saw a great deal of the beautiful French actress Lili Damita. Merle sat at the captain's table with Lili and the South African actor Louis Hayward. One night, a very handsome man appeared at a party and was introduced to Lili and Merle by Hayward. He had crashed in from second class; he was a struggling, obscure beginner named Errol Flynn.

According to British Intelligence sources, at a party in Mayfair Flynn had expressed a strong admiration for the new Nazi government of Germany. An actress, unnamed, but of great prominence, was, as sources revealed, asked to keep an eye on him on the ship. Could this have been Merle? A careful examination of the passenger list shows no other British actress of equal note was on board. Moreover, Korda and Leslie Howard were both, even at this early stage, involved in activities on behalf of Intelligence. Later, Merle was to work closely with Korda on matters connected with Intelligence—in travel arrangements. There is no proof, but it is interesting to speculate whether she was keeping an eye on Flynn. She may not even have understood the purpose of watching him. Shortly before her death, she was asked her opinion of him. She expressed total disgust at the mention of his name and said (inaccurately) that she had met him only once, in Mexico City, and considered him utterly despicable.

Merle traveled with a new secretary, Ruth Fraser. In New York, after giving a press conference on deck, and showing a shapely leg for cheesecake shots, Merle continued with Ruth to the Sherry-Netherland Hotel. There, they were joined by another young attractive woman who was to become Merle's lifelong friend: Tessa Michaels, the energetic, appealing, highly intelligent publicist for United Artists, whom Korda and Joe Schenck had delegated to take care of Merle during her American stay.

Tessa Michaels recalls:

> I'll never forget Merle and Ruth on that first night. They couldn't unglue themselves from the hotel window! The Manhattan skyline was more beautiful in those days than it is today. They were laughing with excitement, like two young kids, completely dazzled by the view. I realized immediately that Merle was totally innocent at heart, that she loved beauty wildly, passionately.
>
> We went shopping together. She *loved* to shop. She would go up and down Fifth Avenue, totally enthralled. She had a knack, an amazing knack with clothes. She wasn't rich in those days. She would buy an inexpensive dress and, with the addition of one single jewel, make it look expensive. She refused to buy costume jewelry; she was wildly extravagant, but with a purpose! And she would plunge her savings into anything that would enhance her looks. I remember she wore two small diamond brooches in rotation.
>
> She hated to get out of bed in the morning. She simply refused to be woken until she had completed her beauty sleep. And yet, I remember one time I was shocked at a sudden change in her. A call came through from somebody and of course I didn't wake her. When she found out, she flew into an absolute rage. She berated me! I couldn't believe it was the same person. It took me quite some time to simmer her down.

Who could the call have been from? Who could have telephoned, who was so important to her that she would tear at her new friend? It could only have been Leslie Howard, madly in love, who is known to have called her constantly from London. He was due to arrive in days, but much to her annoyance, she had to continue to Hollywood immediately.

On one of her last nights in New York, she ran into Ben Finney, the big game hunter who had given her the first chance with Rex Ingram. She saw him across the floor at Jack Rumsey's nightclub. In a characteristic gesture, she slipped behind him, stood on tiptoe, and put her hands around his eyes, whispering startlingly in his ear, "It's a long way from Calcutta, isn't it, you son of a bitch!" He spun around on his heel—it was Queenie! He was dismayed. It was clear she hadn't forgotten his disappearance from Antibes, to judge by her coolness; it was also clear that she had wanted to surprise him.

Merle and Ruth arrived in California by train on December 5, 1934. Doug, Sr., sent Merle a message saying she should come to visit him at a ranch and that he would send a private plane for her. But she was too exhausted to consider the suggestion. Indeed, she checked into the Beverly Hills Hotel and gave one or two magazine interviews, unenthusiastically spinning out her customary fantasies about Tasmania and India and the Monteiths. Darryl F. Zanuck, head of Twentieth-Century Pictures, barely spoke to her and ordered her into complicated makeup sessions. Since she was supposed to be a Eurasian beauty in the picture, the makeup people worked overtime to correct her own corrections of her looks. She wound up resembling a Chinese Christmas cracker in silver lamé, her face so gilded, her eyebrows so artificially arched, that all expression was submerged.

Again, she worked only on alternate days because there was a French version being shot at the same time, starring the international White Russian beauty, the Princess Natalie Paley. Chevalier was a difficult, almost impossibly irritating and moody man who grumbled incessantly to the director that he had to perform all of his scenes twice. Roy del Ruth, who had the build and manner of the average football player, pointed out that Chevalier should be pleased he "got to kiss two different dames for the price of one."

Del Ruth was furious with Merle because, in direct contradiction of her own nature, she refused to express the smoldering passion required by the script in her love scenes with Chevalier. The truth was, although attracted to most reasonably good-looking men, she found him totally unappealing sexually—and no doubt her thoughts were running constantly to Leslie Howard. Since she was not a natural actress, but rather a star who needed to imagine situations before she could act them, she pecked Chevalier gingerly when she was supposed to embrace him with abandon. Roy del Ruth screamed at her, "For God's sake, Merle! You're not a schoolmarm, you're a madly-in-love, tropical, Oriental sexpot! That's why we hired you! What do you think you're doing?"

Merle steeled herself and, clearly mindful of the fact that if she didn't obey this idiot, she might sink herself in Hollywood, went into an act so violent she almost knocked Chevalier out. After many takes, she finally managed to give a more or less convincing impersonation of unbridled lust. But the moment the scene was over, she retreated to her dressing room to nurse a headache.

Merle's nights were totally empty. Whereas in London she would be busy whirling around the night spots with the Plunkets, the Bensons, and the two Dougs, she was now left with nothing except the dubious comfort of the radio. Unlike the BBC, California radio provided nothing except endless music and reports on racing and football. She began to feel she had landed on the surface of the moon. And her misery was scarcely improved by reading that her counterpart in the picture, the Princess Natalie, was going out night after night with a succession of handsome dates to dance up a storm at the Trocadero, the "in" night spot of the day.

She rented an expensive, oversized house, hocking her salary to do so. But no one answered her invitations. Her loneliness became unendurable at Christmas. She wrote, many years later, "The girl whose personal popularity was supposed to be simply terrific found herself completely alone in a big house with nary an invitation nor a phone call to rouse her from her miserable loneliness."

Christmas was an Occasion in Hollywood. In those days, the studios closed down for the better part of a week and everybody who was anybody drove out to the Santa Anita racetrack, in high hat and gray topcoats and fashionable dresses, as though they were at Ascot or Longchamps. That Christmas, Maureen O'Sullivan gave a tea for the British colony headed by dear old Sir C. Aubrey Smith and Ronald Colman, and the other members of the British First XI cricket team and their wives. The famous director Woody ("One Take") Van Dyke gave an open house into which actor John Miljan released twenty stray dogs from a dogcart, and producer Anthony Hornblow, Jr., gave a big do for the Clark Gables, Mary Pickford (who was preparing to divorce Doug, Sr.), Gloria Swanson and her lover Herbert Marshall. Merle was invited to none of these events.

She let her maid go on Christmas Eve and she was alone on Christmas morning when the doorbell rang. She opened it; it was Maurice Chevalier, looking very depressed, on her doorstep. This humorless, miserable man, the opposite of his cheerful, insouciant screen image, had not been asked anywhere either. He was known not to be fun and was scarcely considered as more than the classic example of a party pooper. He told her, she reported later, "Merle, nobody has asked me to join them for Christmas. Everybody else is having a grand time . . . I am desolate." He added, unwittingly, "I came here because I know how popular you are and there will be a celebration at your house. May I stay?" Merle added, "There he was, repeating everything I had been thinking myself. I'm afraid my sense of humor didn't rescue me at that time, and I promptly broke down and wept. But we tried to make the best of it. We raided my deserted kitchen, dining on hamburger, salad, and canned fruit, all that the cook left in the ice chest. That dreary experience taught me never to envy celebrities at Christmas."

Chevalier makes clear in his memoirs that he and Merle seized on their mutual loneliness to become very good friends. But even given their proximity and isolation, it is unlikely that there was an affair. Merle was emphatic in her attitude to men: unless a man was romantic and exciting, she could not enter into a sexual relationship with him. And for all his fame, Chevalier simply wasn't her type.

Besides, her thoughts were still with Leslie, and he was restless for her as well when he arrived in New York for rehearsals of *The Petrified Forest*. Everyone who chronicled his activities at the time agrees that he was even more unreliable than usual. He was notorious for missing rehearsals and disappearing in mid-rehearsal, despite the fact that he was not only starring in plays but was also their co-producer along with Gilbert Miller. Obviously the thought of Merle was distracting this highly sexed man unbearably. He was nervous, irritable, sleepless, and the arrival of Ruth and his children scarcely improved his state of mind.

With amazing impulsiveness, no doubt more conscious of Merle than ever because it was New Year's Day, he skipped a rehearsal on January 1, 1935, and flew out through a blizzard—a highly hazardous procedure in those days—to Los Angeles to be with Merle. Gilbert Miller, his ill-tempered partner, exploded in rage when he heard that Leslie had left town only days before the play was due to open. Dodging reporters at the Los Angeles Airport, Howard made his way to Merle as she finished work on *Folies Bergère*. So intense was his sexual obsession with Merle that he went all that way for a single night with her—one can imagine what an explosive night that was!— and flew back the next morning, another day-long ordeal through violent turbulence, barely arriving in time for the dress rehearsal.

The play opened on a wing and a prayer. Stimulated by his whirlwind, utterly romantic journey to the Coast, Howard gave a performance that electrified New York. As the tragic, doomed intellectual, opposed by Humphrey Bogart's snarling gangster, Howard projected such nervous intensity that he brought the fashionable first-night crowd to its feet. Brooks Atkinson and the other critics were almost uniform in their praise. Yet Howard kept picking away at his own performance, trying to improve it nightly despite its near perfection. Merle had to go through the paces of her far less prestigious effort, painfully aware of the different level of her own career.

As romantic as Howard, Merle did not wait one hour after the final shot of *Folies Bergère* at the beginning of February. Although mortally afraid of flying, which she had never experienced, she undertook a miserably bumpy and protracted journey to New York the night she finished in order to be with Leslie. She checked into a hotel; Howard went through an elaborate pretense of checking in there as well, although he was already in an apartment with his wife and family. Living at two addresses proved to be quite a strain. Moreover, Howard was torn between Merle and the constant presence of his children. Tessa Michaels remembers that Ruth Howard used the clever device of sending her teenage son Ronald over to the hotel at every possible opportunity to remind Howard of his obligation and responsibilities. Ronald remembers that his father took him to meet Merle at the hotel where, with surprising boldness and commitment, Howard introduced Merle to the boy as his future stepmother.

No doubt Ronald conveyed this to Ruth, because she suddenly lost her usual composure and in a totally uncharacteristic gesture decided she had had enough; she flew to California with her children to see if she could obtain a quick divorce. Apparently, she lacked any knowledge of American laws: California had difficult and slow-moving arrangements for divorce; Reno, Nevada, would have allowed her a far better and quicker arrangement. She talked to a number of friends in Hollywood; the result was that she began to cool down and decided to return to New York to fight for Leslie after all.

Meanwhile, Howard was so severely strained, not only by the difficulty of the performance but by the sudden departure of his wife (he dreaded losing the comfort and security of a bourgeois marriage), that he became ill with a mysterious fever that kept him in bed for several days. On February 6, he broke out in a severe and agonizing attack of boils, which covered his body from head to foot, even his nose. With amazing resolution, he managed to drag himself to the theater for all performances; he did not realize he was risking his life since a boil on the nose, comical though it might sound, is in fact extremely dangerous, because there is a nasal vein that leads directly to the brain. Had the infection spread, he would have died instantly. He was in despair at his Job-like illness; there were no proper antibiotics in those days, and the boils had to be lanced painfully one by one. But they kept breaking out again, so delicately balanced was his constitution, so emotionally overwrought was he over Merle.

She attended a premiere performance of *The Scarlet Pimpernel* without him on February 8, followed the next day by an elaborate afternoon tea given by the British consul. Leslie was too ill to attend either occasion. She also went unescorted to the premiere of *Folies Bergère*, which had been rushed out with amazing speed within three weeks of its completion.

Leslie Howard's severe physical condition totally destroyed Merle's affair with him. He rejected her sensitive care and concern because he needed his wife in his extremity. Moreover, Merle could not constantly be seen with him in his suite; gossip columnists were known to bribe maids to obtain information, and even a hint of adultery in those days could jeopardize a career, so ferocious were the women's clubs and other puritanical custodians of moral standards. When Ruth Howard returned to New York, it was obvious to Merle that Leslie was rejecting her. All hope of his obtaining a divorce when he recovered had vanished with the wind.

It was painful for Merle to realize that the man she loved with all her heart didn't need her except on a most superficial level and that he was far more deeply married than she had known. Salt was rubbed in her wounds when a reporter from *The New York Times* cornered Howard as he painfully made his way to a matinee performance. The reporter had gotten wind of the situation and asked him if divorce was in the air. He snapped, "Certainly not. No man would throw away the sort of family I enjoy. My wife and children are essential to my existence!" These were cruel words for Merle to read back in California.

In those days, Alexander Korda, always anxious to exploit his stable of stars, had concluded a deal with the ruthless, semiliterate Samuel Goldwyn to share Merle's contract for a sum of money far beyond her earnings. Goldwyn had admired her not only in *The Scarlet Pimpernel*, but also in *The Battle*. He invited her to a dinner party at his house on her birthday, February 19.

She was naturally impressed by Goldwyn's presence: his tall, thin figure was a fine contrast to the tiny Louis B. Mayer, his former partner, and to many other diminutive Hollywood executives she had met. His face, seemingly made of concrete, exuded a brutal power. His stream of talk, laced with his famous malapropisms, combined a crude humor with a vicious streak that had helped him secure his place on the Hollywood heap. Ironically, this hard-bitten man was under the thumb of his beautiful wife, Frances. It was she, if truth be told, who set the tone of Goldwyn films: technically perfect and glamorous, glossy, romantic, superficial, and drenched in the molasses of Hollywood music. His movies were for the most part exercises in tearful, restrained sentimentality, genteel and civilized to a fault but bloodless and sexless. Goldwyn pictures exuded a kind of pious good cheer; they dealt with tragedy with a velvet touch.

Like most European expatriate Hollywood executives, Sam Goldwyn had a respect for the British and a desire to buy the intellectual respectability the British carried with them. Merle, already dignified by her Korda vehicles, would be an ideal addition to his stable of up-and-coming stars. He watched her closely at dinner, observing her exquisite hair, makeup, and clothing, listening to the diction she had learned from Margaret Yarde. She was everything he wanted in a star. He never once suspected the truth of her origins.

Goldwyn asked her if she had ever heard of the silent film *Dark Angel*, starring Ronald Colman and the Hungarian actress Vilma Banky. She almost jumped from her seat. *Dark Angel*, she said truthfully, was her favorite movie as a child. As she spoke at the elegant mahogany table to the brilliant circle of Goldwyn's friends, she must have been carried back to Calcutta, to a sleazy, flea-bitten theater in the stifling summer heat, with moldering plush and men's hands straying on her legs. She snapped herself together as Goldwyn said, "Would you like to appear in my new version?"

She could hardly believe her ears. Here she was, after only three months in Hollywood, being offered a chance to play the Vilma Banky role in the one movie that more than any other had stimulated her to embark on her career! She told Goldwyn she was overcome, thrilled beyond words, by the suggestion.

Merle was in a buoyant mood. After the misery of losing Leslie Howard, she was young, free, and happy again.

She bought a beach house at Santa Monica to celebrate: it had a white clapboard front and a conical roof in bastard Cape Cod style. It stood up against the crumbling giant sand dunes and shabby palms, looking out across the Pacific toward the Orient. Merle's neighbors were Irving Thalberg, the gifted head of MGM, and his sensitive, genteel, sweet-natured Canadian wife, Norma Shearer. The two women struck up an immediate friendship. Merle was fond of the Thalbergs' son Irving, Jr., and she once again felt a poignant sense of not being able to give birth to a child. She loved skipping rope and playing hopscotch with Irving, Jr. She caught yellowtail and sent them to the boy; delighted, he decided to pay her back.

He instructed his chauffeur to drive him to the fish market at Ocean Park, where he settled upon an alarming and enormous sea creature with a repulsive smell. At home, he packed the beast in a shoe box and dressed it with sweet peas. He wrote a message, *From me to you*, and gave Merle the shoebox with an air of great ceremony at her front door. Touched, she opened it and had to give the performance of a lifetime to pretend not to be overcome by the stench. Late that night, Norma crept to her house and the two women secretly buried the monster in the sand.

That season Merle met a young man named David Nevins—David Niven—whom she had run into at parties in London. Publicity people had created an utterly fantastical version of his early life. Although he was the son of an obscure army lieutenant killed in the Dardanelles in World War I, he was supposed to be the son of an imaginary General William Graham Niven, and an equally imaginary Lady Comyn-Platt. He was alleged to have had twenty different jobs all over the world which had landed him in Hollywood flat broke although cheerfully possessed of a titled background, a fake background that gave him entrée into the top social circles of Hollywood. His perfect British accent, suntan, clean-cut good looks, quizzical smile, crinkly eyes, and flashing laugh made him extremely popular in a Britain-mad Hollywood world.

He was the ideal escort for wealthy and prominent women. He was not a man of any depth or serious intellect; people felt comfortable with him. He didn't question values or analyze them; he skated along the surface of life with few anxieties and a giddy, superficial but undeniable charm. He was a very good dancer and a witty teller of tall tales and "inside" anecdotes, many of them extremely risqué. A fine athlete, he could match anyone at tennis and beach ball. He was at his happiest when deeply tanned and stripped down to trunks on a beach, running in and out of the surf. In short, he was exactly what Merle wanted—the opposite of the unathletic, sensitive, neurotic, and introspective Leslie Howard, who suddenly seemed pallid and weak alongside this happy, uncomplicated, and virile young man.

Their affair began swiftly, without regret or tension. They were both in their twenties, they hadn't a worry in the world, and they were glamorous. The only difference between them was that David was penniless and Merle was already earning thousands a week. Yet although many people think Merle was the one who drew David into social circles, the opposite was true: he had been part of the social set for many months, even though his only jobs had been as an extra or walk-on.

Freed from strain, Merle discovered a side of herself she had never known with Leslie. David taught her riding, surfing, clear-water and deep-sea fishing. Because of his ingratiating personality, he was a frequent guest on yachts whose owners liked to catch marlin or shark; often he and Merle took off in yachting parties around the Catalina Isthmus or sailed south to Ensenada for a weekend of laughter, fun, and lovemaking.

This was the life Merle wanted most: an outdoor life of walking, often along the beach, looking at sunsets and sunrises, listening to the surf at night as she lay in David's arms. She often told friends she helped him overcome a problem he had caused: in the course of his many extravagant boasts, he had claimed to Darryl Zanuck that he was a polo player, a sure mark of social distinction. Unfortunately, Zanuck was a whiz at polo and according to Merle called his bluff by asking him to join a polo team. Niven rashly plunged in, but he proved to be a hopeless failure with a chukka, helping Zanuck to lose the match. Zanuck started talking about blacklisting David. Merle suggested that David go to a Turkish bath at a tennis club frequented by Zanuck and Goldwyn; Goldwyn got into conversation with him and, much to Zanuck's annoyance, offered him a test. Merle, on hearing that David was going into the test, worked with him very closely on it and even talked Goldwyn into giving David the best director and cameraman available.

David was signed. Although his acting ability was limited, as Merle's was, he shared with her a quality that the camera loved: on screen he sparkled with delightful good humor and charisma.

While David began work for Goldwyn, Merle started *Dark Angel* the spring of 1935. She was so excited at playing the part of Kitty, the eager young English girl involved with two men in World War I, that she overlooked the fact that the picture completely failed to capture the look or feel of England, where it was set, and that her co-star Fredric March neglected even to attempt a British accent. The picture was false, artificial, airless, set in a never-never land of White House-sized mansions, bright un-English sunlight, and elaborate breakfasts accompanied by noble self-sacrificing conversations under chandeliers. The characters were of the sort to gladden the heart of film censor Will Hays, a persnickety bluenose of the old school who liked films to be clean, wholesome, and worthy of inclusion in a history of the saints. The movie was pure Goldwyn: everyone in it was noble, distinguished, and utterly lifeless.

Only Merle was able to rise above the script. Whereas today Fredric March and the other leading actor, Herbert Marshall, seem tired and dull, she acted with a fierce ambition and an intensity that went beyond the demands of her role. Her opening scene, in which she is discovered in bed, stretches, awakens, her face gleaming with excitement, and runs headlong down an immense staircase into a breakfast room, is star performing at its best. She conveys a freshness, good health, and innocent eagerness that are touching and natural. Only her excessively precise diction takes away from the conviction of her acting, sometimes giving it an unwonted artificiality.

Merle liked the sentimental director Sidney Franklin, who lay stretched on his couch like Elizabeth Barrett Browning through most of the shooting, suffering from some imaginary ailment and directing the limp goings-on with a languid hand. But she was most fascinated by the cameraman, the lean, quick, brilliant Gregg Toland, later to become world famous for Orson Welles's *Citizen Kane*. Toland, she realized, was her savior: he photographed her with a special technique that involved pouring the whitest and most blazing arc lights directly into her face. The result of this treatment was to make her look almost transparently fair. Not only did Toland remove any hint of her Indian skin texture, but he also brought out her delicate bone structure and the vivid sharpness and directness of her eyes.

For picture after picture, Toland would be her master, her right-hand man. He was as essential to her as William Daniels at MGM was essential to Garbo. Between cameraman and star there existed a relationship as intimate as that of husband and wife. A cameraman had to understand every nuance of a face and figure, the best angles and worst, the way in which a slight flaw (as in Merle's left eye) could be overcome. It says much that though she was a beginner, she instinctively knew this. Unlike Marlene Dietrich, she did not try to control the lighting, but she certainly took immense interest in it and trusted Toland to execute it to her best advantage.

Merle established the beginning of a long relationship with another pillar of Goldwyn's closed community: a big, husky, genial all-American who rejoiced in the stage name Omar Kiam.

He was a costume designer of great taste and skill who preferred timeless fashions that would not seem excessively dated in years to come. Unlike Adrian, his counterpart at MGM, he did not believe in fanciful and extravagant costumes. He designed in simple, clean lines. Merle learned much from him.

Goldwyn acted with unheard-of consideration in the film. He

knew that Merle had a skin problem and that she was highly sensitive to toxic elements in makeup. He permitted her to use a special makeup without those chemicals to which she was allergic. She adored him for that; again, Frances Goldwyn was probably an influence in her favor.

The shooting offered an unexpected pleasure. She had always admired Gary Cooper on the screen. He was making a film called *The Wedding Night* under the direction of King Vidor on another sound stage and Merle, Cooper's co-star Anna Sten recalls, used to visit the set every day in breaks from work to gaze fascinatedly at Coop. From him she learned that screen acting has nothing to do with theatrical acting in the usual sense, but that it is simply an expression of feeling in repose, reaching out of a powerful personality in a love affair with the camera. Knowing that she had limited ability, and a face the camera loved, she learned to act in stillness; she became fascinating because she did not force herself to be so.

The summer heat in July of 1935 was insufferable even to someone who had grown up in the streets of Calcutta. Hollywood heat was not humid or sweltering like that of Calcutta, it was harsh, dry, consuming, like the inside of a furnace. It rendered breathing difficult even in those happy, smogless days. The sound stages at the Goldwyn studios were totally airless. Every door had to be closed to cut out the sound of passing cars or planes that would upset a scene. Air conditioning was unheard of at the time. Fans played between the scenes, and there were frequent rushes to the water coolers, but the strain was constant and harrowing.

On July 6, Merle broke down completely and fainted, sobbing as she recovered; she was taken to a hospital in an ambulance. Doctors examined her. It was evident that her early weakness from the stomach trouble and the heart murmur were acting up. Goldwyn was again the most considerate of producers. Unlike Jack Warner, who treated actors like cattle, he treated his players like thoroughbreds, appreciating that they required the most delicate and sensitive care. He gave Merle several days off and closed the picture. But after only three days more of work, she was ill once again.

Her youth helped her to recover swiftly. She was amused when Korda, bubbling over with his usual roster of ideas for her, telegraphed her to report to work in London for two different roles at the same time. One was Roxane in a version of *Cyrano de Bergerac* with Charles Laughton, and the other the long-hoped-for part of Anne in the full-scale *Anne Boleyn* she had scripted herself. To celebrate, she went off dancing at the Trocadero one night with David. A woman at the door asked for her autograph, along with his as "Mr. Oberon."

His reaction, perhaps fortunately, has not been recorded. Joe Schenck was there, and he and Merle greeted each other warmly; so were Marlene Dietrich and her romantic interest, the director Josef von Sternberg, and the Robert Youngs; they sat in the banquettes under the chandeliers or danced before the great glass windows that over-looked the glittering pinboard of Los Angeles.

Once the arduous shooting of *Dark Angel* was over, Merle really broke loose in Hollywood for the first time. (She was nominated for an Oscar the next year.) The word was out that her performance in *Dark Angel* was sensational and she was invited everywhere. She at-tended a party at the Gene Markeys at which the guests were given fake passports with acid, highly personal accounts of their private lives and statistics (usually unflattering) printed in the front—down to the statistics of their most intimate parts; they were lured to a sofa one by one and talked to a fortune-teller. At the end of the party it was revealed that their most private conversations with the seer had been recorded by a well-known columnist who was hidden under-neath. . . .

Merle had the pleasure of attending the very successful first pre-view of *Dark Angel*. Ida Lupino invited her to a birthday party for Ida's famous mother, Connie Emerald; among the guests were Irving Thalberg and her beloved Norma Shearer.

She splurged on a magnificent dinner party for Alexander Korda at the popular Café La Maze; it made all the columns. Korda, who had with him Sir Connop Guthrie and his business manager, Steven Pal-los, was with typical perversity visiting Hollywood after insisting that she come to him in London.

On the train to New York, Merle received many telegrams of congratulations following the successful opening of *Dark Angel*. Alex Korda, Goldwyn, Jock Whitney, Sid Grauman, Harry Cohn, Eddie Goulding, Basil and Ouida Rathbone all showered her with congrat-ulations, emphasizing the fact that she had overcome the "exotic" category.

The reviews of *Dark Angel* were ecstatic. The *Hollywood Reporter* said, "Audiences will see a new, gloriously vibrant Merle Oberon, whose sensitive performance places her high in the cinema roster." When she arrived at the premiere in New York on September 5, more industry leaders praised her and a huge crowd mobbed her, knocking the policemen's caps off. It was obvious that she had "arrived" in the United States.

Merle sailed for London on the *Berengaria* on September 7. When she landed, she found to her surprise and shock—though she should not have been surprised—that Korda's projects for her were mere hot air, devised to keep the ever-dazzled Sir Connop Guthrie excited and ready with more money. Without warning, Korda wired her from Hollywood that she would no longer play Roxane in *Cyrano de Bergerac* but that Penelope Dudley Ward would play the part instead. As for *Anne Boleyn*, this was so utterly a figment of Korda's imagination that when she went for fittings with the costume designer René Hubert, he literally knew nothing about it.

Furious, Merle was stuck in London without a job. Fortunately, Goldwyn called her and advised her that he wanted her to star immediately in a cleaned-up version of Lillian Hellman's new stage hit, *The Children's Hour*, about a vicious child who exposes two women in a lesbian relationship. She accepted at once after Goldwyn assured her that the story would be changed to conform with the restrictions of censorship.

Perhaps to compensate Merle for her disappointment over *Cyrano* and *Anne Boleyn*, Korda flew to London and threw a lavish reception for her at the Savoy Hotel. A week later, Jesse L. Lasky of Paramount gave an even more elaborate party for her at the Dorchester; she came with Doug, Sr., and Lady Ashley, the Plunkets, Dorothé Plunket's mother, the legendary actress Fanny Ward, and the tenor Richard Tauber, who was engaged to her old, close friend Diana Napier. Her happiness would have been complete had David not been absent; he was trudging through the tedium of making *Rose Marie*, a Nelson Eddy–Jeanette MacDonald boomer-and-screamer, on a sound stage at MGM.

Merle was a guest of Cecil Beaton at his beautiful house in Wiltshire that October; she was seen frequently with the well-known movie executive John Sutro, but there was no question of a romance. Merle returned to New York on the *Berengaria* with her Airedale pup Snootie and spent much of the voyage talking to the dear, grizzled, avuncular Sir C. Aubrey Smith, who had naturally been seeing the cricket at Lords. While she was watching the waves in a giant storm, the window of her boat deck suite crashed on her head, leaving a large gash. She had to see the press in bandages.

David flew from the coast to greet her and they returned by train. Back in Hollywood, she rushed straight into costume fittings with Omar Kiam for *These Three*, the new title for *The Children's Hour*. Her reunion with David was joyous; he told her hilarious stories of the clashes between Nelson Eddy and Jeanette MacDonald off the set once they had concluded their moonlight-and-roses duets. She felt a good deal of anguish over the struggle of Douglas Fairbanks, Sr., torn between Lady Sylvia Ashley and Mary Pickford, to whom he flew in a desperate last-minute attempt at a reconciliation; Merle was again caught between two fires. She adored Mary and had gotten to know her more intimately over the past year; but of course, she owed everything in the world to Doug, Sr. It was painful for her to have Mary crying constantly, heartbroken at Doug's desertion of her; at the same time, Merle sympathized deeply with Sylvia, who was an old friend. It was typical of her that she would suffer as acutely for these friends and their differences and attempts to be happy as though they were her own family.

She started *These Three* on November 21 in a divided mood: thrilled at being with David again, and distraught over the Fairbankses. Perhaps this emotional turbulence aided her portrayal of the unhappy schoolteacher whose life and career are threatened by a monstrous child. For the first time, she was acting under a great director. William Wyler was among the few artists capable of overcoming the false, sickly sentimentality of Goldwyn and his team. So great was his power in Hollywood that he could refuse Goldwyn any degree of influence, and he managed to bring a sense of realism, an approximation of the harshness of life, to the drama in hand. In private—Merle had met him at Goldwyn's dinner parties—Wyler was a gentle, pixieish, almost whimsical little man, with attractive jug ears, mischievous flashing eyes, and a wiry body. This charmer was a different animal entirely on set. A perfectionist, fanatical over detail, he was a brutal martinet, who had a sharp-witted sense of the temperamental folly of famous stars. He believed that if a star was hired it was his or her business to know what to do; he refused to discuss or explain the part. His policy was to drag the players through endless takes in order to force them to be subdued, to remove their tendency to act theatrically. He knew that an atmosphere of extreme emotion would be all the more powerful if conveyed through underplaying, through a skillful suppression of overt feeling. Casting was two-thirds of the battle; once a player fit a part, the player would, Wyler knew, instinctively understand the mind and feelings of the character being played.

But this method was hard on actors, who, almost uniformly vain, self-centered, and deeply insecure, wanted endless reassurance for their fragile, hungry egos. Merle was no exception. Uncertain of her own talent, vulnerable and hypersensitive as always, she missed the soft personality of the much-inferior Sidney Franklin or the adoring attentions of her beloved Alex. Moreover, she had to put up with the intolerable behavior of that overwrought Southern belle Miriam

Hopkins, who stormed and ranted and raged with irritating frequency. Hopkins was known as a holy terror in pictures; her vulgar, unrestrained temper and her sheer lack of sportsmanship drove everyone mad. Only Joel McCrea, solid and phlegmatic, a former football player, managed to survive the director's manhandling with a degree of good cheer. Merle assured the child actress Marcia Mae Jones and gave her great encouragement.

At Christmas, exhausted by the work, Merle was relieved by the traditional holiday break. The Christmas of 1935 was a far cry from her miserable, lonely experience with Chevalier a year earlier. On the holiday afternoon, Merle, though pale and weak, pulled herself together to join the merry throng at the home of the brittle, witty star Clifton Webb and his famous mother Maybelle, for a party in honor of Lady Elsie Mendl. Gloria Swanson and Herbert Marshall, Marlene, John Gilbert, Kay Francis, Cole Porter, and the Ronald Colmans joined Merle and David for wassail and cakes around the Christmas tree, and Porter played the piano and sang. He became a great friend of Merle's from that day on, and she gave him a favorite dog, a pedigree schipperke named Pépin le Bref, for his birthday.

There was another break in shooting on New Year's Eve for a party at the Goldwyns', with Marlene, Cole Porter, Gary and Rocky Cooper, Lew Ayres and his wife Ginger Rogers, Dolores del Rio and her husband, the art director Cedric Gibbons. Merle and David danced with the others until dawn. Joe Schenck was there, but there was no acrimony between them; their friendship continued until the end of his life.

There was party after party in the new year. Nineteen thirty-six was the height of Hollywood glamour and even during so important and taxing a picture as *These Three* Merle could not resist the allure of these events. She would never forget a do at Jock Whitney's at which all the guests came as their favorite nervous breakdown and Carole Lombard, another good friend of Merle's, was wheeled in from an ambulance on a mobile stretcher with her head in bandages. Elsa Maxwell, the dumpy hostess who looked rather like Charles Laughton in drag, gave an elaborate costume party in which the guests changed into paper period costumes behind screens. During the course of the evening, Merle got into a close, eyeball-to-eyeball conversation with Leslie Howard. The carefree David Niven could not have cared less, but several other people started to whisper behind their paper fans. An unnamed actress began drinking up a storm and Elsa ordered the butler to take her a Mickey Finn in a champagne glass. As the silver tray went by Leslie, he grabbed the glass and drank the champagne. He passed out at Merle's feet. He was carried up to the master bedroom where he lay among piles of furs; the actress, who had now been given the same treatment, was stretched out on a bed beside him.

One evening Merle was invited to dinner at the home of her agent, Myron Selznick. To her surprise, the other guests had no escorts: they were Loretta Young and Carole Lombard. Myron had become so tired of their individual complaints to him that he had decided to invite all three so that he could listen to their grumbles at the same time. In the middle of dinner, Merle said suddenly, "Myron, you're not listening to what I'm saying!" He replied, "Merle, I'm so hard thinking about going to bed with you that I can't concentrate." So she said, "Well then, let's go upstairs now so you can get it off your mind!" Of course, she didn't mean it; everyone dissolved in laughter and the party went on.

There were darker moments during the shooting of *These Three*. Mary was devastated by the marriage of Doug, Sr., to Lady Sylvia in January, and Merle stayed up late nights comforting her. Following the death of King George V in London, Merle, so deeply devoted to royalty, went into mourning for a day; the picture had to close down. The death brought her more firmly center stage in the British expatriate community than ever. Her great friends the Plunkets were in town and she and David joined them in the obsequies at the homes of the Ronald Colmans and the Nigel Bruces.

Despite all her misgivings and complaints and attacks of crying, Merle was overjoyed when she finally saw *These Three*. By digging deep into her mind and emotions, Wyler had gone far beyond Korda or Sidney Franklin in discovering her resources as an actress. He made her abandon her clipped Margaret Yarde diction and opt instead for a subdued and convincing mid-Atlantic accent. He was brutal only in order to be kind. He stopped her high-falutin' quasi-Mayfair posing and made her act with an unusual tenderness, delicacy, and warmth. This inflamed his wife, the mercurial, unreliable, maddening Margaret Sullavan, who conceived an absurd and meaningless jealousy of Merle during the last weeks of shooting in January 1936. Totally wrapped up in David, Merle had no sexual interest in Wyler whatsoever and was exasperated when Sullavan, who herself was by no means faithful, perversely kept appearing on the set and staring directly at Merle from behind the camera. Merle said that it was impossible to work because she kept catching Sullavan in her eye lines. As a result, Wyler closed the set. Merle never worked on an open set again if she could help it. Sullavan's irrational jealousy precipitated the collapse of her marriage to Wyler while Merle and David laughed it all off.

David was still being attacked as clinging to Merle's skirts in an effort to further his career; people forgot that it was he who had helped her into Hollywood society in the first place. She was called in more than one column "that lovely couple, Merle Oberon" and he was—again—called "Mr. Oberon." Neither Merle nor David was worried about it. They were secure in their life of the beach, the sea, fishing, sailing, and enjoying quiet evenings together. They shrugged off the tensions of the day. They were like young kids together, and the future looked romantically golden to the essentially simple, ambitious couple.

Chapter Six

Merle was in seventh heaven when the reviews of *These Three* came out. Even so severe a critic as Graham Greene was impressed, calling her acting "admirable"; Lillian Hellman liked her, and it was generally agreed that Wyler had done wonders with her, enabling her to match up to the fearsome competition of Miriam Hopkins.

But the triumph was accompanied by a disappointment. Merle had, for some weeks, spent every spare minute reading books on the life of Florence Nightingale. David O. Selznick had, under pressure from Myron, set the story up as a film vehicle for her; Korda, with his mania for the biographies of the famous, was extremely enthusiastic. Merle decided from the outset that this must not be a saintly, supersweet portrayal; that she would bring out the toughness, resilience, and sharpness of the great nurse. But no sooner had she committed herself emotionally to acting the part than Jack Warner, getting wind of the project, announced without warning that he would make a version of Nightingale's life with Kay Francis. After much argument, Selznick was forced to tell Merle that he had given up the idea. She received another blow when Korda, without telling her, literally sold her to Selznick for a single-picture deal in order to get in exchange the actress Dolores Costello for a British film.

At that moment, a shocking thing happened. Merle had a visitor, someone she knew slightly in England: a cheap crook and chiseler who had attached himself to one of her girl friends. With her usual kindness, she agreed to see him, and he told her that unless she paid him a very large sum of money he would reveal to the press that she was of Indian origin and her career would automatically be ruined.

She showed typical presence of mind. Instead of panicking, she asked him how he knew. He told her that he was friendly with her father's family, the Thompsons, in Darlington. They had told him the truth and he had possession of birth and marriage certificates to prove it.

Merle asked for time to think the matter over. Reluctantly her visitor granted it. Merle went to see Goldwyn. She showed extraordinary intelligence in doing so, since she might otherwise have been paying the man for the rest of her life. Goldwyn paid a fortune to get rid of the man. It would not do to have it get out that he had an "Indian" star.

Merle faced yet another setback. David O. Selznick announced she would do a version of *Dark Victory*, a stage play about a woman stricken with blindness as a result of a brain disease, the film to be shot in Technicolor, then, with typical capriciousness, sold it to Warners. Suddenly, he bought Robert Hichens' novel *The Garden of Allah*, the story of a Trappist monk who abandons his faith in order to take up with a world-weary tourist in North Africa. At first, Merle was excited: *The Garden of Allah* had originally been made by Rex Ingram; how her mind must have flown back, when Myron told her of the project, to those far-off days in India, when she first saw the picture, and to Nice and the Victorine Studios! But when she was given the script, disillusionment quickly set in. It was very disappointing: old-fashioned, foolish, filled with endless moonings about God, the human heart, and eternity. The role called for her to stare endlessly into the desert, musing about her tormented affair with a former celibate. And then came a real insult: conscious of her skin problems, David Selznick asked her to test. This was unheard of for an actress of her stature. But he was worried that she might not look good in color, and he had several anxious conferences about her with the all-powerful Technicolor tycoon Natalie Kalmus and her obligatory cameraman, W. Howard Greene.

Merle was to appear with Ramon Novarro, but at the last minute Selznick replaced him with Gilbert Roland. With the intolerable burning lights required by Technicolor searing her, she sat in the set of a large desert tent with Roland, speaking lines of surpassing absurdity to which she was unable to give any credence. Possibly the only approach was that adopted by Marlene Dietrich, who later played the part with a flat, monotonous, exhausted tone. Merle, clipped and precise, could only be embarrassing. Selznick threw up his hands in despair and instead of letting Merle down lightly, he sent her a cruel letter stating that he didn't think her box-office allure was strong enough to justify her playing in the picture and that Marlene would be taking over at once.

Merle's careful surface of genteel good humor cracked and she flew into a rage, charging Selznick with gross malfeasance. To the great consternation of Myron, she sued Selznick for over $150,000 for a broken contract and hurt feelings, and she hired the fashionable attorney Lloyd Rucker to handle the case for her. Selznick refused to settle and depositions were drawn up.

Merle was scarcely cheered by David Niven's announcement in March that he would be leaving at once for a long and arduous shoot on *The Charge of the Light Brigade*, an Errol Flynn vehicle that fancifully distorted the facts of that famous debacle during the Crimean War. The locations, at Chatsworth and in the high wind-swept peaks of the Sierras, were almost impossible for a woman and David warned her not to go there. Merle defied all rules and in her usual romantic headlong mood drove three times to Chatsworth to be with him. Goldwyn, however, flatly refused to allow her to go to the Sierras. Almost on the first day of David's shooting in the Sierras, she heard on the radio that the mountain inn where cast and crew were staying had been burned down. She frantically tried to get a call through but it was very late at night before she was able to reach David, who assured her he was safe.

She was lonely and fretful through the eleven weeks of shooting of *The Charge*. Preparing the suit against Selznick, with no work immediately in view, was boring. Warren Reeve, reporter for *Photoplay*, arrived at her beach house in early April, finding her wearing dark blue slacks and sitting in the middle of the living room floor directing her maids in packing her trunks for Palm Springs. While telephones rang and messengers arrived begging her for interviews on the suit, she showed herself to Reeve as a feminist before her time: "I believe women have as much right to defend themselves as men! And you know what men do when they feel they've been done an injustice. They fight—and settle details later. But the courts are the only recourse for women. That's why I'm taking this case to law! I'm going to fight this thing through to the finish. I think I'm right." She went on, "Naturally my pride was hurt by so abrupt a dismissal from a contracted picture. But beyond that, I felt that my career would be injured if I left undisputed the rumor that my color tests were unsatisfactory. Color is the big factor in future pictures. An undenied rumor could do me total damage. . . ." She compared herself with John Gilbert, who had allegedly been ruined because of his voice. "It might become legend that Oberon did not photograph well in color. Not one producer in this town would take the trouble to find out the truth."

She continued, in a remarkably compulsive, driven, nervous vein: "I've worked for what I've achieved in my career. I can't stand idly by and watch a mere rumor pull down everything I've worked years to build. Motion picture acting is the most precarious profession in the world. Such little things make for success. Such little things break it! The mere thread of rumor has been known to snap the most solid of foundations.

"And so, if what we have achieved means anything to us, we can't afford to be timid. We can't stand back and be pushed off the rungs of a ladder we have already climbed. Once you give way, you stand back and let Hollywood push you around, you might as well give up. You are beaten. Your prestige as an artist is gone, your importance and value as a personality all somehow damaged. It can't always be the first blow that does the damage—but the first is inevitably followed by others until at last you can shout your lungs out at the bottom of the heap and no one cares. This business is not famous for its second chances. Once you arrive at the top, you've got to fight every moment to stay there. That is why I never have and never will allow Hollywood to kick me around. When the public says they no longer want me, I shall retire, grateful for what I had. But I refuse to be shoved in the discard through freak developments over which I have no control."

Brave words, but Merle proved unequal to them when it came to the case itself. She arrived at the county courthouse downtown in Los Angeles in a state of extreme nervous tension and fear of facing the courtroom. Somehow dodging a crowd of fans and curiosity-seekers that crammed the corridor, she drew her attorney aside and told him to reach a settlement, any kind of a settlement, in order to get her out of it; then she forced herself to go into court.

Rucker had not much of a case since the fine print of the Selznick contract was filled with tiny traps. He did manage to secure about $80,000, but Merle was so dissatisfied that she suddenly fired him and he had to threaten her with another suit before she finally paid his fee.

It was increasingly clear that at twenty-six Merle had developed a certain waywardness and restlessness of character, an impulsive shifting of moods that completely failed to fit with the icy, almost masklike Oriental calm of her face.

But she kept making new friendships. One was with the lovable Marion Davies, mistress of William Randolph Hearst. On May 2, dressed as a Spanish dancer, Merle was at Marion's beach house for a Spanish fiesta party to celebrate Hearst's birthday with an eight-foot by six-foot cake, a replica of his famous ranch San Simeon. The dancer-actress Tilly Losch created a sensation when she came dressed as Goya's naked Duchess of Alba in a skin-colored, skin-tight costume that left nothing to the imagination.

Worn out by the endless partying and the court case and bitter fights with her lawyer, Merle came down with a severe case of influenza and fled to a desert ranch–hotel owned by Herbert Marshall and Ronald Colman, grieving that she had to miss parties given by Cole Porter and Oliver Messel.

Back in Hollywood on May 24, she flung a huge shindig herself. Despite the unseasonably chilly, rainy weather, she and David gave an outdoor lunch in honor of Doug, Sr., and Sylvia. Their closest friends were there: Marlene and her new romantic interest Willard Goldbeck, the Gary Coopers, Herbert Marshall and Gloria Swanson, Myrna Loy, Joan Bennett, Marion Davies, Norma Shearer and Irving Thalberg, and the Charles Boyers.

Merle was very excited because David was to take Fredric March's part opposite her in a Lux Radio Hour version of *Dark Angel*, but at the last minute he had to cancel the appearance. He was cast in William Wyler's *Dodsworth*, and went to work with Merle's dire warnings of Wyler's directorial methods ringing in his ears. But Merle had a consolation prize: Rod La Rocque appeared with her on the Lux Radio Hour instead. His wife was her childhood Hungarian idol, the beautiful Vilma Banky, who had captivated her in *Dark Angel* on the silent screen. She took the opportunity to meet the legendary star and to tell her of her youthful fascination.

Merle worked very closely with David on *Dodsworth* at night, helping him with his lines and interpretation, salving his wounds after the nerve-racking days with Wyler. She arranged for him to be cast with her and Brian Aherne in *Covenant of Death*, a romantic melodrama of the Irish rebellion, later to be titled *Beloved Enemy*. Most evenings, she and David were with Doug and Sylvia; Fairbanks kept them enthralled with stories of his recent trip to the South Seas.

On July 10, Korda cabled Merle that he had cast her as Messalina, the dissolute empress of Rome, with Charles Laughton as Caligula, in a version of Caligula's life; then he cabled her again with typical impulsiveness to say that he had decided to make *I, Claudius* instead, based on the novel by Robert Graves. Emlyn Williams would now play Caligula and write the script, and Laughton would play Claudius. In mid-July, Elizabeth Haffenden, the charming Korda dress designer, came to Hollywood to work with Merle on designs for the costumes for Messalina to be done in London by John Armstrong.

Weekends were happily filled with deep-sea fishing. Merle and

David were out at sea on Sunday, August 1, 1936, when Merle felt a tremendous force tugging at her fishing line. She used all her strength but David had to help her. Together, the rod bent almost to snapping point; they struggled for most of an hour with the sea beast. At last, they won, and hauled up a monster of the deep—a 250-pound shark. They were jubilant as the creatured struggled and died in the net; Merle's hatred of killing living things apparently did not extend to the denizens of the deep. But when they got the beast to the Malibu pier, to their fury, the authorities would not let them take it home.

Early in August, Merle, David, and Brian Aherne began work in good spirits with a new director, H. C. Potter, on *Beloved Enemy*. It was a thinly disguised version of *Romeo and Juliet:* an English girl from an upper-class family and a dedicated Irish patriot brought together across the bitter divisions between England and Ireland in 1921. Once again, at her insistence, Merle was partnered with, more than merely photographed by, Gregg Toland, who evoked every nuance of her beauty with his lighting. Her performance was even more refined and delicate than that in *These Three*. She was ideally cast as a headstrong romantic girl who overcame political barriers. Her big scene came in the middle of the picture when she visited her lover secretly to enjoy a brief romantic tryst before the hotel he was hiding in was surrounded by British troops. She played the sequence with understatement and subtle feeling. Her tenderness, softness, and fineness had not been seen to better advantage. It was a magical, captivating performance that again earned her very good reviews.

Her acting was enhanced by further suffering: in midproduction, the beginning of September, Norma Shearer called to say that Irving Thalberg, overworked and exhausted, had fallen seriously ill with pneumonia. Merle canceled the day's shooting and rushed to Norma's side. With the wealthy and powerful, the elite of Hollywood, she waited in agony in the hallway of Louis B. Mayer's Santa Monica beach house to hear the hourly bulletins. As the evening went on and Thalberg drifted into a coma, she began to cry. Shortly after ten fifteen, the news came that the greatest figure of the film industry was dead. Norma was inconsolable and Merle, although she was suffering herself from severe influenza, stayed with her. Merle did not attend the funeral, probably because she was too distressed, but she spent every moment she could with Norma. She was also under tension because *Beloved Enemy* was dragging on, and she had instructions from Korda to come to London at once for fittings on *I, Claudius*. To reach New York in time to board the *Queen Mary*, she was forced to cancel her train reservations, and fly to New York with David, who was unable to go all the way to England because of other commitments.

In New York, with two days to spare before the *Queen Mary* sailed on October 21, Merle whirled David off on a lightning trip to Philadelphia to see Leslie Howard in an out-of-town matinee of *Hamlet*, and then to Boston to see her friend Noël Coward. Although there was a hectic farewell party in her stateroom, by the time she kissed David good-bye, she was still not exhausted.

Back in London, she was furious to discover that *I, Claudius* was delayed indefinitely because of Charles Laughton's nervousness about playing the part and Korda's uncertainty whether he would make the picture at all. In early November 1936 she was plunged into a series of meetings with Korda, whose fascination with her had increased; he was now more than ever in love with her. He had waited until she was the big star he hoped she would be, and now he could consider marrying her, since she would enter the relationship as his equal. It is doubtful whether she felt more for him than admiration, deep respect for his talent and for his amazing skill as a promoter; certainly, he was not her physical type. In the *Kama Sutra*, the aims of the experienced woman looking for a man of wealth and position are made clear: among them are "Men who hold places of authority under the king; men who are always praising themselves; one who was a eunuch, but wishes to be thought a man; one who is proud of his wealth; a brave man." Korda certainly held a special place in royal esteem; he was boastful and self-advertising to a degree; he was widely believed to be sexually impotent, a fallacy that an affair with Merle would dissipate; he was certainly proud of his wealth, and lived with a remarkable degree of ostentation; and he had the courage of lions.

Yet Merle was annoyed with Korda, not ready for a physical affair with him, and she was still committed to David Niven, who was in Hollywood filming that fall. And Alex was enormously distracted, not only by the complications of preparing *I, Claudius*, but by the crisis over the refusal of the Baldwin ministry and the Dominions to consent to the marriage of King Edward VIII and Mrs. Simpson. At Merle's dress fittings, hairdressing sessions, and meetings with old friends like the Plunkets and the Bensons, there was talk of little else.

And then there was the taxing task of mastering a script that changed from day to day, as Korda impatiently and nervously blue-penciled draft after draft, cutting Robert Graves's original script to shreds, hiring Carl Zuckmayer to rewrite pages, then adding his faithful Hungarian, Lajos Biró, to mirror his ideas.

Meanwhile, Merle was busy moving. She had given up the apartment in London when she left for Hollywood the year before, and her mother, ailing from some mysterious sickness, was living in a comfortable residential hotel. Merle leased a handsome Nash house in York Terrace (around Regent's Park from Korda's house in Avenue Road, St. John's Wood), furnished it with splendid English antiques, and hired four servants, headed by an indispensable spinster, Frances Thurlow, who was to stay with Merle for a lifetime.

From outside, the house did not look particularly large. But it had high ceilings and wide rooms, with an upstairs drawing room reached via a stone staircase with iron banisters. The drawing room was flanked by long windows and a narrow stone balcony. Merle hung cream-colored organdy curtains on the windows. Beyond was a vista of trees and grass with Regent's Park Lake glittering in the pale London light. There were magnolia blossoms on the grand piano. The dining room was in green with modern landscapes and flower pictures. She decorated the library with gaily colored drawings. The bedroom was in rich pink duchess satin with a green boudoir.

In fine weather, Merle enjoyed her breakfast on the balcony overlooking Regent's Park. She would sometimes wake up early, stretch, and walk to the window of her bedroom, where she saw the ink-and-wash picture of barges moving along the Regent's Canal in the pearly mist of morning. She adored the house and told Korda so; in a fit of generosity, he bought it for her.

An extraordinary, complicated, and embarrassing situation arose in London. Marlene was living two floors below Doug, Jr., in a house on Grosvenor Square. She had been quoted making cutting remarks to the press, saying that she had done *The Garden of Allah* only to stop Merle from ruining it. The Bensons and Doug Fairbanks had to go to remarkable lengths to prevent the two actresses from meeting: Merle and Marlene had to visit the Bensons on different nights or weekends.

During those weeks of waiting for *I, Claudius* to begin, Merle decided to have her portrait painted by Gerald Brockhurst, one of the most prominent artists in England. She went to see him at his fascinating house in Tite Street, Chelsea, the former home of Oscar Wilde—following Wilde's disgrace and exile, the house number had been altered to conceal the fact that he had lived there. Brockhurst was charming, a perfectionist like Merle, an intensely private man of the Midlands whose furniture was of rare fifteenth- and sixteenth-century English oak and who had one of the largest collections of very early English pewter in the country.

Brockhurst explained to Merle his specific technique and requirements. He painted only by natural light. His studio had a large north window like Rembrandt's in order to admit the famous north light which created shadows and highlights in the human face. He painted, Merle was fascinated to learn, on an easel that had been the property of Sir Joshua Reynolds, and he used the unusual technique of stretching the canvas on a six-panel board with four holes bored through the panels to enable the canvas to breathe.

All of his portraits were done against either Irish or Italian landscapes. Although he might have chosen Irish for Merle, in view of her father's origin, he preferred to paint her against an imaginary landscape of the green hills of Umbria. Also, he unpredictably elected not to paint Merle in an Oriental costume, as he often painted his wife. Instead, he selected a costume in the Italian mode, with heavily boxed shoulders, fashioned of velvet, and a cap that suggested a Renaissance lady of the aristocracy.

Merle was surprised to find that instead of wearing her own clothes for the sittings, she would instead wear Mrs. Brockhurst's clothes, which had to be refitted for her. She was intrigued to note that Brockhurst began the painting with the inner corner of her right eye. He made no sketches. He believed that by beginning at the core of the human being, the eye, which could least hide a sitter's nature, he could capture the human spirit on the canvas. After he had finished the right eye, and the left, he would begin to work on the other features, gradually increasing the light from the bottom of the canvas to the cheekbone so that the impression was given of a flow below the face. The effect resembled that used by Gregg Toland in photographing Merle: the sculpturing of her features.

A problem, unknown to Merle but greatly vexing to the Brockhursts, was that Marlene Dietrich had commissioned a portrait of herself at the same time as Merle. Like Merle, she insisted that it be done at once. The Brockhursts knew that if either star found out the other was having sittings, there would be a major conflict between them. Brockhurst knew that whereas Marlene was the bigger star, Merle was the greater beauty.

The Brockhursts established a subterfuge whereby Merle would arrive at certain hours and Marlene at others. Since both were punctual, the danger of their meeting was reduced. But since the house on Tite Street was small and narrow, with only one staircase for entrance and egress, there was always the danger that they might bump into each other. Amazingly, their many friends in common, led by Doug, Jr., never let on.

But one day, due to a sudden change in schedule, Marlene and Merle did meet at the entrance. There was a row and both were furious with Brockhurst, whose diaries show that Marlene impetuously canceled her portrait, but later had it repainted from scratch in an almost identical pose after Merle's picture had been finished.

For years, the painting hung in the place of honor in Merle's various homes. The commission cost her an enormous amount of money at the time, $10,000. It captures her better than any other work: the eyes are oblique, unfathomable, mysterious, romantic, and poetic, the eyes of a dreamer and a visionary in search of herself, with an almost mystical strangeness and allure. The pale chiseled features, the high cheekbones, and the disciplined mouth are offset by the formalized gown and the static, dream landscape of Italy behind her.

Marlene's former lover, Josef von Sternberg, was out of work and lying ill in the London Clinic when Korda and Charles Laughton persuaded him at Marlene's prompting to direct *I, Claudius* after Hollywood's William Cameron Menzies dropped out. Von Sternberg was chosen because Marlene knew he could perform miracles with actresses; Merle looked forward very much to working with him. He was very gifted in the art of lighting, and he had made Marlene's image immortal. Korda undoubtedly hoped he could give Merle that same legendary quality. And in his first meetings with her, and in their discussions of the part, von Sternberg made clear, very coolly, very dryly, that he saw through Merle's mask of carefully composed, genteel politeness and good breeding to the ambitious, restless, and daring creature underneath. He wrote in his memoirs, with a characteristic, deadly throwaway line, "Merle Oberon was ideally cast as Messalina." This was of course a heartless slander; Messalina was a corrupt monster and a murderess. But von Sternberg did observe the consuming sexuality and drive of Merle's nature, and a streak of ruthlessness necessary to achieve success. He understood Merle deeply: more deeply than Korda.

Shooting began in February 1937. Shortly before, Goldwyn contacted Merle to advise her he had cast her in *A Kiss in the Sun*, a comedy about a cowboy and a society woman, to be written by Frederick Lonsdale; she was excited by that, since she loved Lonsdale's plays. Also she was in a vibrant mood entertaining George Cukor in London or rushing off to Paris with Brian Aherne and the Wylers. She was in exceptionally good spirits when she began rehearsals for *I, Claudius*; the John Armstrong costumes were dazzling, and her hair had been cleverly redressed in the Roman style. Yet once again she experienced a sudden shift of mood; she became frightened of stepping into Marlene's shoes under the direction of a man who had a well-deserved reputation for sadism and coldness toward stars. At the last minute, she panicked and told Korda she wasn't sure if she could

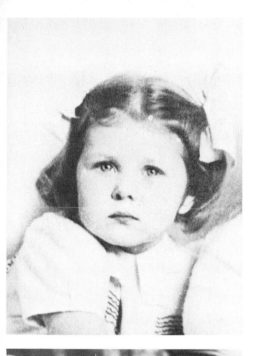

Merle's earrings when she
was three years of age

Above left, Merle at age five in Bombay
(Robert Wolders collection). Above
right, the romanticized painting that
Merle commissioned of her mother
Charlotte (Robert Wolders collection).
Below left, Merle's half-sister Constance
Thompson Soares (Harry Selby).
Below right, Merle's earrings that
Constance kept her whole life
(Harry Selby).

Above, St. George's Hospital in Bombay, where Merle was born (Harry Selby). *Center*, Imperial Mansion in Bombay, where Merle and Charlotte lived in a ground floor flat around 1914 (Harry Selby). *Below*, Merle's apartment on Ripon Road in Bombay (Harry Selby).

Above, Merle dancing as a rose in a
children's pantomime in Calcutta in 1925
(Robert Wolders collection). *Right*, Merle in
Calcutta in 1926 (J. Lee Morgan
collection). *Below*, Merle boating on the
Hugli River in Bengal while attending
school in India
(J. Lee Morgan collection).

Above left, Merle and a friend on their way to England on the *Aquileia* in 1929 (Robert Wolders collection). *Above right*, Hutch (Roy Moseley collection). *Below left*, Douglas Fairbanks, Jr., with Merle and the Countess Dorothy di Frasso (J. Lee Morgan collection). *Below right*, Joseph M. Schenck (J. Lee Morgan collection).

Merle as Anne Boleyn about to be beheaded in Sir Alexander Korda's *The Private Life of Henry VIII* (J. Lee Morgan collection).

Merle and Douglas Fairbanks, Sr., in *The Private Life of Don Juan*, 1934 (J. Lee Morgan collection).

Charles Boyer, Merle, and John Loder in *Thunder in the East*, 1934 (Charles Higham collection).

Merle, Leslie Howard, and Melville Cooper in *The Scarlet Pimpernel*, 1935 (Charles Higham collection).

Merle and Leslie Howard photographed at Paddington, England, on their departure for Hollywood in November 1934 (Culver Pictures).

Left, with her secretary-companion Ruth Fraser on their arrival in New York in November 1934 (Robert Wolders collection). *Right*, with David Niven, Norma Shearer, and Shearer's husband, the MGM producer Irving Thalberg, at the annual Mayfair Club party in Beverly Hills in 1936 (J. Lee Morgan collection).

Above left, with the director William Wyler and Walter Huston in 1936 (J. Lee Morgan collection). *Right*, with her beloved friend Norma Shearer on a fishing trip off the California coast in 1936 (Robert Wolders collection).

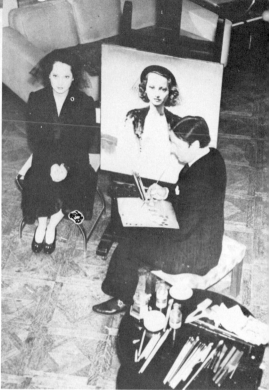

Above left, with David Niven at the beach in 1937 (Robert Wolders collection). *Right*, being painted by Gerald Brockhurst in London, 1937—for the finished painting, see the back of the jacket (Robert Wolders collection).

Left, at Santa Monica in her beach house, 1937 (Robert Wolders collection). *Right*, in front of her beach house with David Niven, 1937 (Robert Wolders collection).

Above, as Cathy with Sir Laurence Olivier as Heathcliff in the film version of *Wuthering Heights*, 1939 (courtesy the Samuel Goldwyn Company). *Below left*, with Olivier and Vivien Leigh in London, 1938 (Robert Wolders collection). Below right, with Sam Goldwyn, Eleanor Roosevelt, and James Roosevelt at the *Wuthering Heights* preview (J. Lee Morgan collection).

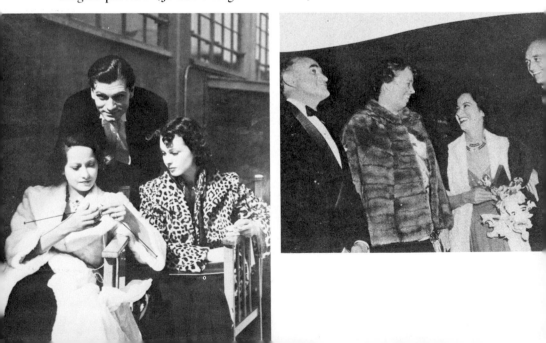

go ahead; he used all his Hungarian wiles on her, flattering her, cajoling her, and finally convincing her of a fallacy she sustained until her death—that the whole point of *I, Claudius* was to further establish her as an international star, although it really was a vehicle for Charles Laughton. It is an indication of her vanity that she believed Korda's lie.

Laughton was the major problem for her apart from von Sternberg. This great actor, the tyrannical Captain Bligh of *Mutiny on the Bounty*, was at heart a soft, gentle, and miserable homosexual who hated himself because of his ugliness and his weight and was a willing victim of male prostitutes. Indulging in an orgy of self-pity, he infuriated von Sternberg and Korda alike with his disappearances from the set and his refusal to remember lines, but when he "came through" in scenes, he played with great authority.

The abdication of Edward VIII in favor of the woman he loved deeply moved and disturbed Merle, who knew them both very well; and Laughton didn't help by constantly playing a recording of the King's abdication speech very loudly from his dressing room day after day, night after night, in an attempt to gain inspiration for his part. Nor did his habit of imitating the stammer of the King's brother, the Duke of York, improve Merle's spirits. Still worse, Laughton would come into Merle's dressing room without warning, place his head in her lap, and start to cry like a baby. She scarcely knew what to do in the face of such pathetic weakness.

Scene after scene was an ordeal to shoot. She had to be frozen, contemptuous, and cruel—contradictions of her true nature. Von Sternberg gave her nothing except ice and fury. She found no responding chord in him; it was not until later that she found out that he was disappointed because she was not Marlene; that he was still in love with Marlene and directing Merle was a torment to him.

Matters on *I, Claudius* came to a head in late February. In his memoirs von Sternberg described a scene in which Claudius had to be kicked into Messalina's bedchamber and then had to grovel at her feet. Merle sat on her bed tapping her foot, dressed in an almost transparent robe of fine silk that showed off her flawless breasts. Laughton was supposed to be pushed into the room in an illusion of being kicked, then grovel to Merle with the words, "This is not how I would have chosen to appear before you."

After thirty attempts, Laughton was unable to play the scene. Suddenly he said to the director, "There's only one way I can do this. If I am actually kicked into the room." It was obvious to Merle that Charles had been maneuvering toward this since he had his eye on a tough, powerful young actor in the line of extras. While she shrugged with despair and irritation, Charles exited. The young man he had chosen pulled back and kicked him into the room. Charles enjoyed this so much he asked if it could be done again. Von Sternberg nearly went mad. Merle turned to stone. Again and again, Charles was kicked into the room.

Another sequence proved to be a problem: Merle had to walk quickly along a corridor, surrounded by an entourage of insipid courtiers and giggling handmaidens; she had to smile with tantalizing viciousness at Claudius, relishing her power over him and the fact that there was little chance that this ugly, miserable man would be able to consummate his longing. Again Laughton proved impossible; again there were endless takes without a satisfactory result. In another scene, for which Merle took many dancing lessons, she had to perform an exotic solo ballet; at the end of the sequence she was to draw a cloak covered in stars of silver over Claudius's bent shoulders. Von Sternberg was delighted with her in the scene, the amazing degree of her sensuality when stripped of the Goldwyn gloss; but again Laughton ruined everything.

Korda kept impatiently ordering new sequences to replace others, which meant that Merle, whose entire wardrobe would normally have been ready at the beginning of the picture, had to be fitted again and again. Because the designer John Armstrong had his own salon in Mayfair, she had to go into town in her Rolls for fittings in the afternoons after shooting all morning, or sometimes drive from her house in York Terrace. On March 16, 1937, a day of heavy rain, her chauffeur, Briggs, inherited from Doug, Sr., drove the Rolls, Alex's birthday present, from York Terrace to Armstrong's. She was late for her appointment and urged Briggs to get there as soon as possible. Either out of irritation or anxiety to please her newly restless, impatient nature, Briggs began to speed as he headed down Portland Place and made his way through a maze of streets to Bolsover Street. As he turned the corner into Carburton Street, Edward Bundy, a motorcar salesman, was driving a demonstration Daimler in the opposite direction. He sounded his horn as Briggs tried to cut in front of him on a left turn but it was too late and Bundy hit the Rolls at a glancing angle.

Merle was flung to the floor. Her head struck the metal footrest provided for the extra folding passenger seat. She was badly cut over the left eye and ear. She lay unconscious, covered with blood, as Briggs and Bundy tried to stanch her wounds. A crowd of people, including the staff and customers of a neighboring barbershop, peered through the windows of her car, calling her name.

The next thing she knew, she was in the ambulance on the way to Middlesex Hospital, moaning brokenly, "Is my face disfigured?" Already, the first-aid team had bound her head in bandages. She was rushed to the outpatients' room and hastily stitched up; to her repeated requests, the doctors replied that her wounds would heal shortly. Alex drove to the hospital with flowers and as soon as the news broke on the radio, David Niven called anxiously from Hollywood, miserable that he could not be with her.

While Merle lay in a concussed state in the darkened hospital room, her nerves in shreds, an official version began to circulate that Korda was going to close the picture in view of her incapacity. Actually, he at once got in touch with Paramount in New York, oddly, Merle's benefactor Mark Hanna, and with Jesse Lasky in Hollywood, and tried to obtain the services of Claudette Colbert, a fact reported widely the next day. But Claudette was busy and could not undertake the trip to England. A carefully disguised fact was that Merle, once she was better, became hysterical, telling everyone, Korda included, that she would not continue with the picture; and Korda had to protect himself with the insurance company. Another hidden fact was that Charles Laughton's contract was due to run out in four weeks and he told Korda he wouldn't wait, that he had formed his own Mayflower Productions and had promised his coproducer, Erich Pommer, that he wouldn't lose a day of work. So Korda had no alternative but to go to Sir Connop Guthrie and the Lloyds insurers and tell them the picture could not be finished.

Merle lay in limbo for four weeks, visited by such dear friends as the Bensons and the Plunkets. The Bensons invited her to stay with them during her convalescence at their beautiful home, Shawford Park. Merle gladly accepted the offer and felt better with a diet of fresh farm produce, fruit and vegetables, freshly laid eggs and fine English beef, lamb, and fish.

While Merle was ill in the hospital, Charlotte also was very sick. She had been suffering for some time from high blood pressure and diabetes. She had been distressed by endless complaining letters from Constance in India; Constance would see Merle's movies whenever they came out, and would return to her room, partly proud of the connection, partly miserable and furious, and rail against her unfortunate children in their tiny space. Why was Merle, or rather Queenie, world famous and rich while Constance had to suffer in poverty?

Merle had continued to give Charlotte the best of loving care, but Charlotte had grown tired of her role as maid and took it into her head to be the mother now that Merle was famous. Charlotte had become fretful and said she was going back to Bombay. Indeed, she wrote letters to that effect to Constance as she began to fade. She was taken care of by an excellent nurse, Gertrude Webb. In a letter sent on June 1, 1937, to Constance Joyce in India, Mrs. Webb wrote of the final hours of Charlotte's life:

> I managed under very great difficulty to see [Mrs. Thompson] for a few minutes. I have some mementos for you and will send them on after I hear from you again. I must find the best way so that you do not have to pay anything on duty although they are very tiny, but they were things Mrs. Thompson valued. Your questions were did her daughter see her? Yes, although she had everyone with her she wished, she wanted to die as she was, so ill she could not enjoy anything in life.
>
> When you wrote her *all* your troubles I would have given anything to have seen you and asked you not to worry her, she would never let anyone know how ill she was. I knew of course, but I did not like to interfere with anything, her mind was quite clear until two hours before she went to the better land, and twenty minutes before, she turned and smiled at me then passed out. Oh, the poor darling.
>
> One thing I must tell you, she had the best doctors there was. Not a thing in the world that her daughter would not have given her, she has been a wonderful child, and you think just about your eldest son's age. She was helping to support her mother, she would have spent every penny on her. Miss Thompson's accident was more serious than her mother knew. She had a concussion and is not working yet . . . She has had bad luck and misfortune.

Charlotte Constance Selby died at the sadly early age of fifty-four, on April 28, 1937. According to a statement Merle made to her second husband, Lucien Ballard, several cemeteries rejected Charlotte on the ground she was Indian. Finally, Merle arranged with the Bensons, who had influence with the local cemetery keepers, that Charlotte should be buried in an unmarked grave in Micheldever, near the Benson home at Shawford Park. The parson at the simple funeral read the words of the Twenty-third Psalm: "The Lord is my Shepherd, I shall not want." Only three or four persons were present.

In India, Constance received word of her mother's death without a tremor. The bitterness of her rejection was still deep. She would see Merle's films and try not to be envious, but then she would return home and cry continuously.

The Bensons took care of everything. Through Charlotte's life in England, they had in every way protected her, had her at their house on weekends, and surrounded her with love and kindness. They had striven to give this simple woman a life that was pleasant and undemanding. Merle had always paid for everything, making sure that her mother was comfortable and free of all responsibilities at all times. Charlotte left very little money but she had no sense of money and therefore could not handle it. Her estate amounted to a saddening £270.

Twelve years later, in 1949, Merle, in an intense feeling of nostalgia, had Charlotte's portrait painted from a photograph. The artist lightened the skin, perhaps in order to sustain the illusion that Merle was not of part-Indian origin. Since Charlotte was very dark, this is certainly likely to be the case. In other respects, the likeness is perfect; the face is haunting, moving and intriguing. The picture hung in Merle's homes in Los Angeles, usually in the libraries, till the end of her life.

While Merle was recovering from her accident in June 1937, Alex brought her a script for a ballet film, *The Red Shoes*, based on the story by Hans Andersen. It was about the ill-fated love of a ballet dancer and ballerina, filmed later as the story of a composer and a danseuse. Merle very much wanted to play in the picture and trained at the barre for weeks with Anton Dolin in order to reach a sufficient standard to be matched in the long shots to a first-class ballerina. Just as the picture was about to start shooting, Korda with characteristic impetuousness canceled it.

David arrived in London during the rehearsals. On June 25, they went to Paris, where Merle had been invited to appear at a gala performance of the Comédie Française designed as a farewell to the Comédie's celebrated star Albert Lambert. Merle was presented to the president of France and gave a pretty speech in perfect French; her La Martinière training was still holding. Later that night, she attended a gala ball at the Palais Royal in honor of the Duke and Duchess of Kent. She again found an instant rapport with the Duchess, the beautiful Marina, a Greek of great style and charm. They remained friends for life.

Recovered from her accident by late summer, Merle made two minor but reasonably entertaining comedies for Korda, which were a way of marking time and of cheering her up as well: *Over the Moon* and *The Divorce of Lady X*. In the first of these, she appeared with Rex Harrison; in the second with the very young Laurence Olivier. *Over the Moon* was the story of a poor girl who suddenly becomes heiress to an immense fortune; *The Divorce of Lady X* was a society story set in Mayfair. Merle played both pictures with easy charm; they made no demands on her resources as an actress.

She was still in London in February 1938 when Marion Davies called her from San Simeon with sad news. Dorothé and Terry Plunket had been staying over the New Year season with Doug, Sr., and Lady Sylvia in Beverly Hills. Merle had promised to fly out and join them for a big weekend party at the ranch; but she was sick and couldn't leave London. Dorothé had called up and asked Marion if she could safely make a flight with another friend of Merle's, bobsled champion Jimmy Lawrence. Marion warned them not to leave Los Angeles later than two o'clock as fog rolled in by four, reducing visibility to near zero. Dorothé promised to remember this and Marion sent her pilot, Tex Phillips, down to Burbank with the plane.

As she went on with the story, Marion began to cry. Merle begged her to continue. Marion said that at four o'clock she became very anxious because the sky was heavy and the fog was rolling in and there was no sign of the plane. Marion called the man at the Teletype to radio the plane. He said he would try. A minute later, Marion heard the sound of a motor and the Teletype man screamed, "Tex is in trouble. I'm trying to call him. He can't get in!"

Marion rushed down to the plaza at the front of the house but she couldn't hear the motor anymore. She assumed the Plunkets were on their way back to an airfield. Then, without warning, the plane shot up out of the fog at an angle to avoid a mountain peak. It plunged sharply and crashed almost literally at Marion's feet. Jimmy Lawrence was thrown clear and survived. The plane snapped in half at the tail end and the Plunkets were burned to death in seconds. Nothing was left except their heads. Marion fainted.

Merle screamed with horror at the story. The images Marion had conjured up, of the fog over the castle, the explosion, the heads of the people she adored lying on the plaza, sickened her and caused a total breakdown. It was the first of a chain of similar events that scarred her life.

She went to New York, spending days with Tessa Michaels, trying to get over the shock. She was depressed, had fits of crying, and only gradually struggled back psychologically to the point that she could see David Niven again. But he was already drifting away from her; perhaps aware of Korda's increasing involvement, he had—according to the papers—taken up with another actress, the blond and beautiful Virginia Bruce, the widow of Marlene's ex-lover, John

Gilbert. It seemed Merle's life was always entangled with Marlene's.

She at last forced herself to return to Hollywood in April. Goldwyn had prepared an elaborate vehicle to mark her return: a Ruritanian spectacle called *Graustark*, co-starring Gary Cooper and Sigrid Gurie. He had built elaborate sets and Omar Kiam had designed fanciful costumes, but Goldwyn lost interest and canceled the picture the day Merle returned. Instead, he went back to the earlier comedy he had planned for her written by Frederick Lonsdale, whose script had been redone. It was now entitled *The Cowboy and the Lady* and she would play a rich woman in love with Gary Cooper's long-limbed Western hick.

But the trouble was that *The Cowboy and the Lady* still had no proper script. Merle gave Sam Goldwyn a magnificent black smoking jacket—and a note in the breast pocket asking him if he couldn't find something better for her to do. He obstinately went ahead, more to keep the assembly line busy than anything else. She found a part for David in the picture—she had quite forgiven him despite his interest in Virginia. It was part of her sporting nature that she always remained friends with her former lovers.

Instead, and since Gary Cooper was firmly married, although having an affair with the Countess Dorothy di Frasso, Merle took up with another lover, the handsome Irish actor George Brent, who had just broken up with Garbo. It was typical of the stars that they were involved in this sexual merry-go-round, cheerfully conducting complicated but lighthearted adulterous relationships under the noses of puritanical film censors, protected by the well-bribed Hedda and Louella from scandal, the fence around them so complete that the public, as usual, was kept totally ignorant of their behavior.

Much against his nature, William Wyler accepted Merle's entreaties to direct her in *The Cowboy and the Lady* to try to save the wretched thing from total disaster. But from the first day of work, the picture ran into heavy weather. Goldwyn, who hadn't really wanted Wyler in the first place, tried to interfere with him, charging him with wasting film in too many takes, although he knew better than anyone this was the way Wyler worked. On June 18, Wyler sent Goldwyn a memorandum reading "I am compelled to work without a completed script. Only one sequence was ready to work with when we started and I didn't get today's work (Monday) until late on Saturday night." He refused to meet Goldwyn in his office to discuss the matter, and on June 19 Goldwyn fired him and suspended him from the payroll without salary. Merle was bitterly disappointed; when Goldwyn asked her whom she would accept as a replacement (Cooper never cared who directed him) she said, furiously, "Nobody!" She demanded Wyler return but he had had enough. He left by plane for New York and by ship for Europe the next day.

Forced to a decision, Merle said she would accept H. C. Potter, whom she had liked on *Beloved Enemy*. They worked together fairly well but Potter himself was removed and replaced by Stuart Heisler. It was obvious from the beginning the film would be a failure and the results were indeed dismal.

During the making of *The Cowboy and the Lady*, Marion Davies gave her most elaborate party ever: an all-American costume party in which the guests appeared as figures in American history.

Norma Shearer called Merle and told her that she was going to go as Marie Antoinette, using a costume she had been wearing in a new film based on the life of the ill-fated French queen. Merle remonstrated with her. Hearst had run into business and political problems in France and had been asked to leave that country, and Merle was sure that he and Marion would be deeply offended if she and Norma were in French clothes. Norma laughed giddily, saying that Marion wouldn't mind. When Norma arrived at Merle's, Merle was astonished to see that her dress was so enormous the back seat had had to be taken out of the car and she filled the whole area, barely able to move. Her wig was two feet high and very heavy and lay in her lap.

Merle climbed in the front with the driver. When they arrived, Norma barely squeezed through the front door. As they reached the library, it proved impossible to get through that door and Norma screamed, "Take it down! Take it off the hinges!" Marion appeared, fuming, along with Hearst, and they glared at Norma and Merle, who wanted to die of embarrassment. Hedda Hopper materialized in a rage and said to Norma, "How dare you come as Marie Antoinette, with a French court, when you know that Mr. Hearst has been chased out of France? You should go right back home!"

Marion interceded and told Merle to go into the library through the ballroom which had large double doors. But even so, Norma had to go in sideways, and when she went to dinner, she had to have four chairs to sit on. Merle had to squeeze into the fourth, sharing it with several yards of satin and wire hooping.

In the midst of all this silliness, Merle received momentous news.

Chapter Seven

The intelligent and well-informed producer Walter Wanger, a friend of Merle's, along with his wife Joan Bennett, had for some years been planning to make a film version of Emily Brontë's celebrated novel *Wuthering Heights*. Wanger had never envisaged anyone else in the part but Merle; with great perceptiveness, he had seen below the carefully lacquered surface of her personality, seen beyond the clipped Anglo-Indian diction and the too-formalized, overbred movements and gestures, to the wild spirit within. Cathy, as Emily Brontë had described her, was a tormented creature, crying in the wilderness of a disordered life. It was Heathcliff, the orphan of unknown, perhaps gypsy, origins, the stable boy with yearnings of far lands and dark, brooding imaginings, who set fire to her nature and drove her to an ecstatic and tormented relationship that took her into the thorn forest of madness. Cooped up in her parsonage on the moors, with a gloomy father and a desolate absence of sex, Emily created this extreme romantic fantasy in a spirit of hopelessness and longing. Cathy *was* Merle Oberon; Merle Oberon was Cathy. She had loved the novel as a young girl; in her own mind, there was no one else who could play it. But she had had no idea that Wanger had her in mind for it; he had never told her because he was afraid that she would be disappointed if for some reason his backers refused to accept her.

When he told her at dinner one night at his house that she would play Cathy, she was even more excited than she had been that night at Goldwyn's when he told her that she would star in *Dark Angel*. But Wanger was forced to admit to her that he had been stumped in making a deal on the picture because he had wanted Charles Boyer to play Heathcliff. Totally blind to this serious mistake in casting, Wanger had provoked only laughter when he had made the suggestion that this elegant French matinée charmer should play the powerful and disordered hero of Brontë's novel. Merle's face fell at the news; but a moment later, Wanger told her that he had sold the package to Goldwyn, without Boyer, and that Goldwyn had of course approved Merle immediately. As the dreary business of making *The Cowboy and the Lady* dragged on, and H. C. Potter finally threw up his hands and Stuart Heisler took over, Merle was sustained by the thought of playing Cathy. She reread the novel again and again, knowing she would have to take a great risk in playing the part. She would have to disclose something of her true nature, for she was not the careful, studied, "aristocratic" figure the public knew. Of course, only Wyler could possibly direct the picture: could possibly have the stature, the fire, the all-out passion and conviction that would be necessary to bring the pages to life on the screen. Yet Wyler was in Europe now; and when Merle implored Goldwyn to bring him back with this new offer, Goldwyn was uneasy. It took all of Merle's charm to persuade Goldwyn that she had to have Wyler. And of course once more she also had to have Gregg Toland, without whom she felt insecure and lost.

She wanted Douglas Fairbanks, Jr., so close to her, and now over a romance with Marlene, to play Heathcliff; she felt that his extreme handsomeness, the fire and dash he exhibited as Rupert of Hentzau in Goldwyn's *The Prisoner of Zenda*, would fit him well for the part; and she was certain that he could simulate Heathcliff's roughness and harshness of character successfully. But his test displeased Goldwyn.

The next choice was Laurence Olivier. Korda was very keen for him to play the part and he went to the extent of sending a print of *The Divorce of Lady X* to Goldwyn, showing not only Olivier's romantic glamour, but also the ease and charm with which he played opposite Merle. Olivier was in Europe and received word of the part with interest. But he was not excited by the thought of Merle playing opposite him. He had nothing against her; they had gotten along well on *Lady X* and he admired her skill as an actress, but he was now madly in love with Vivien Leigh and she, as impassioned and driven and romantic as Merle, longed to play Cathy. But this was before *Gone With the Wind*, and Vivien was not yet an established star in the United States. There had never been any thought of her playing in *Wuthering Heights*—except in Olivier's mind.

Olivier cabled Goldwyn: NO TO WUTHERING HEIGHTS UNLESS VIVIEN PLAYS CATHY. Goldwyn was very disappointed and Merle was savagely upset. Wyler, in London, talked to Olivier, trying to charm him and to persuade him that the role would enhance his career and establish him once and for all as a star in the United States.

Olivier hung back, imprisoned by his own passion and by Vivien's pleas. It was not until October 1938, with much of the production ready to start at once, that he finally yielded to Wyler's entreaties and those of his great friend and fellow actor Ralph Richardson.

It was not a happy circumstance in which to begin a picture. Merle knew that Olivier hadn't wanted her and that Vivien was still waiting in the wings in case Merle should suffer an accident or breakdown in health. He knew that she hadn't wanted him as first choice but had preferred Doug, Jr. Myron Selznick as both Olivier's agent and hers was in an impossible position.

As shooting began the tension was extreme. Wyler scarcely helped matters by proving to be a tyrant, driving the actors unmercifully through rehearsals and preproduction meetings. Moreover, Olivier and Wyler had to fight against Goldwyn's maddening tendency to glamorize, to clean up everything; he objected to tests in which Olivier was shown in rags, filthy and intent, as was proper for a creature of the moors who had an utter contempt for convention, breeding, and cleanliness. He screamed that Olivier was the ugliest actor he had ever seen in his life, a bitter and inaccurate slight for one of the handsomest actors in England, and one which Olivier, superlatively vain like all actors, could not laugh off. Merle herself preferred to wear very simple clothes, with almost no makeup, and she and Wyler had to almost strangle Goldwyn to stop him from smothering her face with contemporary cosmetics and forcing her into glamorous dresses. Over everyone's objections, he absurdly updated the film over thirty years; because the styles of the turn of the century were rather somber and subdued, he wanted the more opulent fashions of a later period.

Unhappy with the gloomy, depressing set of *Wuthering Heights* itself, Goldwyn insisted upon making the modestly pleasant household of the bourgeois Linton family a kind of British version of the White House with chandeliers, glowing white walls, and everyone dressed in breathtaking finery for a ball. It took almost superhuman efforts by his director and stars to stop him from presenting a Hollywood version of England; as it was, the picture was compromised here and there by his fatal Goldwyn touch.

There were comic aspects of the film's making that did not seem comic to the participants at the time. Merle was running through the large bristling broom that substituted for heather on the San Fernando Valley location when she stumbled and twisted her ankle. Simultaneously, Olivier also developed a swollen foot from gout and the very tight shoes given him by the costume department, and the two stars began hobbling about like cripples. Merle had to play several scenes seated, while Olivier quite openly limped when limping was not called for by the script. In another scene, she attempted to cling to a wall while looking admiringly at the Lintons' guests at the elaborate ball. Unfortunately, her arms were too weak to sustain her weight and she fell in a heap in a flowerbed among loudly snapping and snarling dogs. David Niven, cast as Edgar Linton, did not make matters better by calling "Trubshawe!" to one of his dogs. He had a trademark in all his films in which his friend Trubshawe had to be mentioned; he and Merle owned a dog named Trubshawe during their affair. The dog did not respond, and the director ordered the line struck from the sound track. Merle was rescued from the flowerbed.

Between scenes, Olivier hobbled around on crutches, ready to kill Wyler, who kept snapping at him after he had delivered a speech, "You're lousy, you son of a bitch!"

Merle was overcome by the tension of Olivier's refusal to utter a word to her when a scene broke up. She went to his dressing room—according to some sources to try to patch up the problem, according to others to show her attraction to him.

He told her with great coldness to get out of his room, and she was forced to withdraw in a miserable, undignified manner, to tend her wounds in private. She was in those days dangerous, violent when crossed, and from that moment on, making the picture was hell for all concerned. It didn't help that she had to play out scene after scene of passionate embraces with the very man who had rejected her.

It says much for the professionalism of both stars that no hint of their animosity comes through on the screen. Lonely and frustrated, Merle could find no solace in David Niven, whose presence as the milksop Linton she marries in the story can scarcely have helped her disordered nerves. And Wyler! A hundred takes insisted on again and again! Outbursts of temper! Harassment and cruelty at every turn, both to her and her fellow actress Geraldine Fitzgerald! Merle cried often with exhaustion, frustration over everything, and sheer rage; her vanity had nothing to feed on, nor did her sexual appetite; she was worn out, ready for a breakdown.

The ordeal intensified. One scene took place in a violent storm, when Cathy runs out into the night in a transport of romantic feeling. The wind was created by airplane propellers set in the studio walls that sucked in the outside air and blasted it onto the players, herself and Flora Robson, at about seventy miles an hour; the artificial rain created by machines that spun water through blades lashed them and drenched them to the skin. Moreover, it was December now and the weather was chilly; the studios in those days were not properly heated and the temperature was very low. This would not have mattered so much if the scene had been shot only once. But Wyler wasn't satisfied with Merle's playing; he felt that she flinched too much, too sensitively and too obviously, at the studio-created downpour; he wanted his Cathy to confront the storm, to throw herself into it as into the arms of a lover. Cathy, he knew, was a creature who would find herself one with the storm; and he had found out the weaker side of Merle's playing of the part, that her delicacy, her fragility and vulnerability, worked against the strength of Cathy, the vigor of Cathy's romantic self-indulgence. So again and again he made Merle go back, to have her show pain overcome by a longing for nature and for the wildness of the storm; and the agony of repeating the drenching, of suffering it over and over, finally affected her always most delicately balanced health.

She came down with severe shivering, trembling, difficulty in breathing, and delirium; as she was rushed home and thence to a hospital, she vomited with racking convulsions and fever sweat broke out all over her body. Her temperature soared over one hundred and two and she had nights of tormented, sleepless misery. Goldwyn was frantic; not so much because of Merle's distress and possible danger—after all, he was a typical Hollywood movie executive—as because the picture had to stop production or be shot around her. His store-bought flowers and pleading notes were of course entirely in his own interests; and at last she forced herself to go back to work.

But only on condition that special heaters were used to warm the wind that would once again beat on her. The propellers and rain machines were moved to another sound stage where the wind and rain could be heated, and the picture began again along with the rain lashings and the retakes. Now she was in a kind of Indian monsoon—and she was more accustomed to that. But she was immensely relieved when at last Wyler got the effects he wanted and obtained something of the look on her face of passion and abandon.

Crucial to the portrayal of Cathy's character was a scene in which, overwhelmed with a sense at once mystical and physical that she is one with her lover, Cathy cries out in a paroxysm of emotion, "I *am* Heathcliff!" The delivery of the line would have been a major challenge for a great dramatic actress at the height of her powers, and vivid and appealing though she was, Merle could make no such claims for herself. Therefore, she had to reach deeply into herself to find the key to the necessary emotion. Wyler tried again and again but she couldn't reach the pitch of feeling that was called for. Flora Robson, who shared the scene with her, suffered with her in her attempts to "get" the scene. Miss Robson was an actress of consummate power and umplumbable resources, and she reached out in spirit to Merle to will her into achievement.

At first, the line was to be spoken out-of-doors; but Merle's health did not allow for this. There was talk of her speaking the words when flung down on a bed in agony, clutching the sheets, or pacing about the room; but at last Wyler hit on a solution. It was a melodramatic, vividly obvious device that would work with the mass audience. As she uttered the words, thunder would rumble and lightning would flash, and the storm would crudely symbolize her outburst of feeling. And it was at the moment when this decision was made to color the sequence in this heavy but effective manner that at last Merle herself hit on the correct approach. She suddenly realized that it was fear that Cathy felt more than anything else. Fear of Heathcliff dominating her delicate tormented spirit forever. And she played, quite beautifully, the line with fear, not with that sense of challenge and excitement that Wyler wanted. She understood from her own depths of intelligence that she must be threatened by the thought of "being" Heathcliff; she spoke with breathless terror and awe and wonder and the effect was striking and unforgettable.

Yet another challenge was in the death scene. She had to play again with great resources of feeling; she had to wring the hearts of the audience with her terrible weakness and looseness of body; she had to seem as though every ounce of strength had been drained from her by Heathcliff; as though she were dying *of* Heathcliff as if from a mysterious, ineluctable disease. In the over-pretty bedroom Goldwyn infuriatingly insisted upon, her emotion was true and precise. She expressed an anguish and helplessness that were almost unbearably touching. When Heathcliff carried her to the window to look out at the moors, it was one of the great moments of the screen. One wonders if she saw Garbo in *Camille*—surely, she must have—and understood how to convey imminent death: the total surrender of the body and the dreadful sense of lack of strength that makes the limbs feel like water. Although she was not of course anywhere near Garbo's level, she had her own miniaturist's perfection and she was never better on the screen than in this transcendent romantic moment.

When the picture was released, with a rather unusually large number of fake anecdotes in the publicity, including stories of Olivier spitting at her and Niven vomiting over her, all of an unusual fatuousness, the reviews were justly strong. Frank Nugent, the all-powerful critic of *The New York Times*, spared no praise in adjudging her the perfect Cathy, correctly seeing how her own wild spirit, seldom seen hitherto in pictures, had been released in the playing. His fine and expertly written review, repeated in his special Sunday column, was effective in placing Merle in the forefront of her profession. It is appalling—the word is not too strong—that she was not nominated for an Academy Award that year.

Perhaps because of Olivier's rejection of her, perhaps because of her knowledge that David Niven was no longer hers, and perhaps because now she was at the very top, she could marry for the first time a man of equal stature. She drew much closer to Alex Korda in the weeks after the completion of *Wuthering Heights* at the beginning of 1939. Another strong link between them was that with war approaching in Europe and Hitler's plans for conquest revealed in his annexation of Austria, and later Czechoslovakia, she understood more than ever before how important Alex was in the British scheme of things. Not only was he a patriot of his adopted country, but he was passionately committed to fighting the forces of appeasement and compromise symbolized by the outrageous statement of Lord Halifax that he would welcome the prospect of riding in a carriage with Hitler down the Mall, and Prime Minister Chamberlain's presenting of foreign countries to Hitler on a platter. She herself, committed to Britain as only a devoted colonial could be, in love with visions of empire, was addicted to Korda's way of thinking; they had that much in common.

And they had their deep romanticism also. Both loved color, magic, mystery, the Arabian Nights, the myths of sword and sand and saber that flamed through the adventure novels of the late nineteenth and early twentieth centuries. While Merle was making *Wuthering Heights*, Alex's gifted brother Zoltan was in the Sudan, directing with great attack, style, and expertise the boys' adventure story *The Four Feathers*, with its scenes of courage, suffering, and heroism, its vistas of the Nile and the charges of the Fuzzy-Wuzzies, its epic sequences of boats being drawn up the river by slaves in loincloths under a burnt-sienna sky. Merle loved the picture when she first saw it in the rough cuts flown to Alex in Hollywood in early 1939, and this affection she had for his work made Alex adore her all the more.

So here they were: in love with empire, in love with adventure, romance, English traditions, the aristocracy, courage as a byword, love of earth, love of London, love of travel. The lack of a strong sexual attraction, at least on Merle's side, was not fatal. And one cannot underestimate Merle's ambition in this matter. Korda was more than ever the greatest figure of film in England. His power and influence reached into Whitehall and Buckingham Palace. Her Anglo-Indian spirit longed for acceptance at the highest levels of society. To be Mrs. Korda—and perhaps, eventually, Lady Korda—would be the frosting on the cake of her life. There was no question that she could not accept the role of mistress. Wife she must be; and she must be accepted by the King and Queen.

She traveled to England in March, followed by rumors that she and Alex were already married in Canada. It had become obvious to everyone, although they had absurdly tried to keep it a secret, that they were engaged; Merle didn't wear an engagement ring—in order to keep up the pretense. Always nervous of the press, though anxious to please it when she had to, Merle dreaded being overwhelmed by reporters at every turn of her travels; but she could not possibly avoid the swarm of notebook-wielding vultures that circled around her and swooped upon her when she stepped off the *Normandie* at Southampton. In London, she was greeted by friends, headed, of course, by the Bensons, who heaped her with congratulations; and she and Alex traveled on to Nice in the south of France, where there was a society preview of *The Four Feathers* that spring. Exquisite in a white Molyneux evening gown, with Alex smiling owlishly in heavy horn-rims at her side, Merle made a great splash at the opening; and she sat enthralled by the finished picture, masterfully edited, and scored by Korda's favorite Hungarian composer, Miklos Rozsa.

It was typical of her that she should insist that she and Alex stay at the Hôtel du Cap at Antibes, the scene of her relationship with Joe Schenck and, of course, that first wild fling at a career in 1928. Everyone at the hotel knew that she and Alex were sleeping together, but she didn't want to be blatant about it and they did not occupy the same suite.

After two months of an idyllic Riviera spring of joy and laughter, in which Alex was in exceptionally fine spirits, inspecting sketches by his brother Vincent of the glowing romantic fantasy images of the new Korda production *The Thief of Bagdad*, wedding plans were laid down for June. A midsummer wedding was Merle's dream, and indeed it was a perfect choice because it was the height of the season and everyone who was anyone would be on the Riviera. For a while, she and Alex planned to have everyone imaginable present but then these plans were replaced by a sudden decision to have an extremely quiet ceremony on a Saturday at Antibes.

The wedding very nearly didn't happen. Merle and Alex discovered—amusing in view of the fact that Alex had high-level connections in several governments—that they had no proper documentation for the ceremony. They needed identity cards and visas and lacked both. Moreover, neither had a birth certificate: Merle's was buried in a puzzle of files in some sweatbox building in Bombay and of course she had the problem of keeping up her lie about having been born in Tasmania. If the press should find out her true origin by bribing someone—disaster. As for Alex, his own birth certificate was probably somewhere in a remote province of Hungary already under Nazi domination, which would scarcely be obliging to so complete a "British" patriot on the Gestapo special list. Up to 5:00 P.M. on the Saturday set for the wedding, Alex was wrangling in French with the local authorities in the office of the mayor, trying to bulldoze his way through a jungle of red tape. He was also painfully aware that his ex-wife, the farouche Maria Corda in Hollywood, was telling everyone that she had never been legally divorced from him. It scarcely helped matters that neither he nor Merle had the legal papers necessary to cement their own relationship.

However, a determined Hungarian is a determined Hungarian, and by sundown Alex had finally talked the mayor to a standstill; the marriage was performed by that gentleman with dispatch. The witnesses were the Duke and Duchess of Windsor's and Merle's French lawyer, Suzanne Blum, and an old friend from Juan-les-Pins, Henri Guenot.

Zoltan Korda and his wife Joan (formerly the actress Joan Gardner, who had appeared in *The Private Life of Henry VIII*) were significantly not at the wedding although they were staying at the Hôtel du Cap. Zoltan, Joan confirms, did not like Merle at all; he felt that she was using his brother for power and position and that she did not genuinely feel attracted to him and was not in love with him. Zoltan also resented the intrusion of a beautiful and gifted woman into the closed masculine circle of the Korda clan; Vincent's wife, Gertrude Musgrove, had been accepted, and so had Joan, because they were not in any way striking or outstanding personalities; they were pleasant, undemanding women who could occupy the role of housewife as easily as they occupied parts as minor actresses. But Merle was something else again: a big, imposing public personality, a challenge, an exotic jewel in the Korda crown.

Alex presented Merle with a wedding present fit for an empress: a necklace that had been worn by Marie Antoinette and had helped to cause the downfall of the French monarchy. It was the beginning of Merle's stunning jewelry collection, added to prodigiously in the years to come.

The honeymoon lasted two days and one night. Joan Korda re-

calls that almost at once Alex and Merle were locked in tigerish quarrels, with violent words exchanged on both sides. The quarrels
continued as they flew back to London. According to Michael Korda's
book *Charmed Lives* they made their way there by train and ship
because of fears of approaching war. But records show that they took
a plane, for the more humdrum reason that Merle had heard of an
ideal house she could rent in Denham near the studio, for her and
Alex to live in. Alex's home at Avenue Road, London, was not, she
felt, suitable for them both, and she had already tired of her own
house in York Terrace.

She and Alex were met at Croydon Airport by Alex's chauffeur
driving the Rolls. Alex went straight into conference with Vincent on
problems connected with the designs for *The Thief of Bagdad* and Merle
drove on to inspect the house. It turned out to be quite unsuitable and
she had to go to the real estate agents and get another list. The next
few days were taken up with house hunting while she and Alex lived
temporarily in York Terrace.

At last they found a suitable home, after weeks of searching in
the stifling summer heat of 1939. It was a pleasant manor house with
six bedrooms, a large flower garden, servants' quarters for her beloved
maid Frances and the other members of her staff, and stables that
were turned into cutting rooms. Unfortunately, she and Alex made a
very serious mistake. They decided to move the whole family into the
house, Zoltan and Joan, Vincent and Gertrude, the children (David,
Zoltan's son; Michael, Vincent's son; and Peter, Alex's son by Maria),
and all their own servants. The result was something resembling a
zoo. The proximity of Merle irritated the brothers and Alex had to
put up with their endless grumbling. Although the arrangement offered the advantage of having everyone close to the studios at a time of
intensive work and approaching war, it also threatened the family's
solidarity and made Merle an object of hate for what the others considered her uppity Eurasian airs and graces.

And in this stifling atmosphere Merle clearly began to have second thoughts about her new marriage. She soon realized that although
she had much in common with Alex, when it came to living with him
there was much that aggravated her unendurably. She was slightly
paranoid, almost neurotic, about her health, with a strong streak of
hypochondria and a fear even at the age of twenty-eight of looking and
growing old. She was nervous about cigarettes to such a degree that
not only did she not smoke them herself, she found the presence of
cigarettes or cigars insupportable. She drank sparingly, only allowing
herself sips of white wine with dinner; and she usually left a half-full

glass at the end of the meal. She liked to go to bed early with eye pads and cream on her face and could not endure being awakened for any reason whatsoever until her beauty sleep was over. She dieted by eating very small amounts of food in dainty, delicately prepared servings. Her one weakness was Charlotte's recipe for oxtail stew, served on the bone: until the end of her life people were astonished at the sight of this delicate creature with her exquisite slender fingers, guzzling away at a large bone, the oxtail itself, dripping with gravy and oozing heavy meat and gristle.

Alex was the most complete contrast possible. His addiction to large, aromatic cigars was a torment to Merle. The carpets, the curtains, and the furniture coverings were saturated with the cigars' stench night after night, and she had an overwhelming compulsion to send everything out to the cleaners. Alex loved to drink, often heavily. He was a night owl, suffering from lifelong insomnia, whose greatest pleasure was sitting up all night wreathed in poisonous smoke, discussing production plans with his team headed by his brothers. He liked the heaviest possible meals. Whereas Merle would sip a delicate cup of China tea and nibble at a piece of toast for breakfast, he would sit down, his ample belly pressed against the table, to devour a Herculean meal of cold cuts of duck, poultry, and grouse left over from the feasts of the night before, or stuff rich, heavy pâté down his throat, washed by oceans of black coffee. As a result of this diet, he suffered from poor health for most of his life and had an understandably gray complexion, as well as a flabby, out-of-shape physique. He despised exercise of any kind, whereas Merle loved to swim and walk, and he could barely bring himself to rise, crammed and satiated, from the breakfast table to make his way to the Rolls for the short trip to Denham.

One major relief in this difficult period was that Merle could see the whole of the new and magical fairy tale *The Thief of Bagdad* emerging under her husband's impatient, driven guidance. The script had been written by a colleague of Korda's in Intelligence, Sir Robert Vansittart, the actor Miles Malleson, and several others as a kind of compendium, stripped of eroticism, of Powys Mathers' famous translation of *The Thousand Nights and One Night* combined with a reworking of the Douglas Fairbanks, Sr., silent version of the story. Korda, alive with manic invention, cooking up new ideas in the early hours of the Denham morning, kept adding layer after layer to the fables. Sabu, the celebrated Indian star of Korda's *Elephant Boy*, and John Justin played a pair of adventurers whose encounter with the evil Grand Vizier Jaffar (Conrad Veidt) sparks off a series of romantic and mysterious episodes, luminously portrayed in the delicate palette of Georges Perinal's photography. The picture displayed Korda's passionate love of the exotic. Scene after scene mirrored the filigree world evoked by Edmond Dulac's illustrations to the fables. A six-armed figure of a tempting mechanical idol had a disturbing erotic power; the Indian Temple of the All-Seeing Eye, over which Merle exercised influence, offered the great spectacle of Sabu fighting a giant spider in a web stretched through a statue's entrails—a particular invention of Alex's; a genie flew through the air after emerging triumphantly from a bottle swept in by the sea; a beautiful princess was entranced by the scent of a blue rose. *The Thief of Bagdad* remains the most captivating of all children's films; it was wondrous in its revelation of Korda's art.

And day after day, at the studio and at home, Merle was able to see the beautiful artifact evolving, like the smoke that emerged from the green, shell-encrusted bottle that gave the genie birth. For Korda, of course, every day was a torment; this driven perfectionist, maniacally scrapping sets, riding three directors into the ground, screaming at everyone and then beaming unexpectedly with pleasure, never ceased to amaze Merle with his dedication.

Problem after problem marked the production as war crept nearer and nearer and Hitler began clutching at the throat of Poland. Some scenes were shot in Cornwall. When shots were taken along the coast, carefully excluding any pictures of contemporary ships, an excessively zealous Coast Guard team seized Vincent and some other Hungarians including the director Michael Powell and charged them with spying. Fortunately, Alex's influence in Whitehall had them bailed out quickly, but the few days of good weather were lost and everything had to be started again.

Merle was so mesmerized by the adventure in production and design that she even took over a column in the *Daily Mail* of London and wrote about the shooting. She vividly described the shooting of a storm sequence in which Grand Vizier Jaffar summoned up the elements; and she gave an appealingly surrealist portrait of the great ships of the port of Basra riding on the studio grass. She wrote with great affection of Conrad Veidt, a racy charmer of whom it was said that he would have sex with a butterfly, and his attractive daughter; and she also formed a firm friendship with Sir Robert Vansittart, which may explain her later role in Intelligence.

There were more problems still. As Merle wrote in the *Daily Mail* on August 20, two weeks before war broke out, "What with the weather, and the airplanes, locations are becoming very difficult in Britain. At one time you could ask the local airport people not to fly over the studios when you were shooting outside, and your request was courteously respected. Now it's a matter of a national emergency. And as soon as the rain stops, up out of the clouds come the planes."

Despite her pleasure in seeing *The Thief of Bagdad* unfold, Merle became extremely depressed. Even when there was a sudden burst of fair, sunny, almost Mediterranean weather in late August, her gloom did not lighten. With her great sensitivity and capacity to foresee disaster, she was in agony.

And on September 3, the blow fell. Prime Minister Chamberlain came on the air when she and Alex and his brothers were gathered for a meeting in the office. In his slow, halting, genteel voice, the Prime Minister who had sold out Europe disclosed the fact that war had begun. The combination of the pain in Chamberlain's voice, the guilt and anguish his policy of appeasement had brought on the world, and the terrible solemnity of the occasion shattered Merle's carefully built-up composure. She broke into helpless tears. Nothing that Alex could say could comfort her. Zoltan and Vincent showed little sympathy. To them, she was simply an artificial movie queen indulging in a fit of hysterics.

But her emotion was true and deep. She cared desperately that her beloved Britain was imperiled and she knew with piercing certainty the long agony that lay ahead. She was very pleased when Alex decided to rush out a picture that would whip up public enthusiasm for Britain's air power, *The Lion Has Wings*. She was lost in admiration for his decisiveness in suspending work on *The Thief of Bagdad* so as to have a total commitment of his entire company on the spot.

The writers worked day and night to pull together a makeshift script in which Merle would play the wife of an RAF wing commander (Ralph Richardson). Although embarrassingly overemphatic and flag-waving, impossibly dated today, *The Lion Has Wings*, financed by Alex's life insurance policies, was indispensable in time of war and resulted, much to Alex and Merle's delight, in Hitler putting him on his personal Gestapo hit list.

It became obvious to all concerned that *The Thief of Bagdad* could not be finished in England in wartime conditions. Alex was in an agony of indecision about where to resume production. Finally he realized that much as he hated Hollywood, he would have to resume there. He knew he would be criticized for leaving Britain at such a crucial moment—and he was right. But on the other hand he could not leave his beloved production half completed as he had done with *I, Claudius*. He would be ruined financially if he did; already, the Prudential had withdrawn its support and the bedazzled Sir Connop Guthrie was looking elsewhere for investments.

Alex saw another role coming up. He decided to intensify his work for British Intelligence. Precisely what he disclosed of this to Merle at the time is not known, since she resolutely—and rightly—kept it a secret for the rest of her life. Bound by the British Official Secrets Act, neither she nor Alex would be able to disclose precisely what he did in World War II. There is no question that she was not only privy to Alex's wartime activities and aided him in travel arrangements, but also undertook certain missions herself. These missions were apparently not of an espionage character but were of a correspondence character, in which she was a contact, using her high-level connections.

Merle, increasingly uncomfortable at Denham, aware of the hostility of the Korda family, and anxious for new work, accepted a loan-out arrangement to Warner Brothers that fall, succumbing to a weakness for which she would later enormously and courageously compensate. When she arrived in New York, she admitted to her friend Tessa Michaels that she was terrified of bombs and the brutal violence of war; and she was also savagely ashamed that her cowardice was driving her from England.

On her way to Hollywood, she read a script that excited her, that whiled away the interminable plane journey across the continent. It was a new version of Margaret Kennedy's *The Constant Nymph*, a story about a teenager romantically attracted to a middle-aged composer, which had already been filmed with Merle's friend Brian Aherne and the English actress Victoria Hopper. The part was ideal for Merle and offered her the challenge, always appealing to the vanity of actresses past twenty-five, of playing a child. She made up her mind firmly on arrival in Los Angeles, cabled Alex, and he acquired the property and talked to Jack Warner by long-distance telephone to make sure that she would act in the part.

Meanwhile, the household at Denham had been violently disrupted. Vincent went to California to prepare the groundwork for the continuation of the shooting of *The Thief of Bagdad* in the Mojave Desert and in the Grand Canyon. His wife Gertrude and his son Michael came by different routes, dodging U-boats in a painful crossing of the Atlantic. Vincent installed himself at the General Services studio where he built a spider web for a sequence and set himself up in a Moroccan mansion in Beverly Hills. Merle bought a huge English-style estate on Copa de Oro Road in Bel Air, with rich plantings of palm trees and what Michael Korda has described as "an enthusiastic but inexact copy of the abbey of Hendaye, complete with a bell tower and a carillon."

Simultaneously, as she began furnishing the house, Merle also bought a beach cottage not far up the coast from the one she had shared with David Niven. This was her favorite home: it overlooked her beloved ocean, it was very close again to Norma Shearer, and it was compact and comfortable. Alex flew in and out, on mysterious missions to New York and London, working on *The Thief*, locking himself in meetings with Mary Pickford and Charlie Chaplin and Douglas Fairbanks, the all-star board of United Artists. Merle, for her part, began work on a remake of an early talkie tear-jerker, *One Way Passage*, which was retitled *We Shall Meet Again*, and later *'Til We Meet Again*. She was to play a passenger stricken with heart trouble on a Pacific liner: a strange forecasting of her own final illness and death, and a mirroring of her lifelong heart murmur.

Bette Davis, who had played a doomed woman before, could not endure another one and had turned the part down when Jack Warner had driven to New England to offer it to her in person.

As she began work on *'Til We Meet Again*, Merle was not only troubled by fear for her dear friends in England and great concern for Alex and his courageous, bumpy flights across the Atlantic, but she was also gravely concerned with the condition of Doug, Sr., who was suffering (ironically) from severe heart trouble. Playing a woman with a heart condition and knowing of Doug's may have aided her acting, which had an unusual delicacy, fineness and sense of tragic gaiety. The strain told on her, however, and she was in very poor shape for most of the shooting, despite the attentiveness and kindness of her director, the British sophisticate Edmund Goulding.

On December 8, 1939, Sylvia Fairbanks called Merle to tell her Doug had died of a severe heart attack. Perhaps seized by a premonition, Merle had been ill, acutely distressed, all day, suffering from so severe a virus that she could barely drag herself to work. After lunch, at 1:20 P.M., she was talking to George Brent in a scene in the Hong Kong Bar of All Nations when she fainted. The studio doctor was called; he told Goulding that Merle, who was running a high temperature, must go home at once. That evening, feverish and vomiting, she had word from Mary that Doug had died. She broke into tears.

The unit manager, Al Alleborn, tried repeatedly to get in touch with her until late at night, and, with typical studio callousness, insisted that her maid Frances get her to give a decision whether she would insist on charging for the use of her own jewelry. Her agent Jimmy Townsend was furious because the studio would not assume responsibility for the jewels or insure them. Alleborn withdrew supplementary jewels from the bank as a precautionary measure in the event she would not use her own. He wrote in a note to studio manager Tenny Wright, "I am sure she carries insurance on these jewels and I agree that we should not insure them again."

It was finally agreed that her jewels would be used. Meanwhile, on December 9, Merle had another fainting spell. She was overcome by grief over Fairbanks and with the effects of the virus, and Dr. Pressman, Claudette Colbert's husband, could barely console her or get her up on her feet. She was off for a week, but took sick on the afternoon of December 14 and remained home until December 19, tended by Louis B. Mayer's daughter, Edith (Edie) Goetz, with whom she stayed for a time. She was fretting not only about Doug, and missing work and the funeral, but also about the endless discussions over *The Constant Nymph*, which was being delayed in the writing, and which it was her obsession to go ahead with once *'Til We Meet Again* was finished. When at last she made her way back onto the set on December 14, she broke down and started to cry at one o'clock; after two hours of sobbing helplessly in her dressing room, a first-aid man sprayed her throat and a nurse conducted her, exhausted and pale, to her car.

She took sick for another week. At Christmas, she rallied sufficiently to join Edie, Bill Goetz, Louis B. Mayer, and the rest of the Mayer family around the Christmas tree at the Goetzes' house. Edie says, "Merle gave me a small, beautifully wrapped package. I presumed it was a box of monogrammed handkerchiefs as it was flat and square. I opened it with interest but not with wild excitement. Knowing Merle had been sick, I knew she wouldn't have had much time to go out and buy anything. I undid the paper and took out the object that was inside. When I saw it, I literally broke into tears. It was a Renoir!"

Merle had in fact brought the painting from England and had succeeded in hiding it in her bedroom, where no one could find it. It was typical of her flawless taste, Edie says, that she would have chosen such a perfect gift; Edie had a passion for late nineteenth-century French art, and a very strongly developed aesthetic sense.

No sooner had Merle struggled back to work at the beginning of January than Goulding himself fell ill from the same influenza virus and the picture once more ground to a halt. Merle again fell sick when Anatole Litvak took over the direction for a week. By January 10, she had been absent for more than half the schedule of the picture.

She was desperate not so much to finish *'Til We Meet Again* as to be sure she would be fit enough to start *The Constant Nymph* in February. She always dreaded taking antibiotics, which were then in a rather primitive stage. Sulfa drugs had only begun to be fashionable in

1939 and there was always a danger in those days of side effects. But Pressman had used the treatment on her friends, including Goulding, without ill effects and she finally decided that she would have to take a chance and go ahead. On January 29 at the beach house, she took the sulfa injection with great unease. She felt sick almost at once and a swelling developed on her face that made her virtually impossible to photograph. Her fever subsided only slightly, and after struggling through several more days of work, she collapsed again. She wrote to studio boss Hal Wallis in an undated note that was almost certainly mailed on February 1, "I don't know whether you know about this yet or not—but the aftereffects of my infected throat [are] causing my face to break out—which has never happened before—Eddie and Tony [Gaudio] can't shoot me nearer than eight feet—which makes things awful complicated—also this is in my opinion the most important scene I have in the picture—If I have to play it all the time trying to keep one side of my face from the camera—the scene obviously will not be good. I've already asked and have found out that they have something they could shoot this afternoon—in which case I could go to the doctor and have treatment which would make it all right all the sooner. The lights and makeup might aggravate it and make the infection worse. Quite frankly, Hal, I'd be much happier not shooting looking the way I do—it would be better for you, too, as I am afraid you'll only have to retake as things are."

Wallis allowed her more time off, but soon it became obvious that if her absences continued, the picture would have to be canceled—an almost unthinkable possibility in Hollywood. So she went for further shots, and then disaster struck. She woke up one morning in the first week of February and found her face unbearably itchy and sore. Her maid Frances Thurlow reacted with barely disguised shock when she saw Merle sitting up for her traditional breakfast in bed. When Merle looked in a mirror, she became hysterical, almost insane with horror. Her entire face and neck were covered with hundreds of red, oozing pustules. The further shots of sulfa drug and the combination of toxic makeup had finally done their worst. Edie Goetz says, "I rushed to the house. Merle was insane with terror. I couldn't believe what I saw. It was like the disease that sometimes attacks the exquisite white leaves of a camellia. That perfect face, and now just a mass of sores! I couldn't stop crying as I hugged Merle, who could not be consoled. I honestly believed she could have killed herself. She felt the world had come to an end." Her friend Skip Hathaway also rushed to the house. She says, "Merle was totally out of her mind. I don't think she knew what she was doing." The two women and Frances did everything they could to ease Merle's spirit but it was useless. The only consolation was that she had just managed to struggle through her last bit scene in the picture and that rewrites could cover her absences from the story. However, the whole future now seemed doomed.

With a kind of blind, steely determination, the studio even began laying down plans for another picture to come before *The Constant Nymph*, *The House on the Hill*, a version of Somerset Maugham's novel *Up at a Villa*, another script rejected by Bette Davis. Instead of sending flowers and notes of condolence, the studio sent Merle stiff reminders that she was due to appear in *The House on the Hill* on April 1.

Alex was informed of her plight in London. Although he had been there only just over a month, he immediately flew back to join her. He was severely attacked in many quarters for having left Britain in time of war, but of course he couldn't give the reason for his departure since the public must not know that Merle's beauty might be destroyed. After a violently turbulent flight, Korda rushed straight to her bedside at the end of February. He was distraught, berated Dr. Pressman, and started calling every specialist he could think of in Los Angeles, New York, and London to find out what could save her.

He learned that the only possible chance lay in a treatment known as dermabrasion. This was an almost unendurably painful procedure to be used only in drastic circumstances. The best practitioner was a plastic surgeon, a woman in New York. There was no time to wait for a train. Alex called Tessa Michaels in New York and told her to fly to Chicago at once to meet Merle at the airport. He dared not go with Merle as it would attract too much attention from the press; instead, Merle had to go alone and completely incognito, wearing a heavy black veil. Alex made the necessary arrangements with the airline.

Unrecognized by the other passengers, Merle arrived in Chicago and Tessa flew with her to New York. Merle was barely able to speak. Tessa checked her into the Sherry-Netherland Hotel. She says, "Merle went to bed. She was in a terrible state of nerves. She seemed to take no interest in anything. She just used to cry and cry. I had to go on with my job at United Artists. The only thing Merle seemed to want was the occasional woman's thing. I took my lunch hour for her every day to buy things, and after work hours, before the shops closed.

"At night, Merle would say, weakly, 'Tessa, I've just got to get out of this room and have a walk.' She loved walking almost more than anything. Fortunately, it was spring by then and not too cold. We used to go through Central Park. Merle was still heavily veiled and in pain. No one ever recognized her. I think it gave her little pleasure to get the exercise and fresh air. Poor darling! It was unbearable to see her suffering so!"

After a few days, Merle was sufficiently strong through the rest and exercise to face up to the ordeal of dermabrasion. Tessa took her to the plastic surgeon's clinic. The surgeon must have warned her of the misery she would experience. But nothing would stop Merle if she saw a chance to rescue her face, even though, as sensitive as ever, she deeply dreaded pain.

She was seated in a chair while the nurse degreased her skin with a special astringent. The surgeon marked each portion of the skin that was to be treated with a purple dye and sprayed the skin with a substance that froze it. When each portion of the skin was thus hard and fixed, the pain became extreme. There was no way to desensitize it properly.

The surgeon took a small hand-held machine with a diamond burr on its head, similar to a dentist's drill, and began the ghastly process of literally abrading the skin's surface in its frozen state: actually grinding it off with the whirling drill.

At the same time, to ensure that the skin was completely removed, the doctor applied a peeling agent, an acid in jelly form; and the pain of the burning and scraping was so great that Merle had to have a fan in front of her face to ease it. After this gruesome experience, the effects on Merle's delicate sensibility were almost impossible to imagine; her face was an exposed and bloody mess of flesh. Wrapping it in bandages was perhaps the worst ordeal of all.

Close to collapse, Merle went with Tessa back to the Sherry-Netherland. Lying in bed, she had to go through days of still further suffering as the skin began to grow back and there was the inevitable severe and maddening itch that went with it. Merle's hands had to be tied to the bed by the nurse so that she would not tear at her face in the night, and she had to be fed through a glass straw. After a week of misery, Merle managed to return to the surgery. The surgeon clipped off the bandages and peeled off the lint. It was a suspenseful wait, to see whether the hell she had been through was worth it. The results were shattering. She would have to go through further peels because the marks in the skin were too obvious and would show up in photographs.

Incredibly, with amazing determination, Merle went through two more of these horrendous treatments. The result was a disaster—a visible pitting and indentation of the skin, particularly around her mouth, and it was years before all trace of it disappeared through constant and fanatical beauty treatments. Her only consolation was that Cole Porter came by to give her solace; he had been through agony for years from legs smashed in a riding accident. And he played the piano for her. In March, she returned to Hollywood in very poor shape. *The House on the Hill* was canceled completely. On March 29, she and Korda (who was busy completing *The Thief of Bagdad*) and Myron Selznick had a meeting and it was agreed that as soon as her face was in shape she would start on *The Constant Nymph*.

It was early June before she was able to get to a point at which she could do tests for *Nymph*. But a note from Hal Wallis to legal chief Roy Obringer, dated June 6, shows the disappointing outcome. He wrote, "In connection with the Oberon matter we made a test of her for the part of Tessa in *The Constant Nymph*. The test was very good so far as action and her youthfulness were concerned and we would definitely put her in the picture but for one thing. . . . Her face has not as yet healed up and the closeups in test reveal a very bad skin condition which makes it practically impossible to properly photograph her. Consequently, we cannot use her in *The Constant Nymph*. I don't know when the condition of her face will permit satisfactory photography but in my opinion it may be a matter of months. I have asked Jimmy Townsend to come over and see the tests and then to discuss the matter with me and at that time I would like to have you present. I see no solution to the matter except to suspend her contract until such time as she is physically able to work and be photographed and at such time we will have to reach an agreement on a story. In the meantime, it is our plan to make *The Constant Nymph* using someone else in the part. Confidentially, Oberon, according to David Lewis [a producer], is insistent that if she does not do the picture, Korda will want the property back, but in view of the fact that we are willing to make the picture with her and that our inability to do so is because of her physical disability, I'm sure we can proceed."

Jimmy Townsend of the Myron Selznick Agency drove over to see the test. He told Merle of the results, and she insisted she have another chance. She said she would come to the studio any afternoon and wait until Bette Davis was through for the day and then have Tony Gaudio make a photographic test; if her face still showed blemishes she didn't want to do the picture. Reluctantly, Wallis agreed to another test. It was done under the direction (as the first one was) of Michael Curtiz. Wallis wrote, "It can be much the same as the one Mike shot before, except that we don't have to spend so much time in the long shots. As a matter of fact, I see no necessities for making long shots. Let's just shoot close action, two shots, and big heads of her, and get some movement in the scene so that the test will be made as nearly like actual shooting conditions as possible. In other words, don't have Oberon planted in one spot so that Gaudio can spend an hour lining her up and lighting her, and then not have her move at all, as this is not a fair example of how the picture will be shot and we should have this protection for her own good as well as ours and make a fair test."

The results were shockingly disappointing. On June 24, the studio manager sent a message to all departments, a curt "This is to notify you to do no further work on *Constant Nymph*. Stop all preparation on this picture and spend no more money."

The picture finally went to Joan Fontaine, who appeared opposite Charles Boyer.

Merle faced an even greater disappointment that June. She went to see a well-known gynecologist, Dr. Leon Krohn. Perhaps fearing that her career might be over, and suffering from the anguish of her scarred face, she desperately wanted to have Korda's child. As a mother, she could work off her frustrations and give the child the best of everything. She could not forget the misery of the earlier operation, but did not know its severity. She told the gynecologist she wanted to have an examination to see why she had not become pregnant.

He conducted an examination that revealed to him that in all likelihood both fallopian tubes had been surgically removed in 1932. He told Merle, however, that only by an operation could the truth be known. Already worn down to the point of total exhaustion, she could not face that extreme measure. It was not until several years later that she went to the famous Dr. John Rock in Boston and learned the shattering facts.

Chapter Eight

Those long months of recovery were miserably drawn out and painful. Merle went everywhere in Hollywood in a black veil, her press agent "placing" her at various parties and nightclubs in the gossip columns in order to give the unsuspecting public the illusion that she was still in circulation. One pleasure in that dreadful year was in knowing that Alex, so restless and shiftless in his emotions, was genuinely concerned about her and that he was doing everything he could in his constant flights to and from Hollywood to reassure her. But he still hated California and was restless and bored at the beach house; with no interest in swimming or lying in the sun, he occupied himself irritably with the endless stream of problems on *The Thief of Bagdad*.

William Hornbeck, the editor of *The Thief of Bagdad*, recalls: "I will never forget that summer of 1940. I used to drive over to the Kordas' night after night and bring them the day's rushes. They would sit hand in hand in the private projection room and Merle would make suggestions. I could see she was captivated by the film."

Hornbeck is right: even in her anguish Merle continued to love *The Thief of Bagdad*. There is no question she exerted influence upon that most exquisite of romantic fantasies. She was horrified and mesmerized by the sequence in which Sabu fought with the giant spider inside the hollow goddess of the Temple of the All-Seeing Eye. The scene was shot entirely in Hollywood, miraculously realized in Korda's direction and the design of his brother Vincent. Merle had retained her mother's horror of killing insects; she shuddered when Sabu severed the giant cobweb strand that sent the spider to a watery death in an improbably placed octopus pool. She covered her tortured face—Korda had to remind her that it was only a movie.

Meantime, Merle busied herself with the art of interior decoration, trying to distract herself from her isolation and pain by learning techniques of blending colors from various specialists, among them William Haines. Haines was a witty, charming friend who had been a well-known motion picture star of the silent era. Merle was very much influenced by him.

She was also dependent on the kindness of her friends, Norma Shearer, Edie Goetz, and Skip Hathaway, wife of the director Henry Hathaway. They helped her and the devoted Frances in preparing meals, painting, cleaning, and keeping house. Somehow, she struggled through.

Despite his care and attention, Alex was never completely at ease with his position at United Artists and he often left Merle alone to disappear to New York or Europe. He was involved in British Intelligence work, not as a spy himself but as a cover for espionage activities, including those of the celebrated "Intrepid," Sir William Stephenson. He liaised with Colonel William Donovan, who was preparing the basis for the Office of Strategic Services which was set up two years later. Alex's chief purpose was to determine American attitudes toward Hitler in this period before Pearl Harbor; and to investigate Japanese activities on the West Coast; there is no question that he supplied a great deal of information to Whitehall in the matter. It was extremely important for the British government to be kept advised on the isolationist activities of certain members of Congress who had vested interests in Germany and German-related companies.

Merle, Alex's friend and Intelligence colleague H. Montgomery Hyde confirms, was privy to all of Alex's work on behalf of England. Very often, because of the Official Secrets Act, even wives were not kept informed of what was going on; and there is no question that Alex kept from her any major secrets that he may have known. However, she did know of all his movements and indeed acted as a liaison with Stephenson and Hyde in arranging them. She also knew what the purpose of those missions was and her extreme secretiveness and recessiveness proved invaluable to Alex. After all, she had managed to conceal her entire childhood and almost all of her private life from the press and even from most of her friends. So it would be a simple matter for her to keep a closed mouth about his activities; and anyway, she was scarcely seen out of the house until the late fall of that year.

She missed Alex bitterly during his absences, and was relieved when Churchill asked him to make a film in Hollywood that would completely turn around the anti-British sentiments present in large areas of the United States. It would counteract the general feeling that it was a serious mistake even to consider joining Britain in a destructive war that would lead to the deaths of many young Americans. The plan was to make a film about the love affair of Lord Nelson and Lady Hamilton, which would illustrate British bravery and give Americans a clear parallel to the present war in its portrait of the struggle between Britain and Napoleon, who stood in rather improbably for Hitler in the story.

For months, Vincent Korda slaved away in the Spanish-style downtown Los Angeles Central Library researching the period. Merle, with her newfound knowledge of antiques and her existing deep knowledge of paintings, made suggestions as to which works of art should be included in the home of Sir William Hamilton, the British representative in Naples who was married to the doomed and tragic Emma Hamilton. Merle would have been ideal as the wayward, romantic, passionate, and voluptuous heroine of the story; and one recalls that Korda showed her being painted by Romney in her introductory scene in *The Scarlet Pimpernel:* Romney had done the most famous likeness of Emma Hamilton, and it was reproduced in the film. But her skin condition simply would not allow for this and she was plunged into deep despondency over it. Instead, Vivien Leigh was cast in the role opposite her husband, Laurence Olivier.

Merle decided to help Alex over his financial difficulties in preparing *That Hamilton Woman.* With all support withdrawn by the Prudential, he was desperate for money, and the British government could not afford to advance him anything for what would be a propaganda picture; therefore, Merle offered to pay for the initial costs of production—it is remarkable that she had shown such shrewdness in investments that she was already close to being a millionairess at thirty years of age. Despite Merle's investments, and the fact that he had plunged every spare cent that he had into the production, Alex was forced to cut every corner, to use the most spare and cleverly designed sets that gave an illusion of luxury; and he was compelled to go to amazing lengths with Vincent in order to evoke on his minimum budget the Battle of Trafalgar and the arrival of the fleet at Naples.

When Olivier learned that Merle had backed the film, despite the fact that she had surrendered the part to his wife, Vivien, his feelings of distaste toward her provoked by the making of *Wuthering Heights* disappeared forever. And she conveyed through notes and phone calls that she too was happy to be a friend. For years afterward, their famous differences on *Wuthering Heights* followed them like shadows, and people were afraid to invite them to the same parties, but in fact they became lifelong friends.

The picture was in every way a triumph. Alex came home to Merle late at night after hard days of shooting, filled with glowing accounts of the work in hand; often, he would run the day's "rushes" or uncut sequences for her at the house, and she would make comments. Without jealousy in her nature, Merle was fascinated by Vivien's beautiful acting as Emma: Vivien's was a delicate and touching portrayal of frustrated love and isolation to which Merle vibrantly responded. And she was captivated by Olivier's genius once again: his superb looks, his magnetism, his bearing as Nelson.

That Hamilton Woman was finished in just under six weeks—a miraculous revelation of Korda's genius. Immediately, both its making and its planned release were severely attacked by isolationist journalists who correctly saw it as the propaganda picture it was. But when it was finally shown it achieved the effect that Alex and Merle longed for. It gave the American public a strong sense of Britain as an embattled power, and it made it possible, through the symbolic treatment of an earlier war, to bring home the realities of the present conflict in a way that even newsreels and news reports could not do in this era before the jet age. Alex had to field the onslaughts of isolationist senators Burton K. Wheeler and Gerald Nye as well as Nazi Consul General in Los Angeles George Gyssling, who knew from his own agents what Korda was really up to.

Winston Churchill long regarded *That Hamilton Woman* (called *Lady Hamilton* in England) as his favorite movie. Indeed, he even contributed a speech to the film with an obvious connotation in which Napoleon was denounced as the man who intended to master the world ("You cannot make peace with dictators, you have to destroy them . . ."). As a result of such propaganda, Alex was summoned over a year later to appear before a special Senate committee investigating the work of foreign agents in the United States.

By November 1940 Merle was up and about again. Alex knew how much she loved comedies, and Edie Goetz would borrow movies from her father Louis B. Mayer that would be guaranteed to cheer Merle up. She adored the Marx Brothers and Jean Harlow, and she laughed ecstatically at their goings-on. This use of laughter as therapy was typical of Edie, who had a strong streak of the healer in her nature.

Alex, in his role as director of United Artists, searched around for a correct vehicle for Merle; and knowing how much she wanted to laugh, he made an arrangement for the world's leading director of comedy, Ernst Lubitsch, to direct her. He chose a vehicle entitled *That Uncertain Feeling*, in which she would play a giddy, excitable girl caught up in a series of madcap social situations. She adored Lubitsch, whose *Ninotchka*, with Greta Garbo, was a favorite picture of hers. Lubitsch was a marvel, a small man with slicked-down, black patent-leather hair parted in the middle, sharply twinkling black eyes, pink cheeks, and a rotund, joyously potbellied body. His only drawback so far as Merle was concerned was that, like Alex, he smoked cigars around the clock; and when they had meetings, she had to sit at the far end of the room, stifling her coughs with a lace handkerchief.

Lubitsch delighted her by serving tea from a silver service to the cast at four o'clock every afternoon. It was a habit she herself adopted. She also greatly enjoyed the company of Melvyn Douglas, her leading actor; she was lost in admiration for his expert comedy technique. But she was nervous and edgy during much of the shooting because of her face and the still obvious deep pits around her mouth; every time she put on makeup she was afraid of an allergic reaction.

Immediately after making *That Uncertain Feeling*, Merle rushed into another Warner picture, *Affectionately Yours*, with Dennis Morgan, who became a friend, and the ravishing young Rita Hayworth. Again, this was a comedy designed to cheer her up. However, there was a disturbing mishap during the shooting: a taxi that was being driven on the set went out of control and ran into a group of people that included Merle. She was thrown to the floor and narrowly escaped serious injury. Sensitive as always, her nature precariously balanced, and suffering from severe nerves about her face, Merle became hysterical as a result of the incident and had to be taken home immediately. She did not return to work for several days.

She recovered sufficiently to attend the world premiere of *That Hamilton Woman* at the Four Star Theater in Hollywood on March 19, 1941. She was dazzling in a costume designed for her by Omar Kiam. She went straight into work that month on a film entitled *Lydia*, directed by the French Julien Duvivier, the story of a woman who, from spinsterhood and old age, looks back through the past from her position as a patron of blind and orphan children to the men who loved her and with whom she could never share her life. She appeared with Joseph Cotten, George Reeves, Alan Marshal, and Hans Jaray. Walter Plunkett and Marcel Vertès designed the excellent costumes.

Duvivier was thoughtful and highly skilled but Merle had little or no rapport with him. Perhaps because of her increasing insecurity over her looks and her constant tension, she began to exhibit a characteristic that became distressingly emphasized during much of the rest of her career. She was exceptionally difficult to work with. The cameraman Lee Garmes, who, with his charming wife Ruth, had known

Merle in London when he worked for Korda on the ill-fated *Cyrano de Bergerac*, found her, he reported later, drastically changed from the romantic, delicate creature he had known. Photographing *Lydia* was a torment to him because of Merle's endless fussing over makeup, hair, and costumes. He recalled an example of an incident in which Merle's fretfulness even temporarily overcame her sense of patriotism. He said:

> While we were making the film, Duvivier was heartsick, depressed almost to tears by the knowledge that France had given up the struggle against Germany so easily, and had allowed itself to collaborate with the enemy in the form of a Vichy government set up under Pétain. Duvivier felt he could no longer be a Frenchman in the circumstances: he could not be a citizen of a country that had betrayed itself.
>
> One morning, we had a late call at ten because Duvivier had driven downtown for an appointment. Merle hadn't been notified. She had come in at 5 A.M. for hours of complicated makeup as an old woman. Duvivier wasn't there when she emerged from the makeup room. He came in smiling with news for us all. Suddenly, without warning, Merle, in her old woman's guise, fronted up to him and shouted before us all, "What happened? Why are you so late?" Duvivier replied, furious, "Merle, I went down to the Immigration Department to take up my papers as a citizen." And I remember the remark she made in reply, a remark that flabbergasted all of us and turned us against her for a long time. She snarled, "Julien, why would you want to do that?" He shook his head and he said, "What else is there left for me to do, Merle?" She turned on her heel and went to her dressing room.

The relationship did not improve. There was a difficult scene of a ball in a mirrored room, with mirrors on all four walls. Even the ceiling had mirrors. It was almost impossible to film without showing the cameras. The camera had to be hidden in a black cloth dressed with a dummy figure covering it, the operator hidden under the "skirt." For some reason, this device irritated Merle; and she was also upset by the endless images of her face, reflected to infinity, reminding her of her skin condition. Again and again she flubbed her lines, and the orchestra had to stop playing and the dancers broke up. Duvivier became more and more restive. Finally, he confronted Merle, accusing her of an outrageous lack of professionalism. She responded with a violent and characteristic outburst of rage.

She was also unhappy with Korda's casting of her leading men who, with the exception of Cotten, a fine actor of the Orson Welles school, were very poor in the film. She blamed Alex for weaknesses in the script which emerged only as the film went on.

Another distraction occurred when Maria Corda, Alex's first wife, suddenly attached part of Alex's bank account for unpaid alimony, sent the sheriff to look for his car, which Alex hid in a studio-owned garage away from prying eyes, and once again threatened him with declarations that his marriage to Merle was illegal. By now, so grave was the jeopardy of Britain that the Chancellor of the Exchequer had frozen even Alex's money in London. He was very short of cash. *Lydia*'s shooting was very expensive and protracted, and the board led by Charlie Chaplin and Mary Pickford at United Artists was grumbling and insisting Alex put his own money into the picture's completion.

As a result of all these problems, *Lydia*, which could have been a picture of great importance for Merle and Alex, was a failure at the box office and, following the only so-so results of *That Uncertain Feeling* and *Affectionately Yours*, provided a major setback in Merle's career. In her bitterness, Merle turned against Alex; she could not forgive him for the pictures' weaknesses. For some time theirs had been a marriage in name only; they had not slept together in months and during much of the ordeal of the recovery from her skin disease, she had withdrawn from him. She had never really found him physically attractive to begin with; her fondness for him had been intellectual, and she had now discovered that that was not sufficient in a marriage. In order to sustain a marriage, there had to be a physical rapport and mutual desire and admiration. Without that, the marriage was sure to drift into companionship or even separation followed by hostility. Her romantic dreams began to dissolve.

Zoltan Korda's dislike for her intensified. In the summer of 1941, Zoltan was busy shooting *The Jungle Book*, one of her favorite children's works, and set in her native India. He had refused to allow her to have any say in Vincent's designs or even in the costumes. She wasn't allowed to come out to the location at Sherwood Forest, forty miles from Hollywood, where a ten-acre tract of land was converted into a tanglewood of tropical flowers and creepers. Bamboos, trees, vines, elephant grass, water hyacinths, and ferns were transplanted under Alex's guidance into an imitation jungle and native village while a near replica of Angkor Wat was constructed with mysterious stone faces and moss-grown archways and minarets. Elephants, panthers, bears, buffalo, monkeys, and wolves, plucked from several zoos, roamed around under an army of keepers. Sabu had a wonderful time cavorting about in a loincloth or swimming with Kaa the snake in the water. On one occasion, an elephant got loose and knocked over the camera; on another, a black panther savaged one of the crew. A forest fire was a tremendous event, with plaster-of-Paris trees and smoke and flames pouring out.

Merle was determined not to be precluded from *The Jungle Book*. Since Zoltan refused to talk to her, she befriended the assistant director Andre De Toth, a vigorous and virile young Hungarian of great good looks and energy and temperament. She told him of extras' costumes, saris and turbans and robes, that were wrong; she guided him on how to direct the women in terms of posture, the way in which they would carry vases on their heads; the way the mother of Sabu (played by Rosemary DeCamp) would carry her baby. Without Zoltan knowing, De Toth followed Merle's advice.

And at night, after the shooting, she would tell this sympathetic Hungarian friend of hers something she had almost never told anyone else: about her childhood in India. She told him of Charlotte's love of her and she urged him to make sure that Rosemary DeCamp treated her child, the little Mowgli, as she had been treated. Thus, her influence infiltrated itself subtly into the film and helped to add to its potent magic. It is a sadness that Zoltan Korda would not allow her a deeper and more overriding influence and that Alex, constantly in movement, constantly distracted, did not overrule his brother and let Merle have a say in a film which would have owed much to her guidance.

The film was beautiful, nevertheless: wrought as beautifully as a *poa* or Indonesian house tapestry, with its images of temples and bells and wild creatures, its emerald jungle landscapes and its climactic blaze of fire. In one performance at least, Andre De Toth makes clear that her influence was paramount: Frank Puglia's as a mean, degraded thief. Merle worked with Puglia behind Zoltan's back and with De Toth's collaboration, advising him on every stingy, secretive actor's gesture, on every detail of his clothing and shoes. It is the best performance in the film.

Before shooting of *The Jungle Book* was ended, Merle traveled to New York. At great risk to herself in isolationist criticism, she insisted upon working very hard there for the British war effort. A reporter from *The New York Times* followed her along streets in the Greenwich Village area as she, in the company of the huge, lumbering former Postmaster General Big Jim Farley, walked from house to house subscribing sums of money for the British War Relief Fund. Unsuspecting housewives opened the door to Big Jim's powerful fist or thrust on a doorbell and stood there gagging at the sight of the famous motion picture star on their doorstep with notebook and pencil in hand and a cardboard box to receive a subscription.

The heat in New York was typical of July: sweltering, airless, oppressive. Merle suffered despite her early years in similar conditions or worse in India; but she loved walking more than ever and greatly enjoyed the experience.

It was in those weeks in New York that she heard after some lapse of time from the dreaded Constance Soares in Bombay. Constance was begging for more money again, and although Merle had been sending small amounts through her accountant and manager, Wallace E. Hunt, she was greatly irritated by the note. She wrote from the St. Regis that July, thanking "Joy" for her letters and saying that she would have written before but had been "frightfully busy doing war work." She said, ". . . have given up films since July last to do this work—so I haven't been too flushed—therefore haven't sent any money—when I return to Los Angeles I will try and arrange to send you something every month." Merle was in fact "flushed": her earnings were tremendous. But clearly she was irritated and bored by this obscure person and her family putting pressure on her and she wanted to forget everything possible about India.

At the same time, Merle started a new affair with a man who was to influence her life profoundly.

Richard Hillary was born in Australia; he was twenty-two years old when Merle met him. He had been a star athlete at the British public school Shrewsbury, and at Trinity College, Oxford; early photographs show a man of extraordinary handsomeness and fineness of physique, with fair hair, vivid blue eyes, and ruddy cheeks. He was quick, eager, highly sexed, and passionate; women found him irresistible. His mixture of Spanish, Irish, and Australian blood made him volatile, restless, nervous, and capable of flashes of violent anger. He was as mettlesome as a young stallion.

Consumed with hatred of Nazism, Hillary volunteered on the first day of World War II and joined the Royal Air Force. Mastering the pilot's task in record time, he performed with great gallantry in the Battle of Britain. On the anniversary of the outbreak of war, September 3, 1940, a Nazi gunner shot down his Spitfire over the North Sea. Rescued by boat and taken to a Margate hospital, he was found to have severe burns on his body; his handsome face was badly charred and his arms and hands were twisted and scorched to the bone.

He was taken to East Grinstead Hospital in Kent, where the New Zealand plastic surgeon Archibald McIndoe was in charge. Operation after operation, and months of lying in agony in a dark room, made Hillary bitter and introspective. With infinite cunning McIndoe took skin from Hillary's arms and thighs and fitted them over his face with visible seams; his eyelids, eyelashes, and eyebrows had to be replaced with skin grafts and hair transplants. His hands had to be stretched on meshed frames like tiny tennis rackets to straighten them.

For a young, healthy, handsome athlete, the suffering of this loss of looks and body was almost unendurable. Even though Hillary would have given his life for his country, he was now enduring a kind of living death that twisted his psyche. He had to do something still. In the spring of 1941, he suggested to the British government that he should travel to the United States to talk to the workers on the aircraft assembly lines—to stir up propaganda against Germany, to show what could happen to a young athlete at German hands. He arrived at the Plaza Hotel for a press conference and was a great success with the reporters. Just before he met Merle, he had traveled to Washington for dinner with Lord Halifax, the ambassador for Great Britain. Halifax poured an icy douche on Hillary's hopes by telling him with unthinkable cruelty that his appearing before the American workers would only create a problem that would hinder instead of help the war effort. American mothers would feel that this must not happen to their sons and that they would lose influence in keeping America out of the war.

Halifax's decision was a devastating blow to Hillary, and when the State Department, ever neutralist, confirmed Halifax's decision which was supported by officials at the White House and the *Washington Post,* he was shattered. All of the carefully wrought-up optimism of the past few weeks was wrecked. The *Washington Times-Herald,* right wing and strongly isolationist, wrote: "The presence in Washington of Flight Lieutenant Hillary is not as good propaganda as the British may think . . . No doubt he shows how well Britain can take it but all-American mothers who see him will say, 'Heavens, this may be my son!'"

Hillary went to New York in July 1941 in a state of almost suicidal depression. He stayed first with the banker Edward Warburg and later with his close friend the publisher Eugene Reynal, who encouraged him to overcome his depression by writing a book that was to make him world famous: that classic of war literature, *The Last Enemy* (called *Falling Through Space* in the United States). Reynal, a man of great charm, with a gifted painter daughter, was a friend of

Merle's through Alex Korda and introduced her to Hillary at a party. She saw before her a tall, broad-shouldered man who was so terribly scarred that the nose was merely two holes in the face and the mouth was a twisted indentation to which lips had been artificially attached. The once square, rugged, and masculine hands were merely claws that could barely pick up a knife or fork. Watching Hillary take a drink or a meal was almost unbearable for his friends and he attracted stares whenever he appeared in a public place. Yet beneath the twisted relic of a man was the gallant tortured spirit that burned through the almost lidless eyes. Only the voice remained as a reminder of the beauty Hillary had been. It was rich, full, and warmly masculine. A voice that touched the heart of anyone who heard it.

Merle immediately felt an overpowering sympathy and warmth toward Hillary. She herself had known what it was to see her face destroyed; she knew in the essence of her being the pain of loss of looks which only a beautiful human being could know. And she had been lucky. She had regained her looks, with only slight scars left behind to mark the torment of her ordeal. Hillary could never be healed.

Tessa Michaels testifies and other friends confirm that Merle was overwhelmed by romantic longings for Hillary. He brought out the frustrated maternal element in her nature as well as the healing element she had inherited from her mother, who had begun as a nurse. She wanted, Tessa remembers, to give Hillary back a sense of his lost manhood; to show him he could still be attractive to a woman of great allure. She knew that by reawakening his dampened and suppressed sexual fires she could give him back his virility and self-confidence. Her instinct told her that, without her really knowing, Hillary had withdrawn from sexual contact with women following his crash and that women must have shrunk from him in horror, at the idea of embracing his tortured and charred flesh. Tessa says, "Merle told me she knew he was very much a man, still, and she had such a great, good heart, that she could breathe her power, her strength into him. It was a beautiful, beautiful thing for her to do."

One day at the Sherry-Netherland Hotel, Merle drew Tessa aside and instructed her to clear away all appointments, everything, even war work, for two full weeks, which she would devote to Hillary utterly. Alex was in England, but there must still be no gossip and Tessa in her role of press agent must make absolutely sure that not a soul among the columnists and gossipmongers obtained even a hint of what she was planning. Tessa proved to be a tower of strength in the matter.

Merle spent nights with Hillary in a hideaway apartment in the

Ritz Towers. From what she said later to Tessa, it is clear that she restored Hillary's virility, that he obtained intense pleasure from her body. Her fineness of spirit overcame what must have been an agony in seeing his naked flesh. Hers was a true heroism, a true expression of total romanticism. Hillary's biographer and intimate friend, Lovat Dickson, a retired London publisher, says today:

> Merle was just what Richard needed at the time. You must remember that Richard was still very attractive, even with his terribly injured face and hands, that his eyes could still twinkle. And Merle helped him to laugh and have fun. She *gave* him laughter—he always said, and he had many women, that their affair was not heavy and major, but it was lighthearted, cheerful, and it took his mind off that dreadful thing Lord Halifax had done to him: that upright monster of rectitude with his straight back and rolled umbrella who had lost a great war hero his chance to talk to the assembly workers.

She and Richard had much in common apart from their shared disfigurement, the experience that made them resemble the hero and heroine of *The Enchanted Cottage*. They had both been treated by McIndoe at East Grinstead and could talk about that; they both loved England, and Merle could overcome his bitterness with their shared patriotism; they both loved the Warburgs and the Reynals. According to Dickson, Richard was a frenzied, driving lover, and we already know Merle's intense sex drive; there is no doubt that their nights together were ecstatically abandoned and fulfilling.

During those weeks with Merle, Hillary was inspired to the poetic beauty of his book, *The Last Enemy*, much of which he wrote in her presence. He would show her passages in it, and with her love of poetry, her romantic nature, she would respond with suggestions and deeply felt praise. Simultaneously, she poured all of her radio earnings from performances in New York into the newly developed fund for the United Service Organization which was being put together at the time as a basis for troop entertainment.

It was a painful separation when Richard Hillary returned to England that fall. But he told Merle he had to get back into the Air Force, and she, fearful of what would happen, became nervous and tried to dissuade him. She knew objections were futile since he longed to serve England, and now that he had been denied his chance by Lord Halifax, he must assuredly return to the air. Back in England, the Air Force leaders knew that it was a risk giving this man with his maimed hands and impaired eyesight one of the extremely rare and valued airplanes to fly. But they could not deny him the opportunity; and he went into special training for the injured in manipulating a joystick and observing enemy or friendly signals.

His letters to Merle disappeared in a fire in 1960, whereas those to his later girl friend Mary Booker have been preserved. It would be correct to assume that his correspondence to Merle was of a similar character: filled, despite his condition, with the lust and joys of youth. Knowing her character, it is easy to see that she would have responded in kind. She longed to travel to England to join him.

Back in Hollywood, Merle joined the cast of another propaganda film, *This Changing World*, later retitled *Forever and a Day*. It was the story of a British house through several generations from the early Victorian era to World War II, played by an almost all-British cast which gave its salary less a five-dollar token fee to the British War Relief. The producer was Sir Cedric Hardwicke, who with enormous energy and vitality and a passionate commitment to England pulled all of the strands together. Merle's episode was directed by her old friend Edmund Goulding, who had made *'Til We Meet Again*. It was the story of a GI, played by Robert Cummings, the son of a runaway household servant, who is billeted at the home which has become a private hotel and who falls in love with the secretary, played by Merle. The episode took three weeks to shoot because Goulding rehearsed the cast in full. Robert Cummings says: "Merle was marvelous to work with. It was just as if I had known her all my life and yet it was the first time we had ever met. She said to me, 'You're so typically American. That's why we picked you.'"

The "we" is interesting. It suggests that Merle had a hand in the production: that she helped Cedric Hardwicke pull together the cast and the many elements that resulted in an exceptionally beautiful motion picture, marked by great sobriety and elegance.

During the shooting, Merle dropped by the set of Alex's new picture, *To Be or Not to Be*, directed by her friend Ernst Lubitsch, and starring Jack Benny and Carole Lombard. Merle's relationship with Alex had by now disintegrated. Their marriage had been eliminated in her mind by the affair with Hillary. Alex shrugged and accepted his fate. He must have known that there was no way that a man of his years and looks could hold on to an all-out romantic beauty like Merle. He had already begun shifting all of his possessions to London in a symbolic move that betokened an eventual divorce. It was not a particularly happy time and once more it was not aided by his brothers' attitude toward her.

She was compensated by forming a very intense friendship with Jack Benny. She also adored Carole Lombard, whose giddy, inspired, antic wit and charm captivated her. Lombard was an object of envy and awe to Merle, who could never be a great comedienne and whose comedies had been disappointing to her, as well as to everyone else. It was marvelous to watch Carole effortlessly sailing through *To Be or Not to Be,* her lovely back arched ironically, her eyes alive with intelligence and humor.

It therefore came as a devastating shock in January 1942 when Merle heard on the radio that Carole Lombard's airplane had crashed in the mountains near Las Vegas while Carole was on a bond-selling tour. Merle and other friends called Clark Gable, Carole's grief-stricken husband, in a foredoomed attempt to comfort him. Merle must have been reminded in those desolate hours of the death of Lord and Lady Plunket in the mountains near San Simeon. It says much for her resolution that only a week later she forced herself to fly through storms to New York for more war bond sales.

On February 5, 1942, rules and precedents were shattered when the New York Stock Exchange opened its doors to her before 3:00 P.M.: she was the first woman ever to appear in the Exchange at that hour. Followed by Mrs. William Vanderbilt and Betsy Cushing Roosevelt, she walked up to a table on the floor at which she sold tickets for the Navy Relief Show at Madison Square Garden on March 10. Master of ceremonies George Jessel also broke tradition by wearing a derby hat; hats were always forbidden in the Exchange. Merle circled the floor with Exchange president Robert L. Stott for several hours and as night fell, she took off to nightclubs with Mrs. Vanderbilt and Mrs. Roosevelt to sell more tickets.

Next day, February 6, Merle was given a tour of a new battle cruiser at the Manhattan docks. She listened to everything carefully and then went to Alex, who was in New York, and told him that she had been given far more information than any citizen should have, even if that citizen were connected to Intelligence. Here, she said, was a severe security leak which could lead to ships being sunk; and she knew very well that certain people who might be given such a tour were highly suspect. She told Korda that this laxity in security must be immediately stopped, and with his blessing and cooperation she personally volunteered to launch the new issue of Button-Your-Lip posters, sold to the public to emphasize the dangers after Pearl Harbor of giving possible enemy agents access to useful Army, Navy, and Air Force information.

In a speech at Town Hall in Manhattan on the day before her

thirty-first birthday, February 18, 1942, Merle drew attention to the danger of careless talk by shipworkers and men and women on the assembly lines; briefed by Korda, she referred to the intelligence leak that had caused the sinking of one of her favorite ships, the *Normandie*, on which she had twice sailed to England, and had provided secret particulars to the enemy about Pearl Harbor. "Be smart, act dumb," she said, in an agreeable lapse from her usually impeccable English. "Loose talk can cost lives." She concluded the speech by selling a large number of posters to help support the British and American ambulance corps.

In June 1942, Alex and Merle received the exciting news that he had been made a Knight Bachelor in reward for his services to the Crown. He would travel to London later that year for his investiture by King George VI. There can be no question that the award was also intended for Merle in recognition of her efforts on behalf of British War Relief. Two months later, on August 7, after litigation lasting more than five years and costing the equivalent of $30,000, the British House of Lords decided that Briggs, the chauffeur who had crashed Merle's Rolls-Royce in 1937, was entitled to recover some $25,000 from Merle's insurance company. During the five years of litigation, the court of appeal had originally reversed a high court decision in his favor. Merle was privately pleased. Over the years, she had sent many messages to Briggs reassuring him that she had no animosity against him and was sorry he was being financially punished for the mishap.

That August, the United Services Organization and British E.N.S.A., the London equivalent, were planning to send a group of performers to entertain United States and British troops in Britain. Merle instantly volunteered to be on the first list to travel there. She was to accompany a small troupe including the gifted singer and actress Patricia Morison and the well-known Warner Brothers character actors Frank McHugh and Allen Jenkins. The star of the show along with Merle would be Al Jolson, who had just returned from entertaining U.S. Army, Navy, and Air Force troops in Alaska.

Merle was overjoyed when she was accepted immediately. There would be the added advantage of being able to stand alongside Alex at Buckingham Palace when he received the insignia of knighthood. Soon she would be Lady Korda! It was a romantic dream fulfilled, and the thought of serving her country at home quite overcame her fear of the Atlantic crossing, the enemy aircraft and warships which would make the journey a considerable hazard in time of war.

She and Patricia Morison, who knew each other slightly in Hollywood, found themselves billeted at the St. Regis Hotel in New

York, where they were to wait until they were given clearance to leave on their perilous journey. The FBI was working closely with the Korda office in security matters related to espionage. Merle, because of her husband's work, checked in on August 17, with Agent L. A. Hince of the Bureau, who was to take care of any problems she might have. She flew to Washington on August 21 to see Hince and told him she had already run into some problems. The U.S. Army Public Relations people were supposed to have arranged everything for her, but when she arrived in Washington nothing whatsoever had been done to help her. She had no reentry permit, and no visa; the War Department had failed to take care of anything. Evidently, the old problem of the absence of her early records had blocked her again. Hince said he couldn't do anything to help her as the FBI had no control over travel documents. It is a complete mystery why Sir William Stephenson, who was in charge of British security coordination, had not taken care of these matters for her.

She went to see the Immigration authorities. The local chief under the Immigration boss, Major Lemuel Schofield, savagely criticized her, saying, "Why, you are just a buck passer! You have always had people to do things for you, and you don't do them for yourself!" Why was the Immigration Department so hostile? The answer may be found not only in the problem of her papers but in the fact that Immigration was at the time, almost a year after Pearl Harbor, harboring Nazis in the country while at the same time in collusion with the Visa Division of the State Department in precluding the entry of Jews. In fact, Major Schofield was involved in a scandalous affair with the Princess Stefanie Hohenlohe, a prominent Nazi agent.

In these circumstances, it is scarcely surprising that Merle was given the runaround in Washington. Hince, on her second visit to him, contacted Colonel Wren of the Army and asked him if he would speak to Merle. He did, and he proved to be very helpful. Hince wrote in a report to his superior, Clegg, on August 22, 1942, "Subsequently everything was fixed up, and she is all set to go."

The FBI also contacted Patricia Morison. An FBI agent who also worked at Universal Pictures asked Pat if she would seduce a prominent figure of the American government to find out if he was a Nazi agent. She declined the assignment. Could that figure have been Major Schofield? We may never know.

In the last week of August, Merle was back in New York with Patricia. They were not to be told at exactly what hour they would leave, nor was it announced even in interdepartmental correspondence. Nevertheless, subsequent events show that their every movement was given away to the Germans. How was this possible?

There was no one in Korda's office in New York who could have been a spy. A careful check of the personnel shows no records on any of them. Sir William Stephenson, however, was unwittingly nourishing one particular viper in his bosom. This was an Australian named Charles Howard Ellis, formerly in charge of the passport office in New York and specifically in charge of British citizens in the United States who might be useful for Intelligence contact purposes.

In a recent book, *Their Trade Is Treachery*, by the British journalist Chapman Pincher, Pincher has disclosed the existence of a sworn confession in which Charles Ellis admitted that he was a Nazi spy. Undoubtedly, his true character went unsuspected both by Stephenson and by H. Montgomery Hyde, who was also on Stephenson's staff. Ellis's presence might explain why Merle was not given satisfactory arrangements for her trip and why her passport and visa were not in order. It might also explain why, on a brief visit to Canada the previous year, she did not have a correct reentry permit and had been threatened with internment at Ellis Island before Korda personally stepped in and fixed everything.

Patricia Morison, who was strongly pro-British, and clearly was considered to be a first-class contact for use in Intelligence, was made privy to the fact later on that their entire journey across the Atlantic and through Great Britain and Ireland was tracked by the Germans. Ellis was the only possible leak.

Why, one might ask, would the Germans be interested in tracking the course of a simple entertainment tour which at the very most would be a harmless example of morale-boosting for the troops? Why would Merle's death be considered advantageous? Clearly, it was the fact that she, like Leslie Howard, had been at the forefront of War Relief efforts and that she was at the least assisting Alex.

In the after-midnight hours of August 22, 1942, Merle was awakened by a telephone call in her modest room at the St. Moritz. A U.S. Army Air Force commander told her to report immediately and with the darkest and most inconspicuous clothing possible at the entrance of the hotel. That sticky, sweltering and thunderous morning, Merle, Patricia, Frank McHugh, and Allen Jenkins appeared at the doorway and were quickly bundled into a large car driven by plainclothes Army men. They could take only one suitcase each because the presence of heavy luggage might alert agents to their identity.

They arrived at the airport while it was still dark. Tired after several nights of little sleep, not knowing when she might be called, Merle walked up the gangway of the huge flying boat and sat down in a bucket seat. The entire inside of the aircraft had been stripped bare for the transatlantic crossing.

It was stifling in the plane; there was no air conditioning and very little ventilation. She and Patricia and the two men made themselves as comfortable as they could. Minutes later, FBI men arrived and introduced themselves, followed by Army Intelligence people and George Meany, the union leader.

The last to enter the plane was Al Jolson. Merle had never met him: she fixed her eyes on him with fascination. Even in this extreme situation, he acted like a star. Not satisfied with being the last aboard, he said, looking around him with icy fury and contempt, "Who the hell are you? I don't need you! I've just been to Alaska on my own and that was good enough for the boys. Why the hell did they send you on this trip?"

Merle and Pat and the two men froze, hardly able to believe their ears. Not only was Merle a major star, but everyone had given his services to the Allies free of charge. It was unthinkable that Jolson would behave in so atrocious a manner.

At last the flight took off. The flying boat vibrated alarmingly, bumped violently about in turbulence, and offered virtually no refreshments. Merle and Pat had two mattresses to sleep on and, feeling rather uncomfortable, had to lie down and try to sleep in front of the men. Patricia Morison recalls:

> We were flying very low because of German planes. It was clear that we were being tracked by the enemy shipping as well. Indeed, our whole trip was under constant surveillance and it's a miracle that we managed not to be shot down. But the pilot was wonderful and kept changing directions. The direction changes made the trip extremely rough and uncomfortable. I'm sure Merle was afraid of enemy gunfire hitting us but she never showed her fear. She kept calm and looked wonderful throughout the trip which went on for well over one day and into the following night.

The flying boat at last reached Belfast on August 24. Merle and the others went to London for briefing. The day they arrived, Merle heard that an old friend of the prewar days, the Duke of Kent, whose wife, Marina, was very close to Merle, had been killed in a Sunderland flying boat when it crashed on the way to a military mission in Iceland. Merle called the Duchess from her room at the Savoy and offered her condolences. It was yet another in the chain of deaths by air crash that haunted her life.

The troupe left for their first performances in Buckinghamshire several days later. The Duchess of Kent, grief-stricken, was in retreat at her house Coppins, in the village of Iver. Merle went to see her immediately, trying to give her some comfort.

That same weekend, Merle said to Pat, "I have an appointment with someone. I want you to meet him." They went together to an inn, an ancient structure with low ceilings, where a crowd of servicemen was drinking. They waited at a table; suddenly, Merle glanced up and saw a tall figure in Air Force uniform in the doorway. It was Richard Hillary.

Theirs was a joyous reunion. Patricia Morison said:

I'm afraid I may have shown my shock at his appearance. There was no face. The hands were twisted into claws. But the voice was magnetic and irresistible and the physique was big and impressive. Something came through the horrifying twisted flesh: a quality of warmth and fineness of character. Merle greeted him with incredible tenderness.

All through lunch at the inn, Merle was exquisitely sensitive, pretending she didn't notice Hillary's desperate efforts to cope with a knife and fork. During a brief interval when Hillary left the room, Merle told Pat that she and Hillary would be leaving for the whole weekend; that she wanted to give him two days and nights of complete happiness. When Merle returned from the weekend, it was obvious that she had achieved her purpose. But Hillary was in love with a friend of the mid-1930s, Mary Booker, to whom, ironically, Merle had introduced him, and he could not commit himself to Merle; nor, as Korda's wife, could she commit herself to him. Their romance was doomed; there could be no chance of permanence and it is not entirely certain whether had they been free they would have entered into a long-term relationship. They were restless spirits; it was part of their empathy that they both had this wildness.

The performances at the bases took place day after day, night after night. Merle acted as m.c. and also recited British verse, including Rupert Brooke's sonnets of World War I and Alice Duer Miller's fashionable romantic-patriotic poem "The White Cliffs of Dover." The troops were glad to see this glorious woman. They cheered and wolf-whistled her as she came on the makeshift wooden stage. Pat Morison sang beautifully and danced contemporary numbers, Frank McHugh and Allen Jenkins did a song-and-dance act, and Jolson, in blackface, his lips painted white like Little Black Sambo, wailed energetically through his hit tunes including "Mammy" and "Swanee."

Kneeling, his arms flung wide, tears streaming down his cheeks, he was electrifying, and even Merle, who hated him, was transfixed by his vivid, schmaltzy attack and style.

Patricia Morison says:

> One afternoon we were entertaining at a big estate near an air base and the GIs and U.S. Air Force men, about 2,000 of them, were seated on the grass under the big shade trees around our stage, which was a converted veranda. It started to get cloudy as Merle went up for her introduction. Within minutes, black clouds began moving across the pale English sky. Frank McHugh and Allen Jenkins went on and did their comedy routine. Jolson went over to Merle and whispered, "You'd better cut into their act. There's a storm due." And he added, "And make sure Pat cuts her act, too." Frank and Allen obliged and so did I. Then Jolson went on after us and said, "Well, guys, the others may be afraid of a little rain but I'm not and I'm going to give you one hell of a show." And he went ahead and performed for twice his usual length of time. When the rain got too heavy, he took the thousands of troops into the main hall of the mansion and continued without a break.

Merle was furious with this upstaging by Jolson of his fellow actors. She snapped at him in front of everyone, "Al, this isn't a show just for your vanity. It's for all of us and for the men out there. None of us is important individually. We are supposed to be helping the war effort and this is no place for star behavior."

Patricia Morison adds:

> On another occasion, we went to a hospital. It was set up in crude Nissen huts. Merle and I went around the wards. Much to her own shame, and sorrow, she couldn't control her tears when confronted by the sight of these young men who were so horribly wounded. She simply broke down and had to leave in anguish. I took her aside and begged her not to show her feelings as it would make the men suffer unendurably. She understood at once, pulled herself together and went back in with smiles. When we came out, Jolson was sitting in the front seat of our car. He had refused to go into the hospital. He said to Merle, with bitter jealousy, "Why the hell have you been in there? Don't you realize you might catch something?" And this was in the full hearing of wounded men who were standing around. Merle completely

blew her stack. She shouted at him, "Al, don't make me ashamed of you!"

One night, Merle and Pat were at a Red Cross facility established in the house that Nelson had built for Lady Hamilton. As they were leaving, the driver picked up two GIs and Jolson got into the front seat. Merle said to the GIs, "Where are you going?" They replied, "We're going down to the village to have a few drinks." They still didn't recognize her or Jolson in the dark. Merle said, "Did you see the wonderful show this evening?" "No," one of the GIs said. "Who was on?" "Al Jolson," Merle replied. And the GI said, "Jesus! I'm glad we missed that!" The two girls screamed with laughter.

Another night, the girls were driving back to London in an Army car when enemy aircraft began tracking them very low overhead. The Germans dropped flares on both sides of the little procession of automobiles. The drivers pulled in under heavy oak trees that concealed them completely. The enemy marauders roared back and forth looking for them. It was clear that they had been alerted to their whereabouts; later, in London, Merle and Pat discovered that indeed this was the case; that Royal Air Force Intelligence knew that their positions had been given away.

On a damp afternoon, Merle and Pat went for a walk through some of the places Merle had known in her younger years. They crossed through Leicester Square. Merle was looking for the Café de Paris where she had been a hostess long ago. Suddenly she stopped and saw a hole in the ground and a crumbling wall. It was all that was left of her alma mater. She broke down and cried helplessly, seized by uncontrollable sobs, and became almost hysterical when Pat was compelled to tell her that many of the people she had worked with including the famous maître d', Charles, had been killed when the nightclub was bombed. From Britain, the troupe traveled to Ireland for ten days of appearances. One night the driver got lost and almost crossed over into the Republic of Eire. When they went into a restaurant on the border, they were shocked to hear people speaking in German; they left at once and drove as fast as possible back through the darkness.

A curious episode took place during the tour of Ireland. Merle and Pat went to visit the seventh Marquess of Londonderry at his country estate. They spent a pleasant day wandering around the grounds and enjoying lunch with the Marquess and his wife. It was not until later that Pat learned that Londonderry was forbidden to come to London during the war and was under close surveillance. The reason was that Londonderry had been a pronounced Nazi sympathizer who had been a guest of Ribbentrop and Goering; Goering had stayed at Londonderry's estate. Londonderry had been a member of the Anglo-German Fellowship, which was noted for its support of German fascism. Why would Merle have allowed herself to visit such a person? Is it possible she was investigating him for Korda? Or was she ignorant of his background?

The schedule chopped and changed all the time because the troupe was being followed by enemy agents. They would return to the Savoy Hotel again and again and wait for orders to leave in the middle of the night with no preparation and so little time to pack that they left their belongings in their suitcases. Pat says:

> Even in these straitened circumstances, Merle managed to be elegant. Her makeup case was exquisite, her silver brush and comb set was perfection. She just had one suit on and one off and one evening gown and one spare pair of shoes. Her most precious possession was an antique silver box with tiny partitions, tiny little drawers, in which she kept her vitamin tablets. She used very little makeup. Just a very soft pencil for her eyes, almost like soot, the kohl used by the silent stars which very subtly framed the eyes.

Merle received a letter at the Savoy which touched her deeply. It was from a man called Ginger in the Royal Navy and enclosed four eggs, which were as precious as diamonds in Britain at the time of major food shortages. The letter read, "I want to send you this little present to thank you for coming to us. We feel it was your own idea, and we love you for it. It is people like you who help us boys go to sea. God bless you."

The troupe was never given any indication where they were going. Many of the bases were hidden. Some of Merle's journeys were so secret that they remained unknown. It is possible that she was visiting Intelligence contacts at the time for assignments. It is certain that she visited Winston Churchill on several occasions, a surprising fact in view of his deep commitment to the war effort. But his passion for Korda and for *That Hamilton Woman* resulted in his inviting Korda to dinner on several occasions to run the film and Merle was present on those occasions. Merle had a special driver, an older woman, for these secret visits and contacts.

A great pleasure of the tour was meeting Generals Eisenhower and Marshall at one of the bases. Eisenhower warmly greeted Merle; he was there with all his aides at his headquarters, although he wasn't very happy about having actors performing for the troops and told Merle, with an unpleasant touch of racism, that he was very worried about the "colored" troops because they weren't "integrated" and were running off with English girls. But he did express his personal admiration for Merle and Al Jolson and the others and the effort they had made in coming across the Atlantic at great risk to their lives.

For once, meeting the Chief of Staff, Jolson behaved himself. But back in London, following a performance for the Eagle Squadron, Jolson suddenly lost his temper and announced that he was returning to the United States; that he was tired of performing with second-raters and could no longer endure the trip. Another quarrel took place at an airfield and a third at a railroad station. Jolson wanted to accept an invitation to appear at the Palladium in London with the troupe, but Merle was against it, saying that they were there to entertain the troops and not the general public. Jolson was furious. On September 16, after just three weeks less one day, Jolson took a clipper back to Manhattan.

The tour continued with the others. They were supposed to go to North Africa but the tour was finally, much to their disappointment, canceled.

At last came the magnificent moment when Merle and Alex went to Buckingham Palace for the official ceremony of knighthood performed by King George VI. It was unarguably the most exciting moment of Merle's life up to that time. She must have known, although she would be the last to tell anyone about it, that the honor was as much for her as it was for Alex. It was an extraordinary event for both of them. As Michael Korda points out in his family memoir, Alex was Hungarian, Jewish, and had divorced his first wife; he was a highly controversial figure because his absences from Britain were so extensive in time of war and the public knew nothing of his work for Intelligence. The others on Merle's tour, led by Pat, now kidded her by calling her "Your Ladyship." She giggled, but privately she was overjoyed.

The flight back to New York was also charted by enemy planes and was equally perilous. In New York, Merle worked closely with H. Montgomery Hyde to ensure Alex's safe passage following her return. She bypassed Ellis and dealt with the loyal and reliable Hyde instead. A telegram from her in Los Angeles dated October 6, 1942, refers directly to William Stephenson. It reads: DEAR HARFORD. WOULD YOU PLEASE ASK BILL TO SEE WHAT HE CAN DO ABOUT ALEX'S RETURN PASSAGE. HE WANTS TO RETURN WITHIN FORT-NIGHT IF POSSIBLE. KINDEST WISHES. MERLE.

She was also influential in assisting Lady Glendevon, then Mrs. Paraviccini, Somerset Maugham's daughter, whose husband was Swiss and therefore neutral. But in America he was believed to be an Italian enemy alien. The fact that he was born in Rome proved to be a problem, too, and they were both suspected of being foreign agents. One morning, when Mrs. Paraviccini was working at the British Library of Information in New York and applied for an extension permit to stay on, she was told that she and her husband were to be deported via Ellis Island. She went to Merle for help. Merle called Montgomery Hyde and told him what had happened. He said he would have to meet Lady Glendevon first. Merle took her to Hyde's apartment. As a result of Merle's intercession, she had to go to Ellis Island only briefly and was told she wouldn't have to take a suitcase. That night she was released to her family.

Chapter Nine

In Hollywood after his return, Alex and Merle began to entertain lavishly with the financial rewards of *That Hamilton Woman*. Michael Korda recalls that studio guards absurdly addressed Merle as "Your Highness" and headwaiters referred to Alex as "Your Excellency." The Kordas joined Sir C. Aubrey Smith and Sir Cedric Hardwicke at the summit of Hollywood-British society. Titles were automatic guarantees in Beverly Hills and Bel Air of invitations to the finest parties. The couple were also very close to the amusing Sir Charles and Lady Elsie (de Wolf) Mendl; Sir Charles was a contact of Korda's in Intelligence. The rift between Merle and Zoltan was as extreme as ever and Joan Korda, who like Zollie had no interest in society or in high-toned events, had no more rapport with Merle than she had had before. She recalls how angry she was when she saw Merle order Alex to open or shut a window or pick up dog dung from the carpet, like a sultana talking to a slave.

At a party given by Sir Charles and Lady Mendl, Merle arrived late with Alex. As the butler announced them and they descended the steps to the living room, a large, handsome man in his middle years stepped forward. Merle looked at him and felt an overwhelming sense of shock. The man was Colonel Ben Finney, the big game hunter who had given her her first break with Rex Ingram, who had stood her up at the Hôtel du Cap at Antibes, and who, most horrifying of all, knew the truth of her racial origins. She had to be assisted to a chair. Then she went home.

Although she and Alex shared pleasure in such friends as the Mendls, their unhappy marriage was marked by insuperable problems. Not only did Alex continue to eat food that Merle found repulsive, and to smoke the cigars to which she was allergic, but he also kept conferring through the night in meetings with Zoltan and Vincent, planning an elaborate version of *War and Peace* in which Merle was to play Tolstoy's heroine Natasha. When Alex wasn't mulling over the script for this proposed epic, he was gambling into the small hours, sometimes until dawn, for stakes that ran close to half a million dollars, with Louis B. Mayer, Darryl F. Zanuck, and Harry Cohn. It was Cohn who expressed an interest in Merle's making a picture for Columbia, the studio of which he was the manic and foul-mouthed mogul. When Cohn met Merle, he was overwhelmingly attracted to her and undoubtedly nourished dreams of making Alex a cuckold. Stubby, square-faced, with an air of nugget-hard virility and power, Cohn was a particularly dangerous beast of the Hollywood jungle, a classic example of a male chauvinist who believed that any woman who was lucky enough to appear in his pictures must automatically be available to him for sex. Indeed, he was said to have had a private corridor built from his office to certain actresses' dressing rooms and he had an alarming tendency to turn up at unexpected moments, exhibiting his male member and asking the actress what she intended to do about it. So crude was his approach, so utterly devoid of polish or romanticism or even good manners, that most of the women who worked with him hated him and deeply resented his attacks on them. If rejected, he was known to blacklist lesser female performers, preventing them from working in Hollywood again. He would stride about his office screaming at everyone when he was frustrated. His viciousness stood out even among his peers.

He fell madly, passionately in love with Merle who, needless to say, was totally unattracted to him. She was clever enough to find ways of using him for her own purposes, while politely declining his advances. There was no way he would dare to try to blacklist Lady Korda. In late November 1943, she began a picture for him on loan-out from Korda and Goldwyn: *First Comes Courage*, a story of the Norwegian resistance movement in which she played, in a curious echo of her real life, a secret agent married to a Nazi commander in order to find out details of his activities. She was directed by the famous lesbian Dorothy Arzner.

Cohn had a rule, which never changed, that all performers were forbidden to park their cars on the lot. Merle, who still did not drive, refused to have her chauffeur cool his heels outside the studio gate and insisted that she be allowed to park the Rolls close to the sound stage and the dressing room. When she was forbidden entry on her first day at work on *First Comes Courage*, courage came first and she said she would go home at once and never return. The gateman called Cohn's secretary and told her what Lady Korda had done. Cohn bawled the gateman out unmercifully and from that moment on Merle was the only actress permitted the use of the lot.

Cohn stocked Merle's dressing room with her favorite butterfly orchids, gazed in rapture at her rushes every night, instructed Miss Arzner to make sure she was gently and carefully treated in the shooting, and in every way doted on her like a lovesick college boy, accepting with resignation (for the first time in his unpleasant life) that he could not hope to obtain a conquest.

Merle was fascinated by Dorothy Arzner. A memorable photograph shows the director, looking like a man in drag, gazing intently from a standing position into the seated Merle's clearly disconcerted eyes; Arzner's attraction to Merle is almost embarrassingly obvious in the picture, and Merle's annoyance is equally evident. Nevertheless, Merle admired Arzner's pictorial skill and style; and very much enjoyed the part of an espionage agent opposite her old friend of the prewar years, Brian Aherne.

During the first weeks of shooting, and at Christmas, Merle had an occasional letter from Richard Hillary in England. Then, on January 8, 1943, in the middle of the making of *First Comes Courage*, she received the news that Richard Hillary had crashed to his death—like the Plunkets, the Duke of Kent, and Carole Lombard. At first the newspapers stated that he had been killed while engaged in action against the enemy. Merle knew this was most unlikely since he had been grounded for some time because of his horrifying injuries. She made inquiries and found that he had gone down in his plane on an icy, moonlit winter night, taking with him his navigator, the very young and well-born Walter Fison. According to Hillary's friend Arthur Koestler, Hillary had apparently committed suicide; he was no longer able to endure his uselessness in time of war. According to another close friend, his biographer Lovat Dickson, Hillary could not have done something which would have cost the life of another man; he was painfully aware that whereas he had been rescued from his earlier crash in the North Sea, others in his crew had died.

Dickson has always maintained that Hillary was killed by accident: that he took up his plane, mistook certain signals due to his impaired eyesight and the intense darkness, and that his ravaged hands could not sufficiently control the plane's joystick. Whatever the explanation, the death was a shocking blow to Merle. She left work for several days and remained in seclusion, hysterical and inconsolable. There is no doubt that Hillary had touched her more deeply than any man; that he had worked his way through the vanity and self-satisfaction of the star in Merle and brought out the tenderness, giving, and impassioned romanticism that lay at the heart of her nature, the best part of that nature. There was no hope of her going to the memorial service in St. Martin's-in-the-Fields in London or to the funeral in Buckinghamshire, where he was buried close to the spot where she had spent that last unforgettable weekend with him. Her one consolation in her agony over Hillary's death was that he had published *The Last Enemy*, or *Falling Through Space*, to overwhelming acclaim some eighteen months earlier; that she could feel she had inspired part of that masterpiece herself; and that the book would be with her forever, as a reminder of Hillary's tortured, headstrong, romantic spirit, so much like her own. She read later that his will contained the request, "I want no one to feel sorry for me in an age when no one can make a decision that is not dedicated from above. It was left to me to make the most important decision of all . . . In my life, I had a few friends, I learned a little wisdom, a little patience. What more could a man ask for?" She would always be a part of the man who had written those words; but she was sorry and saddened despite them.

The shock of Hillary's death gave an extra edge to Merle's playing in *First Comes Courage*. The day after she heard the news, she acted her biggest scene, in which, in a cellar with Brian Aherne, she expressed a burning hatred of Nazism. Her performance notably intensified from that moment on. Inspired by patriotism, she never looked more beautiful than in this film.

In the wake of Hillary's death, Alex drifted even farther away from Merle. He was in London during most of the filming, selling through proxies his stock in United Artists; and Merle's escort on evenings out was, oddly enough, Joe Schenck. She was fond of her nephew, Vincent's son Michael, and invited him to her house; in a famous *Life* magazine spread about Hollywood, she was shown, pretty and slender at thirty-two, playing with him on the lawn at Bel Air; they were accompanied by Zoltan's son David. Michael was a fair, plump little boy who tended to be clumsy and lacking in athletic coordination; and Merle had a house crammed with delicate, fragile china bric-à-brac which suffered from Michael's rather awkward attentions; like many Orientals, she had a strong concern over preserving objects, and she was extremely upset, although she didn't really show it, when Michael shattered a teacup from one of her English bone china sets.

Merle had several pets, including a Chow named Luke with a noble pedigree allegedly going back to the Ming dynasty. The chow was one of four animals, Matthew, Mark, Luke, and John; the others had been given away to friends. Merle also had a beautiful cat, named Amber because of its eyes; Amber was a comedienne by nature and loved to hide behind various expensive ornaments, disappearing seemingly into the woodwork and then jumping out without warning, an evil grin on its face, to unsettle unsuspecting guests. Even in Bel Air, Amber managed to find mice and rats, but instead of burying them in the garden, she carried them into the living room at the height of social events and deposited them with great ceremony before the feet of some lady of distinction who would, since this was Hollywood, say several rather unladylike words and kick Amber out of the room. At one piano recital given by José Iturbi, Amber scratched the ankle of a young actress who was known for her ladylike airs and graces, but whose language in private resembled that of a Marine. Just as Iturbi reached a complicated passage in a Chopin Prelude, Amber jumped up from nowhere and attacked the actress. Everyone froze; and Iturbi could barely continue playing. The actress took a deep breath and said very sweetly to Merle, "My dear Lady Korda, would you be very kind and remove that goddamn animal from the room?"

At the end of shooting, Merle flew to Seattle, Portland, Denver, and Minneapolis to appear at hospitals. With Patricia Morison's advice in mind, she had long since learned to conceal her anguish when she saw men suffering from horrifying injuries. She read to them, recited, comforted, and cheered. Her tours were totally unpublicized, and Hedda Hopper and Louella Parsons kept their promises not to reveal her whereabouts. She did not want to make capital out of suffering, and her great sense of privacy prevented her from having reporters present on these visits.

Just before she left, Alex returned to pack up the last of his belongings. Their parting was friendly and resigned; he had made a deal with Louis B. Mayer to run the British operation of the studio and was very anxious to leave Hollywood forever. His physical relationship with Merle had long since ended and no doubt the knowledge that she was still in love with the dead Richard Hillary was painful to him. Back in London, he could rule the roost once again, and whatever Merle had achieved as an actress after the first flush of her success owed very little to him. For months before the summer of 1943, he had been moving his possessions to London; and following the bombing of his house on Avenue Road, he moved into a suite at Claridge's and continued as a liaison with Sir William Stephenson at that exposed location.

Although she and Alex were separated, Merle worried about him constantly. She also fretted over her other friends in England and wondered if they were in danger from the bombings. She put as many calls as possible through the Korda or Stephenson offices in New York, but it was extremely difficult to make connections to London in wartime.

According to Montgomery Hyde, Merle made at least two more journeys to Europe in 1943. Given her shooting schedule, they could only have been during the summer of that year. She was evidently on special propaganda missions like other stars since no mention of her movements appears in the press at that time nor is there even a reference in the FBI file on her; this means that, as was the custom of the Stephenson office, J. Edgar Hoover was not automatically advised. Contrary to the picture drawn in *A Man Called Intrepid*, there was by no means a satisfactory meshing of the British and American intelligence services during World War II.

Hyde confirms today that Merle flew to Lisbon and then to London, but he is unable to disclose the nature of her journeys, perhaps because of the formal restrictions of the Official Secrets Act. It is likely that as before she was simply a useful contact and that she served much the same purpose as other actors at the time in proving to be a useful morale support in neutral countries where British staffs were resident. Lisbon was a particularly sensitive area because the Portuguese were obtaining Hitler's looted gold in large quantities and because a liaison was maintained there between German diplomatic sources and the Duke of Windsor in Nassau, capital of the Bahamas; in 1940, the Duke had been in discussion with Nazi representatives in the matter of a possible negotiated peace with Hitler and his return to the British throne.

Whatever the precise purpose of Merle's mission, she was—if Montgomery Hyde's description of her movements is correct—fortunate that she was not caught or shot down. Her former lover Leslie Howard was not so fortunate. Once again she was stricken by the tragedy of a violent death: Howard, who had been more overtly on a mission to Lisbon, possibly in connection with work for British Intelligence, was shot down in June in a Dutch plane flying from Lisbon to London that she very nearly took herself. There were rumors that he had been mistaken for Churchill, that a well-known passenger was thought to have been on the flight, and that the Germans assumed Churchill was the man. There is no evidence, however, to support this contention. As Ronald Howard, Leslie's son, discloses in a recent biography of his father, Leslie was more certainly involved in contacting diplomatic personnel in Portugal and helping with local propaganda work against Germany. Another possibility suggests itself: Portugal was locked in a struggle over the export of vital war materials, including wolfram, a form of the metal tungsten, to Germany; attempts were being made by the British and Americans to buy her off. It is conceivable that Howard was seeking to obtain influence over the Portuguese in the matter. The records show that several previous flights of the KLM airline from Lisbon had been fired upon unsuccessfully.

The news of Howard's death when she was in Lisbon and her desperate efforts, all foredoomed, to learn the truth from Alex, seriously affected Merle's health on her return to California and caused a breakdown in which her immune system gave way and she had a series of severe colds and skin problems. Oddly, Alex himself mirrored those symptoms in London, where he was no more happy or content than he had been in Los Angeles. The rationing and the shortage of good liquor wore down the spirit of this all-out *bon vivant*; he hated the dank gloom of wartime London, the soot-encrusted buildings, the misery of badly staffed restaurants, and the fact that it was possible to obtain Scotch salmon or lamb only on the black market. Merle received a stream of complaining letters from Alex, which she wearied of at last, but then she was jolted into an awareness of Alex's real problem when she learned that he was suffering from a heart murmur, as she had from birth.

The parallels between her and Alex seem extraordinary when contemplated: their restless spirits, their passion for luxury, their shrewdness and expert use of confidence tricks, their concern with a glamorous front, their fanatical emphasis on perfectionism, and their obsession with the beautiful also had an undercurrent of bad nerves, indifferent health, poor skin, digestive upsets, and severe breakdowns.

Like Alex, Merle used her time with extreme dedication to herself. She grew tighter with money as the war years went on. It was said, unfairly, that she was never known to have paid for anything; the truth was that she had invested heavily in Alex and in fact, at the war's end, she discovered that she had made deposits in London banks which amply rewarded her; but she was known to keep receipts for everything, to maintain cash entry books or ledgers small enough to fit in her purse, and the slightest overcharge would drive her into transports of rage. She invested her considerable savings—she was far richer than Alex because, as a woman, she had had to spend much less—in real estate. In this, she was advised by Henry Hathaway, the director, and by her business manager, Wallace E. Hunt, as well as by

Hathaway's attractive and clever wife, Skip. Hathaway himself, while quite out of the ordinary as a contract director, first at Paramount and then at Twentieth Century–Fox, was a wizard with investments at a time when buying property was possible, with interest at something like 3 percent, and income tax so low that one-third of an income could be saved. Merle had bought or leased a number of buildings which, through her contacts with the local government and city council, she then leased or subleased to the Los Angeles post offices. Hathaway showed her that, smart though the investment undoubtedly was, it was yielding her only about 8 percent on her income, so although he told her to hang on to the buildings, which by the 1960s were earning her close to 16 percent, he found a much better source of income for her. He and Hunt put her into tract housing. At that time, in the mid-1940s, Los Angeles was still limited in its expansion, and indeed Bel Air, where she lived, was considered to be out of town, rather like living in the country. In the south and east of Los Angeles, itinerant workers from Mexico were pouring in to fill the gaps left by the hundreds of thousands of young men of the blue-collar class who were at war overseas. These workers were desperate for housing and needed roofs over their heads immediately. From this need sprang the first tentacles of the giant Los Angeles housing boom which continued until the overbuilding period of the mid-1950s. Cheap homes made of wood or inexpensive stucco were flung up and sold for a few thousand dollars. Merle made probably over $1 million in this field, and not with an absentee's disinterest either. She went to business school night after night as she recovered from her breakdown; the other students were astonished to see her and were barely able to keep their minds on their work. She brushed off date after date.

Merle also built up her legendary jewel collection from the foundation laid down by Alex. Apart from the magnificent diamond-and-emerald necklace originally owned by Marie Antoinette that Alex had given Merle at their wedding, he had also given her as a kind of parting gift a spectacular necklace of cabochon emeralds the size of pigeons' eggs which had been presented by Napoleon III of France to Baroness Haussmann in reward for her husband's brilliant work in redesigning Paris.

To these invaluable treasures Merle added pearl-and-ruby earrings worth a king's ransom, bracelets fashioned of 17-carat diamonds and pearls, necklaces of amethysts, turquoises, and sapphires, watches studded with rare gems. Whenever she traveled, except on her war missions, she took the jewels with her, each ornament contained in an exquisite velvet box. The jewels were then put in locked pigskin or leather cases which she handled like luggage. Her friends were horrified when she arrived in New York or Washington, D.C., carrying this priceless collection with her.

She also invested heavily in paintings. Alex had a slightly excessive taste in art; she preferred more delicate works. She was particularly fond of Raoul Dufy, whose shimmering, dancing evocations of the sails, brown bodies, white houses, and azure waves of the French Riviera reminded her of her first vision of Europe when she left the ship in Marseilles in 1929. She also loved the works of Utrillo. The gentle colors and rhapsodic lyricism of Utrillo and Dufy filled her spirit with joy and she found a deep affinity with them. When she could not wander along the beach at Malibu, where she still maintained a cottage, and see the sun setting in the Pacific, or the fierce brilliance of the sun at noon, she could find magical moments of the day and evening entrapped forever in her favorite canvases.

Her house on Copa de Oro Road, Bel Air, was frequently redecorated by her in her recurring periods of despondency and sickness; she strove always to purify her environment aesthetically. Whereas most Hollywood houses were vulgar and showy to a degree, with interiors that smelled Decorator and were arranged rather like store windows, Merle was almost unique in having an austere and spare environment with cool, subdued colors, pale, off-white walls, pastel or beige carpets, and tall windows that admitted the light. She liked rooms to be drenched with light; and when guests came to see her, they felt they were in the home of a French or English lady of the aristocracy.

In the summer of 1943, recovering more or less from her enfeebled condition, Merle accepted a part from her friend Darryl Zanuck at Twentieth Century–Fox. She was to play Kitty Langley, a showgirl in Victorian London, in a new version of the celebrated period novel *The Lodger*, by Marie Belloc Lowndes, a reworking of the story of Jack the Ripper. In the accomplished script by Barré Lyndon, the Ripper was portrayed as a soft and sensitive, haunted and artistic man whose obsession with his dead brother offers more than a hint of incestuous homosexuality. The perverse strain in the writing was enhanced by the casting of the homosexual star Laird Cregar in the title role. Cregar, an actor of great resourcefulness and power, was ideally cast and gave the performance of his lifetime under the inspired guidance of the German director John Brahm.

With its crawling fogs, its spectral darkness, and its atmosphere of mounting terror concluding with the extraordinary sequence of the

Ripper's suicide in the waters of the Thames at night, *The Lodger* remains a masterpiece of the macabre. Yet making the picture was an ordeal for Merle. Soon after she accepted the assignment she realized that she was merely a support to the real star, with whom she had no empathy at all. She had other gay friends, most notably Cole Porter and Noël Coward, but they sparkled with keen intelligence, with an antic wit and style, whereas Cregar, for all his extroverted rash flamboyance on the screen, was bitter, murky, and private. He was tormented by his sexual needs and was frustrated in fulfilling them because he was grossly overweight and therefore ruled out from the fiercely competitive, body-oriented, and maniacally sensual world of homosexuality. His only recourse was to buy the sexual favors of men, which inevitably left him more frustrated than before. Merle tried hard to establish some kind of friendship with this difficult, unhappy man, and in order to cheer him up she told him that he was basically very handsome and if he would lose forty pounds in a diet that she recommended of vegetables, light proteins, and no fats, he would look wonderful and still be acceptable in leading character roles. As a result, Cregar suddenly became convinced he could turn from the gloomy restricted life of the homosexual to the more optimistic world of the heterosexual and perhaps could attract a woman and find fulfillment with her. During *The Lodger* and his next film, *Hangover Square*, he began to diet according to Merle's prescription; and he found a young actress with whom he hoped to establish a normal sexual liaison. But unfortunately he overdid the diet and it weakened his heart. He died at the age of twenty-six.

Working with this doomed, immensely gifted actor not only cast Merle in despair for him, but for herself, since she could not hope to match him as a performer; and indeed she hated herself in *The Lodger*, with good reason: she was at her worst in it, stiff, mannered, expressionless when expression was called for. She looked uncomfortable and in one instance, her behavior was inexcusable. She fastened her attentions on a young and extremely good-looking carpenter with blond hair and clean-cut, all-American features. She invited him home to Bel Air to dinner. The conversation was awkward and strained because the youth was totally unsophisticated. In fact, he was quite inexperienced in the art of discussing anything. After dinner, Merle made it clear to him the real reason that he had been invited: incredibly, he hadn't cottoned to it. When she made a move, he suddenly started back and said he would have to leave at once. Her mood changed to fury and she asked him what he thought he was doing. He replied later that he was a recently baptized Christian and that he would never go to bed with any woman until marriage. Next day, he was missing from the crew.

This behavior was not at all characteristic of Merle and suggests a desperate loneliness for male company. Long before Alex left, there had been a hollow in her life; and it says much for her strength of character that, conscious of her position as Lady Korda, and working against the strain of gossip that turned her into a tramp, she had hardly spent so much as a night with a man since Richard Hillary. She was ripe for a new romance and oddly discovered it right on her doorstep with the cameraman of *The Lodger*, Lucien Ballard.

Lucien Ballard was thirty-five years old when Merle met him and he started conferring with her on the lighting of her still-scarred but beautiful face. He had been born in Oklahoma in 1908. Devastatingly handsome, he was over six feet tall, with a football player's shoulders, a flashing smile, cheerful blue eyes, and curly hair. He was part Cherokee Indian, and this gave him a quality of calm, silence, security, and strength. He was slyly witty, elegant, fastidious, a superb dresser—a man of great style, charm, and grace of manner. He also had a ruggedness and an uncomplicated masculinity that were just what Merle wanted at the time.

The romance between Merle and Lucien was electric. They were both of mixed blood, passionate, longing for fulfillment, and possessed of many interests in common. Inspired by the relationship, Lucien developed a new light named after Merle, the Obie, which he patented and which thereafter became generally accepted in the industry. It had the effect of removing any hint of scarring; it whitened the features even more completely than Gregg Toland's lighting had done in the 1930s for Goldwyn. Ballard, more in love every day, spent hours fiddling with tiny arcs and fill lights in order to decorate Merle more sumptuously than ever before. Inspired, he gave his best to the film as a whole, and it remains one of the high-water marks of black-and-white photography in the history of the screen.

With great strength and determination, Lucien overcame Merle's nervousness at the scenes in which she had to dance a rather awkward version of the cancan, described by one English critic rather rudely as the can't-can't. Merle had, as we know, danced in her adolescence, and she came from the strain of Maoris on her mother's side who were themselves beautiful dancers and singers. And, of course, in 1937 Korda had flown the dancer Anton Dolin from France to London to train her in that version of Hans Andersen's *The Red Shoes* which he had abandoned. But to imitate an experienced French cancan performer when Merle was in her thirties and had been seriously ill was to ask too much of her, and she was ineffective in her scenes in a London music hall. Obstinately, she insisted on using a dancing stand-in only in a very few shots, with predictably poor results. She also had to climb flights of stairs made of metal, which formed a crucial visual role in the action. This was not good for her heart and she suffered from strain and palpitations.

Despite her newfound relationship with Ballard, she quickly established her superiority over him by arguing furiously with him on the set. But, encouraged by her friend Joan Bennett, who admired Ballard after working with him in the film *Wild Geese Calling*, she gradually learned to respect Ballard's judgment.

Of course, no hint of the new relationship must leak to the public. Merle was furious when the gossip columnist Ruth Waterbury disclosed in the magazine *Photoplay* that Lady Korda was romantically involved with her professional inferior. Adultery in those days could prove extremely damaging to a career. The women's clubs could easily put an embargo on the films of a star discovered to have strayed from the marital path. The studio publicity machine ground into action and Louella and Hedda were showered with gifts by Zanuck in order to keep their mouths shut.

Merle and Lucien would drive to the beach and watch the sunsets, always an obligation for any lover of Merle's. She began to relive the affair of the late 1930s with David Niven. Alex, with his portly, unathletic figure, heavy diet, and hatred of exercise, had always restricted Merle; now at last she could have fun with a young outdoorsman, a jock who liked gardening, exercise, swimming, walking, running, and beachball. She became rejuvenated by Ballard. She learned to laugh again and let her hair down. All weekend, she and Lucien lived in an old beach house she bought and worked with him to fix up; they wore bathing clothes, sandals, and little else. They rose at seven and went to bed at nine. They ate breakfast on a patio with metal chaise longues and tables set up for food, swam through much of the morning or gardened until noon, and then spent the afternoons loafing or puttering about. Lucien was a man's man who enjoyed fixing things, taking care of wiring problems, carpentry, and even plumbing; Merle joined in everything like a trouper. He built an annex to the house himself. He also enjoyed driving in his run-of-the-mill bright red Ford with Merle up the coast to visit friends like Norma Shearer, to whom she was close even now. They saw Cole Porter whenever they could on his visits from New York. Frances, ever devoted, lived with Merle at the beach house, and so did another beloved maid, Vene Benham. But unlike sober, dignified, secretive, and reliable Frances, Vene was nervous, neurotic, edgy, and seemed to have a nature incapable of keeping peace with itself. She was not at all Merle's type of person; Merle liked to be surrounded by calm, measured perfectionists. Yet she was sorry for Vene; her tender nature reached out for her.

Merle dubbed the pink stucco beach house Shangri-La and with Lucien redecorated it with Mexican motifs. Everything seemed to be perfect for them; but from the beginning there was a problem of great magnitude. Her close friend, Louis B. Mayer's daughter, Edie Goetz, explains what that problem was:

> Of course, we all adored Merle. But it became impossible to entertain her or to be entertained by her once she took up with Ballard. We all felt she had made a most serious and ghastly mistake in becoming involved with him. For instance, Merle was used to going to parties given by Father or by Sam Goldwyn or by any other of the topflight people in Hollywood. But they could not possibly be expected to entertain a mere cameraman! Like all societies, we had our social levels and rules and it would have been totally embarrassing if Ballard—admittedly a charmer—accompanied her to a major dinner party. Gifted artist though he was, he was simply too low on the totem pole. I think some of us tried to point this out to Merle but she would hear none of it. She was completely besotted and of course Ballard did wonders with her face. They walked out of the whole Bel Air–Beverly Hills world and went off to the beach for years. I think she resented our attitude—but what could we do?

Many friends of Merle's agree with Mrs. Goetz in their judgment of the situation. In the light of the built-in social elitism of the time, weird and antiquated though it may seem today, that attitude is understandable. Also, again there was the problem of exposing an adulterous relationship to the harsh light of the social columnists who eagerly covered every party; and even though Hedda and Louella had been bribed, others might not have been bribable. The position was made worse by the fact that Merle was Lady Korda; that she was supposed to maintain her position at least while the marriage to Alex lasted.

In London, Alex began to change. After being totally devoted to Merle and everything she stood for, he began to be bitter about her, yielding to those members of his family who described her as nothing more than a tramp and a user who had married him for position and fortune. He overlooked the fact that she had bailed him out financially, not the other way around; and his bad-mouthing of her in future years was to become a torment to her. After all, he himself had never been a saint; he had had his own reasons for marrying her, which were not entirely pure. But now he began saying that Merle had pestered him to make her a star; that when he had said it took time to do so, she had driven him almost insane with her insistence. Yet of course her relationship with Ballard proved that money grubbing was not her line of business; Ballard had much less money, though he advised her on investments, and in fact she deliberately wore her least expensive jewelry when she was with him, knowing that his masculine vanity would be wounded by the fact that he could not afford to buy her expensive ornaments.

Indeed, Merle set out to reduce the opulence of her life, to become a "simple" person, living a more or less rustic life, on the beach with Lucien and quite cheerfully accepting her social exile as being of no consequence. It does seem extraordinary that within less than a year of acquiring her title, she would so completely have abandoned the privileges it brought her, and which she had so painstakingly aimed for; and yet so wayward and romantic was her spirit that she clearly could not resist this new physical and emotional adventure.

After her first few months with Lucien, she looked better than she had in years. But differences began to emerge, apart from those of income and social position. Merle was prone to daydreams, reveries, and romantic abstractions, whereas Ballard was tough and without interest in mysticism, spiritualism, which was beginning to fascinate Merle, or a study of comparative religions. For years, she had kept up her scrapbook of verses and read them to herself or aloud; Ballard had little interest in poetry, and was happiest tinkering with a car, chopping logs, or riding horses.

Ballard says:

> Merle very much wanted to marry me. She wanted Alex to give her a divorce. But I didn't want to marry her, to be very frank about it: I was enjoying our affair and didn't want to spoil it by marriage. I dreaded being thought of as Mr. Merle Oberon. Finally, I got so tired of Merle asking me, fond though I was of her, that I went to San Francisco to visit with the girl who is now my present wife. Merle followed me there and became so insistent that I finally said yes. She did ask Alex for the divorce.

At the time, Andre De Toth, assistant director of *The Thief of Bagdad* and *The Jungle Book*, made a deal with United Artists to direct a picture called *Dark Waters*, based on a script by Hitchcock's associate Joan Harrison; Korda had suggested De Toth for the assignment. One night, De Toth bumped into Merle at a party and asked her if she would like to play in the picture. She was intrigued, liked De Toth enormously, and asked him for the story line. He told her he wanted her to play a girl, raised in the East Indies, who, arriving in New Orleans after being torpedoed in time of war, has a nervous breakdown. Resting on a plantation in the Louisiana bayou, she is gradually victimized in a plot to deprive her of her fortune.

Merle, nervous, romantically innocent for all her sophistication, and herself a victim of nervous breakdowns, was fascinated and asked to read the script. She was disappointed when it arrived, so De Toth engaged John Huston to rewrite it. Huston had had a hot tip at the Santa Anita racetrack and rewrote the entire screenplay overnight so that he could lay the bet. He lost the money.

The opening scene was so well written that Merle accepted the part on the basis of that alone. It showed her discovered in a strange railway station, not knowing where she has come from; she is seen later in a hospital, hysterical and out of control. DeToth decided not to use a glamour cameraman on the picture: Lucien was busy on another production and he wanted a harsh and realistic look for the film. Merle was not very pleased with the choice of Archie Stout, better known as a location cameraman, for the job and yet she kept her counsel.

Discussing the script with Merle, De Toth said to her, "Look, you just came from the sea. You were *plucked* from the sea. You mustn't be a Hollywood glamour girl. I want the scene to be totally harsh, frightening. You will grow enormously if you shoot without makeup and forget all about being beautiful."

De Toth says:

> It was very difficult but I wanted people to see her talent, not just her beauty. She had to sit up in the hospital bed and say—I wrote the line myself—"Have you ever been at a funeral at which the minister forgot the words of the service?" It was a reference to her amnesia; she had lost her memory because of the sinking. I explained to her that I had seen amnesia victims and I tried to depict to her their bewilderment, their emotional disassociation. We have a defense mechanism, I pointed out, in our bodies with which we react to fear by cutting off unbearably

tormenting memories through simply forgetting them. I said to her, "You have to think of yourself as lost. *Lost*. Have you ever in your childhood been scared, deprived, unable to have something you wanted, suffered so intensely that you blotted the whole thing out since then?"

Merle asked me to close the door of the dressing room. She talked about her childhood with great meaning. She described the Indian children, the deprived, the hungry, the desperate. She spoke of the horror of violence, deprivation, cruelty, and mental suffering. She said she had indeed cut all that off from her memory: that all her life she had hidden everything even to herself in a kind of amnesia, a block in the brain. Having released that block, to me alone, and I have never spoken of it until now, she could *play* amnesia.

They started into the scene. But then her courage began to fade a little. Merle started to panic that her face, without makeup, would look too horrible; that it would be too visibly scarred. De Toth begged her to let the scars show: that the effect would be thrilling and horrifying and would raise her level enormously as a performer. De Toth describes what happened next:

She did the scene courageously, without the makeup, with the scars showing, and she was so frightened, genuinely, that it gave added emotional weight to the scene: There were tears actually streaming down her cheeks. I said, "That's wonderful, darling! We'll print it!" Merle said, to my horror, "I'm not happy with it. I'd like to do it once more." I agreed. But the second take wasn't as good as the first and the third wasn't as good as the second. We did a fourth take. The first was still the best, but I lied to her and said we would print take four. She pleaded, "Can't I have it once more?" I thought, My God, what's the matter with her? But the results were great.

Making the picture was unpleasant in the extreme. Much of it was shot in a fake swamp and a quicksand made of mash, hog feed, coffee beans, and wet corn flakes. Merle had to flounder about in the bayou, fall off a balcony, splash around, and tumble down stairs. Franchot Tone, the leading man, didn't like her particularly and slapped her very hard in a scene where she became hysterical; so hard that she couldn't resist it and slapped him back. He was attracted to her, and jealous of the handsomer Ballard; he lost a bet of his macho male friends that he could seduce her. Merle, always so fastidious, would go home filthy from the day's work and take a shower; then she would get dirty again cleaning out the chicken pen in the backyard or repainting the beach fence or scraping down rust from keyholes and metal window fixtures.

The result of this harrowing work was worth it. Merle gave one of her best performances in *Dark Waters:* sensitive, delicately shaded, excellent in the scene of hysteria in the beginning over which Andre De Toth had labored so long. The direction has great Gothic flair, using all-out melodramatic effects as the heroine cowers in fear before banging shutters, a sudden plunge of a room into darkness, an echoing voice in the swamp calling her name, sinister relatives bent on charming her at a candlelit table in the plantation house late at night.

During *Dark Waters*, Merle began to institute divorce proceedings against Alex, who was deeply despondent in London. He realized that Merle had never really loved him as a man but rather had respected him as a father figure and mentor. He was tortured by the failure of this second marriage, and his misery was not aided by the fact that Maria Corda was crowing with delight at his grievous state and saying that she knew all along that the marriage to Merle would not work. Meanwhile, the studio publicity department at United Artists was working overtime to set up a smoke screen between her live-in relationship with Ballard and the ladies of the women's clubs, who were beginning to suspect her of being an adulteress. The forces of moral righteousness were constantly and nerve-rackingly threatening, but Merle managed to fend them off with various bond-selling and lecturing appearances as Lady Korda.

In 1944, Merle received an offer from the ever-enraptured Harry Cohn to make a version of the life of Chopin in which she would play Chopin's lover, George Sand.

At first, Merle was reluctant to play a somewhat masculine woman. Harry Cohn was determined she would act it, and so was Korda. They put their heads together and decided on a ruse. They told her that Marlene Dietrich was very interested in the part. She accepted on the spot, her old rivalry with Dietrich, going back to the episode of the Brockhurst painting, again flaring.

Cohn offered her a quarter of a million dollars, a tremendous sum at the time, to play the part, and gave her director approval. He called her to his office and told her that he would like an old friend of hers, and Alex's, the Hungarian Charles Vidor, to direct the picture. She was delighted. She had known Charles Vidor as a warm, outgoing, charming man, a *bon vivant* who enjoyed singing Hungarian songs or performing czardases on the piano at the very Hungarian parties that Alex favored. This robust, cheerful man was also a director of great talent, and Merle had admired his "British" films, *My Son, My Son!*, with Brian Aherne, and *Ladies in Retirement*, based on a play co-written by her old friend of Elstree days, Reginald Denham. He had just had a great hit with the entertaining musical *Cover Girl*, in which Gene Kelly had performed a marvelous dance sequence matched to his mirror image in a street scene. Merle loved the film; she was intensely musical and for years had been devoted to Chopin. She had often listened to his piano music at night on records and longed futilely to find the time to play the piano herself.

She read the script for the Chopin story, *A Song to Remember*, with great interest. The author, Sidney Buchman, had been an assistant stage director at the Old Vic Theatre in London and was an intense Anglophile; at the time of *A Song to Remember*, he was a production supervisor at Columbia, and Harry Cohn, not suspecting that Buchman was a former communist, was devoted to him and admired him deeply. He had written very fine scripts for such classics of the screen as *If I Had a Million*, *The Awful Truth*, *Holiday*, *Mr. Smith Goes to Washington*, and *The Talk of the Town*, and he had worked happily with Zoltan Korda on a Humphrey Bogart vehicle, *Sahara*. Zoltan swore by him.

Merle made a point of meeting with Charles Vidor and Sidney Buchman in order to feel her way into the part of George Sand. The screenplay was handicapped by some excessively overblown dialogue and highly melodramatic situations, and it deserted history at every turn of the plot. While recognizing these disadvantages, Merle was impressed by the all-out romanticism and passion of Buchman's approach. She liked the way he used Chopin's patriotic love of Poland as a theme, and that he showed the conflict between Professor Elsner, Chopin's idolized music teacher, and George Sand for Chopin's soul: in Buchman's version Elsner wanted Chopin to devote himself to militant music, whereas George Sand urged him to devote himself to romanticism.

Always the romantic herself, and a liberated woman who had lived her own life, chosen her own men, and refused to be subservient to the male ego, Merle could identify profoundly with George Sand, who had refused to use a feminine name, had worn men's clothing in the nineteenth century, breaking every possible rule and custom of the period, and who had dared, when women were supposed to have no intellect and stay home to mind their households, to be a creative artist, pouring out a succession of inventive and striking novels with prodigious energy.

One of the problems Merle faced in the interpretation was that George Sand, at least to modern eyes, was quite unattractive. Merle spent hours gazing at the subject's portraits, much as she had done when preparing for the part of Anne Boleyn in *The Private Life of Henry VIII* eleven years earlier: She saw the horsy, bold face with the prominent nose and broad forehead, and she started to read about Sand in biographies, learning of her domineering, aggressive, powerful manner. She learned that Chopin needed Sand's strength of purpose and almost masculine vigor and strength; he himself was tubercular, frail, and hollow-chested, his body consumed by his genius. The relationship between the couple was a kind of reversal of the conventional picture of a male-female relationship. This reversal fascinated Merle.

She decided that she should make no attempt to imitate George Sand by making herself up to eliminate her looks. The effect on screen, though accurate, would seem ridiculous to an audience. But she did with enthusiasm decide right from the beginning to wear male attire, and she had fun working with the costume designer on her clothes. She selected rakish black silk top hats, cutaway coats, a range of cravats and white silk pants. The fittings were long and arduous as she sought to cut down her ample hips and broaden her shoulders. The shoulder lines were padded and the trousers cut in folds under the coats. She even, despite her horror of smoking, managed to brandish a cigar in the color tests; but for all Charles Vidor's persuasions, she could not bring herself to smoke it in the film.

Vidor cast Cornel Wilde as Chopin. Wilde himself was three-quarters Hungarian, the son of a cosmetics salesman from Hungary. A national champion with the saber, Wilde had reached Olympics standard by 1936. He had been Laurence Olivier's fencing instructor in the stage production of *Romeo and Juliet* and had played Tybalt in that production. Olivier had expressed admiration for him, and despite his unsatisfactory early screen appearances, Charles Vidor was convinced he would make an ideal Chopin. They talked about the part in Hungarian at preliminary discussions; not for the first time, Merle was irritated that she hadn't learned the language which seemingly every second person close to her was fluent in. Amusingly, while Merle was doing her best to turn herself into a masculine woman and remained the most feminine imaginable of women, Wilde, the most masculine of men, was trying to turn himself into a physical weakling. Like Merle, he had to fight to overcome a problem of physical miscasting. While Merle was having her shoulders broadened, he was having his narrowed with special coats that were cut in such a manner they reduced his appearance of strength. The makeup artist gave him an intense pallor and put shadows in his cheeks and dark rings under his eyes. He began weeks of studying the piano. Vidor, with his passion for music, was determined to make the audience think that Wilde was actually playing. Vidor sent two pianos to his house. One of them was a silent piano in which the keys had been disconnected from the strings; the other was normal. Victor Aller, an experienced concert pianist of the second rank, went to Wilde's house to teach him the fingering, phrase by phrase, through four hundred hours of exhaustingly rigorous instructions. Not only did Wilde have to finger correctly but he had to match the "touch" of José Iturbi, who was going to match the performance in the recording studio off-screen. The Polonaise in A flat, used as a patriotic theme illustrating Chopin's love of Poland, sold a million copies on record after the film was released.

Cornel Wilde describes how impressive he found Merle on the first day of work. They had never met before. He says:

> She was, of course, at the height of her beauty then. Her face was as finely carved as an ivory mask. She exuded the atmosphere of being a great lady: not merely a star. The ribald remarks among the crew which usually occurred when beautiful actresses were on the set stopped dead in her presence. Even the bawdiest "grip" or electrician was silenced by her extraordinary presence. Everyone recognized that her character was of a great fineness.

> Although, of course, like any man I found her immensely attractive, I did not have sexual fantasies about her. I felt as though I had walked into a museum and was looking at a masterpiece of sculpture. She was a work of art or nature so fascinating I couldn't imagine having any intimate physical contact with her.

> We had intense rapport from the beginning. I was very impressed with her talent and became more so as we continued to work together. She was, of course, as far removed from George Sand in looks as it was possible to be, but she brought out a crucial element in George Sand's character: She understood the strength in Sand that Chopin needed to lean on in life. I responded to that degree of understanding and we often discussed our roles in breaks in the shooting. I began to believe as we went on that she *was* George Sand, and that helped me with my own

interpretation. We grew used to our idealizations. What fascinated me particularly was the fire in Miss Oberon, very controlled, but banked strongly under the surface; oh, yes, I was aware of that! And the warmth, also not obvious but expressed in her many kindnesses to me . . . She was not ostentatious, she was extremely reserved in her feelings and thoughts, very private; but working with her was a dream. There was great communication in just looking at her, speaking with her, getting responses from her. I had not known that in my previous films and this was my first major part. She helped me more than I could have imagined.

By contrast, Paul Muni, who played Professor Elsner, was insufferable. He was atrocious in his behavior.

Wilde recalls that Muni was selfish, thoughtless, egomaniacal. He tried to steal every scene he was in and ignored the necessary give-and-take of work in a picture. Whereas Merle and Wilde helped each other constantly and devotedly, Muni used endless gestures, parodies of those learned by him in the Yiddish Art Theater in the early part of the century, unnecessarily shooting his sleeves out, shrugging, frowning, fiddling with his glasses, making little tricks of speech in a symphony of fussy actors' gestures. He had an unnerving habit of not looking other actors directly in the eye, which threw them completely off character: Merle or Wilde would deliver a line to him and he would seem not to have heard it. This ruined scene after scene, which had to be reshot; and indeed his scenes are the worst in the picture. Wilde confirms that Merle, though under intense control, was furious with Muni; not since Charles Laughton had she been more exasperated by an actor. On one occasion, the cameraman, Tony Gaudio, who had photographed her in *'Til We Meet Again*, deliberately left the film out of the camera on Vidor's instruction as Muni improvised a speech.

There were problems with Charles Vidor once the work began. Although Merle continued to admire him, she and Wilde were sometimes irritated by him. He was extremely volatile, temperamental, and nervous. His weakness was procedural: he relied too much on the inspiration of the moment. Whereas Alex, who was also extremely high-strung, would always be prepared for the day's work, with his brother Vincent's sketches and with copious notes, Vidor would walk on the set, all fire and brimstone and Hungarian charm, scratch his head as he looked at the players—and then everybody began to realize that he hadn't the slightest idea what he was going to do.

He had been up all night partying and drinking and singing

Hungarian songs and now suddenly he was confronted with expensive stars, costumes, cameras, and sets and had no more idea of what he was going to do than a driver at his first lesson. He would roam about, snap his fingers, shake his large mane of prematurely gray hair, and suddenly exclaim the equivalent of "Ah! I've got it!" in Hungarian. None of the three principal performers was amused, even though in their various ways they all adored the director. Once he started work, he proved to be the infantry lieutenant or *Gauleiter* he had been in World War I. Sometimes he would break off to sing a Wagner aria, and when he lit up a cigar and brooded and ran onto the set to fix something, everyone had to scatter. Maddening though he was, he created an electricity that stimulated everyone and inspired all to their best.

He had violent quarrels with Muni, so violent and so laced with gutter language that Merle, her face a steel mask, would lock herself in her dressing room until the fights were over. Matters deteriorated still further when Muni tried to bring his wife Bella onto the set. Harry Cohn had it in Muni's contract that Bella must never appear on the set. Hal Wallis had warned Cohn that on every picture she would sit in an extra director's seat behind the camera and nod or shake her head at every scene. If she shook her head, which was most of the time, Muni would drive everyone mad by stopping the scene and insisting on doing it again. Muni was irritated by her absence; he felt like a cripple without a crutch. When one day the crutch arrived, Vidor had it forcibly removed. Muni walked off the set and didn't come back for a day.

So the stormy, difficult production went on, with rows and makings-up and hugs and inspirations and absurdities and madnesses. Some of the dialogue was almost literally unspeakable. When Merle was talking to Wilde, expressing her desire to have Chopin take a vacation, she had to say, "You could make miracles of music in Majorca." On another occasion she had to issue the peremptory instruction: "Discontinue that Polonaise jangle you've been playing for days." Lines like these became the butt of movie buffs everywhere. Merle protested them but she was overruled by the director.

A Song to Remember was Merle's greatest triumph at the box office since *Wuthering Heights*. The critics tore the picture to shreds but the public loved it, and it became one of the most successful pictures in Columbia's and Harry Cohn's history. It was a time when musical biographies were enormously popular and women by the millions, deprived of their loved ones in war, found a marvelous escape in its romantic, daydream version of great and impassioned lives. The glowing colors, the rapturous music track excitingly played by Iturbi, and the all-out energy and charm of the central performances swept the United States. Whatever wounds were caused by the reviews, Merle could salve with an unguent: she was once again at the very top as a star.

Chapter Ten

Merle had a major problem at home at the time. Of her two maids, who had been with her since 1938, Frances was always calm, measured, supremely efficient, utterly devoted to Merle, with no private life of her own, at least so far as anyone knew; she never fussed or grew nervous, expertly conducting Merle's private affairs, fielding questions from inquisitive journalists, supervising the entertainment of friends, carrying Merle's confidences in the locked box of her decent heart, and nursing Merle through collisions and crises with Lucien or her directors and fellow players. Frances kept every inch of the house at the beach (the Bel Air house had been virtually abandoned) spic and span, each ornament and tabletop dusted and polished until it gleamed. A benign Mrs. Danvers to Merle's Rebecca, Frances would brush Merle's hair, tend to her clothes, lay out her bed, set out her drinks for guests—Merle still never drank—take care of a long stream of gardeners, and make sure that rust, that deadly enemy of oceanside dwellers, did not affect the metal fittings in the house or the many locks.

She remained what was known in British families as a Treasure: she always had a cup of tea ready for Merle when she returned at night, woke her up in the morning as regularly as an alarm clock, shopped with quiet expertise, and was a dream on the telephone. She was never known to lose her temper and seldom if ever took a day off. Merle meant more to her than her own life. Sober, subdued, tweedy, utterly British, she was Merle's conscience and her guiding light.

Everyone remembers Frances; everyone who knew Merle will never forget her. But almost no one except Lucien Ballard remembers the existence of Merle's second maid, Vene. Vene was a nervous, difficult person, edgy and off-key, but, undoubtedly, devoted to

175

Merle. Perhaps—we will never know—a sense of inferiority to Frances ate into Vene, because she grew increasingly morose during the shooting of *A Song to Remember*.

On March 15, 1946, she left Universal Studios after visiting Merle on the set to pick up a masseuse to drive to Merle's home at Trancas Beach. She left the studios shortly after 7 P.M. With her she had a bundle of fan mail and grocery purchases. She drove to the house and dropped off the masseuse. Merle was out of town for the weekend. In her absence, two termite fumigators, Ralph Findley and Lester M. Perriguey, whom Frances, who was also absent, had engaged to check the house, smelled a strong aroma of exhaust from the closed garage. Unable to open it, they also found the door connecting it to the house had been locked from the inside. They broke it open and found themselves choking in the midst of heavy fumes.

With damp cloths over their faces, they opened the door of Merle's car and found Vene stretched out on the seat, the shopping basket beside her and pressed against the dashboard. She had been dead for days. The autopsy established suicide. The news came as a severe shock to Merle.

Lucien Ballard says:

> The reason for Vene committing suicide had nothing to do with Merle. Vene's daughter was a would-be actress, very pretty but with limited talent. Merle had sweetly arranged for a screen test for the girl with Selznick. Unfortunately, the girl proved to be a failure in the test. Vene had pinned all her hopes on the girl being successful and had told everybody in town her daughter was a genius and would soon be a star. The rejection drove her into such a depression that she could no longer endure life. Merle and I only learned about this later.

Merle was very depressed by the episode. She had another shock when Alex suddenly collapsed following a heart attack, or perhaps a severe attack of indigestion, while dining at Romanoff's with the actress Gracie Fields and her husband Monty Banks. Conveniently, a doctor was present and Alex was rushed to a hospital in record time. He was saved, but became increasingly moody, aware that his days were numbered. As it happened, he was to live for more than a decade, sustained by his manic energy and colossal ego and love of life.

In the wake of *A Song to Remember*, Merle seemed to be in the best shape personally and professionally that she had been in for several years. But unfortunately, she made a serious mistake at that moment. She signed a contract with Universal, and that studio failed to prepare for her the kind of grand and glamorous vehicle called for at the time. Inexplicably, she accepted the starring role in a very minor and medium-budget picture, *This Love of Ours*, in which she was cast with another unknown actor even more obscure than Cornel Wilde, the Czech leading man and former documentary filmmaker, Charles Korvin, who had made only one other film, *Enter Arsène Lupin*, in which he had played the famous French detective. Merle was protected to some extent by the selection of the director, William Dieterle, who had had a vivid career at Warner Brothers, where he had made *The Story of Louis Pasteur*, *The Life of Emile Zola*, and *Juarez*, and at Paramount, where he had made *Love Letters*, a romantic movie starring Jennifer Jones which Merle admired. Dieterle was borrowed at her behest, but he proved to be a mixed blessing when she started working with him.

The story of *This Love of Ours* was based on a play by Luigi Pirandello which played with time in its complex dramaturgy; the script, written by several writers headed by an FBI undercover man named Bruce Manning, was unhappily sentimentalized and softened. Merle was to play a tragic woman, wrongly suspected of adultery by her husband, who becomes hard and bitter in middle age and takes up a theatrical career; she finally achieves reunion with her lost family. Merle gave a subtle and intelligent performance against heavy odds in this soap opera, particularly in the early scenes in which, jaded and depressed, blowsy and overweight, she is seen in a seedy nightclub; she conveys an atmosphere of world-weariness, of corruption, with great stylishness. She is touching and fragile as the young, innocent bride; and effectively hardened and cold in the middle portions of the film.

From the beginning, she had major differences with Dieterle, who nevertheless gave the picture an expert fluid movement and a strong romantic flavor until the script sank him in the final sequences. He proved to be a martinet: Extremely tall, over six feet six inches, with formidable shoulders and a barrel chest, he was a vigorous German of the old school who had had his training in the German theater and cinema. He treated Merle like a WAAC on her first detail. She fought back with chilly politeness, barely holding her temper until once or twice she exploded with startling violence. It became a struggle to cope with this difficult man. Worse, Charles Korvin hated her. A sophisticated Middle-European of great charm, Korvin was miscast in the picture and looked notably uncomfortable throughout. He was a chunky, cleft-chinned, quite handsome man of medium height who matched up well physically to the tiny Merle, but lacked the romantic forcefulness called for by the director. Korvin's views of Merle are the exact opposite of those expressed by Cornel Wilde:

> She was absolutely impossible to work with. She was only interested in her makeup, hair, her costumes; she was so over-dressed, with elaborate hats, that it was horrible trying to make love to her in a scene. She refused to allow anyone to have closeups done on the same day that she did; even me, and I was supposed to be her co-star.
>
> She hated the young girl who played her daughter in the picture. She had scenes cut involving the girl because she didn't want to be seen with her as a woman in her thirties. She acted like a movie queen all the time and gave me nothing, nothing in return.

Merle gave as good as she got in an interview posthumously published in the magazine *Films in Review*, in February 1982. In the interview, which took place in the early 1970s, she said that Korvin was a bad actor; that Dieterle gave him a very hard time and she tried to build his confidence by lying that he was marvelous; that after a while, he started to believe her, and then became impossibly haughty and supercilious as the conviction that he was first-rate went to his head.

Korvin insists that throughout the shooting Merle was atrociously rude to Lucien Ballard, who had been brought in to photograph the film as a further protection of Merle; Korvin says she treated Ballard abominably, that she would literally scream at Ballard in front of the whole cast and crew if there was the slightest objection to his handling of her; Ballard denies this emphatically. And, Korvin adds, "God knows he lavished enough attention on her; hour after hour would go by while we all twiddled our thumbs and waited as he worked out her lighting to cover the flaws in her face." Korvin adds that Merle's hatred of Dieterle was unjust; he says, "They fought bitterly because in the scenes when Merle was a young bride he wanted her to be completely deglamorized, simple and subdued, and she wanted always to look far too glamorous and well dressed for a woman who had no money and no position in society. They never did iron out the problem and Merle's appearance in those early scenes destroyed their reality."

This Love of Ours was a flop in the United States, but it became an enormous hit in Latin America, and in Spain after the war; and

Merle's performance in it ensured her increased fame in those areas. The picture's extreme sentimentality and romantic gloss appealed hugely to Latin audiences. She could have written her own ticket in any studio from Mexico City to Buenos Aires.

This awareness of her vast popularity below the border turned Merle's thoughts increasingly to Mexico. She had always been fascinated by the country and had made occasional trips there, returning with pre-Columbian art, the foundation of a collection that would ultimately be of classic proportions. She went to Mexico for the premiere of *This Love of Ours* and was given a rapturous reception. She began to discover new friends in Mexico City.

Another connection with Mexico was established at the time. In the final week of shooting of *This Love of Ours*, Merle married Lucien Ballard by proxy in Juarez. They had been unable to get away from the studio because of the pressures of shooting and had barely received the Mexican divorce from Alexander Korda. At the last minute he had been reluctant to sign the final papers, and this temporarily caused a problem. One Alejandro Muñoz represented the bride and an attorney named J.T. Fortillo represented the groom. Oddly, these two men swore their eternal fealty before the judge and the matter was concluded. Errol Flynn and Nora Eddington were married similarly.

In Hollywood, toward the end of World War II, Merle embarked upon her most absurd film to date: *A Night in Paradise*. She began it because the first few pages of the script described her as a Persian princess being drawn in a carriage by white horses. As a child, her most persistent fantasy was playing a Persian princess in a film version of a romantic fairy tale; and her love of *The Thief of Bagdad* undoubtedly stemmed from these early daydreams.

The director of *A Night in Paradise* was the genial Arthur Lubin, whose most notable work on the screen had been directing Bud Abbott and Lou Costello in such trivia as *Buck Privates*, *Hold That Ghost*, and *Keep 'Em Flying*. He had shown Claude Rains with acid-scarred face and flying cloak whirling around the upper reaches of the Paris Opera House in *Phantom of the Opera*, and the delicious Gale Sondergaard making sinister plans in *The Spider Woman Strikes Back*. Merle suddenly had descended from the heights of a major screen career to the nether regions of Hollywood Camp.

She was co-starred in the film with the king of the yashmak-and-saber pictures, Turhan Bey. Born Turhan Gilbert Selahettin Saultevey in Vienna, of a Turkish father and a Czech mother, Bey was a swarthy, coarsely handsome, muscular, and sexy leading man, the idol of the swing shift. Merle first saw him dressed as a very old man with white hair and beard, hobbling about in disguise. After three days, his makeup was removed and he emerged looking spectacular in a Persian costume. Arthur Lubin says:

> Merle took one look at his bulging biceps and immediately changed her mind about him. Fortunately, Lucien Ballard was not working on this picture but was on vacation at the time. Merle definitely had a steamy romance with Turhan behind Ballard's back. She was very nervous that it would be too obvious in their scenes together. Everyone, me, cameraman Hal Mohr, and her old friend Travis Banton, who did her costumes, was sworn to secrecy.
>
> One problem we had during the picture was that Lana Turner was herself madly in love with Turhan Bey. She would suddenly appear on the set at odd moments when least expected. Since she was Lana Turner, nobody dared refuse her admittance, but she would come from MGM, and she would stare at Turhan and Merle in order to unsettle them and make sure that Turhan didn't act out of turn. It became nerve-racking for everyone as the spying went on. Of one star on another. There's no question that Lana was very jealous! Merle always insisted on a closed set. When she finally did succeed in closing it and Lana was asked to leave, Lana peeped through the scenery! It went on and on!

Lubin says that at times he was a little nervous in handling so big a star as Merle. One time, he recalls, he expressed his unease and Merle snapped back, "You've just made a picture with Maria Montez! If you can handle that bitch you can handle me!" He was astonished at this outburst of an icy, ladylike creature and from that moment they worked well together.

A Night in Paradise is virtually unwatchable today. Merle's career had reached its lowest point: her romantic attraction to the story had sunk her completely. She recovered with Temptation, her next picture, a cleverly written, intricately fashioned version of the famous old movie Belladonna, which Pola Negri had made in 1922. Based on a novel by the once popular Robert Hichens, it was the story of a London woman of ill repute who marries a British archeologist and travels to Egypt, where he is excavating the tomb of the pharaoh Rameses V. Restless and lonely in Cairo, she encounters a worthless chiseler and blackmailing Egyptian crook, Mahmoud Baroudi, who encourages her to destroy her husband's life by poison. She begins by administering small doses of arsenic but relents and, discovering that Baroudi intends to hand her over to the police, takes his life instead. At the end, she escapes arrest by a providential accident in the excavations—a tiresome imposition by the Breen office.

In adapting the story, the writer Robert Thoeren provided many excellent scenes that Merle could get her teeth into. The edgy, uneasy but erotically charged encounters with Baroudi were written with great wit and style, and Merle responded to them in the playing. The planning of the murder, its attempted execution during a genteel tea party in the desert, and her witnessing her husband's collapse during the supper party in a tent late at night offered some of Merle's best opportunities as an actress, and she seized them with relish. The performance is subtly graded, worked out with infinite care; it is like the fashioning of a pattern of Brussels lace. Every tiny gesture, every expression in the eyes has been thought out with great experience and cunning.

And the film itself was cunningly executed by the neglected director Irving Pichel, an intellectual who contributed learned articles on film aesthetics to movie quarterlies, an actor of skill who had appeared in many important films, and a man of great integrity and charm. Pichel delighted Merle; they got along famously. But contractual pressure forced her to accept Korvin again as her leading man. He still hated her; and he recalls today how the problems of *This Love of Ours* were increased in this new picture.

The Australian designer Orry-Kelly, who had worked with Merle at Warner Brothers, created one of the most stunning wardrobes seen in any film for Merle: a different costume for almost every scene. Korvin hated the long hours spent in holding up production while the fittings took place and he blamed Pichel for being as weak as Dieterle was excessively strong; he felt that Pichel was totally under Merle's influence, and that may have been true, because the taste, craftsmanship, and style of the film undoubtedly owe a great deal to her. Korvin still feels a strong sense of irritation as he describes coming to grips with Merle in their love scenes, struggling through her yards of lace, huge hats in the style of 1900, and even at one stage kissing her through an elaborately worked veil. He misses the point which she and Pichel worked out together. When Baroudi first kisses Belladonna through that veil, it indicates that she is deliberately using him, keeping herself at a distance from him; when she removes the veil later on, it is a subtle hint to the audience that she has surrendered.

Critics failed to appreciate the skill of *Temptation* (one reviewer dismissed it in a sentence: "*Temptation* is to be resisted"). Merle herself would have preferred the film to have been in modern dress: paradoxical since the period atmosphere was ideally realized, and appropriate for the highly charged melodramatic content of the story. And had the picture been made as she wished, she would have lost the chance to look more attractive and striking than in perhaps any other film; she was "made" for the clothes of the turn-of-the-century, with her hourglass figure, her small shoulders, and emphatic hips.

At the end of 1945, Merle, who was now thirty-four, decided she wanted to have a child with Ballard, to cement their crumbling relationship. She traveled to Boston with Ballard to see Dr. John Rock of the Harvard Medical School's Department of Gynecology, but he said to her agonized distress that she could never have children.

In 1947, Merle signed to make the film *Memory of Love*, later retitled *Night Song*, at RKO for Howard Hughes. It was a story originally written for Loretta Young by the admirable DeWitt Bodeen, of a composer who has been deeply embittered by being blinded in an accident. Merle was to play a wealthy woman who tries to have his sight restored. It was in many ways a reworking of the theme of *A Song to Remember*: of a strong woman and a weak man to whom she gives her strength. She was intrigued, and glad to be working with the director John Cromwell, one of the big romantic filmmakers whose *The Enchanted Cottage* was a film she could identify with, remembering her relationship with Richard Hillary: the story of two people, the man horribly disfigured and the girl simple and subdued, who are transformed by the ennobling power of love. Cromwell's beautiful Selznick production *Since You Went Away* and his richly entertaining *Anna and the King of Siam*, a non-musical precursor of *The King and I*, were among Merle's favorite pictures. She was pleased also that her agent, the tough and hard-bitten Jennings Lang, and her business manager Wallace E. Hunt had managed to get her an excellent $12,500-per-week contract with the studio, and a guarantee that Ballard would photograph not only this picture but all others she would make there.

Dana Andrews, the excellent, intelligent star of *Laura* and *The Best Years of Our Lives*, was cast as the pianist. Like Cornel Wilde before him, he worked with great intensity on the fingering, made more difficult by the fact that he could not seem to be looking at the keys. He says today that he was slightly disconcerted by the fact that Merle made moderately subtle advances toward him in front of her husband, who was photographing them. He felt greatly embarrassed because the slightest indication of feeling might be known to Ballard. Interestingly, Charles Korvin makes the same observation, concurring with Andrews that often Merle liked to make it seem to Ballard that she was attracted to her leading man. Indeed, Merle used to whisk Andrews off to lunch, leaving Ballard behind; Andrews was dismayed by this, and it canceled out any desire he might have had for Merle. Furthermore, their worlds were far apart: his friends were mostly down-to-earth characters like Harry Morgan, who later became a huge hit in *M*A*S*H*. Merle's friends were those few members of the social set who remained loyal to her in her reduced station in life as Ballard's wife, most notably the lovable Skip Hathaway.

In June 1947, Merle signed a new contract for three pictures starting with *Berlin Express*, the story about postwar problems in Germany, and again Ballard was set as the cameraman. Shooting began in September and, after several weeks on the set, was shifted to Europe. Merle was once more cast with Charles Korvin, but his part was subsidiary. The real star was Robert Ryan, a big, rugged, powerful man who for years had held Dartmouth College's heavyweight boxing championship and had worked at a number of jobs, all extremely macho, including ranch hand, ship's stoker, and field laborer; he had had a stint in the Marines in World War II.

Ryan was a modest, subdued, private man of great integrity; a keen supporter of the ACLU. At the time he appeared in *Berlin Express*, he had already given an impressive performance in *Crossfire* as a psychopathic, soft-spoken Jew-hater; he had earned extraordinary reviews for his portrayal. Merle, cast in the unrewarding part of a French schoolteacher caught up in espionage in *Berlin Express*, walked through the role without any visible interest and scarcely bothered to manage a French accent, but Charles Korvin remembers:

> She fell madly in love with Robert Ryan. He was just her kind of man's man. I know that she slept with Ryan both in Hollywood and in Europe and I thought it unfair and cruel of her. Incredibly, Ballard, who undoubtedly knew about it, accepted it all with good humor.* He was almost too good for this world. But I objected to the affair and so did everyone else on the picture.

Merle traveled with Ballard to Paris, staying at the Ritz. For a time he had Merle to himself, as Ryan was to join them on the train to Berlin a little later. Merle kept such meticulous records of every single

*Ballard absolutely denies this account.

franc she spent, even on a white belt she intended to wear in the picture, that her accounting figures fill page after page of the studio files. The hotel cashier at the Ritz advanced her 100,000 francs on studio arrangements and she even managed to winkle 30,000 more for a brief vacation in the south of France.

Korvin remembers that as she joined Ryan with Ballard for the trip to Berlin, she resumed her affair with Ryan. He recalls that she would literally leave Ballard's room on the train and go to Ryan's during the night. This created shock waves in the company as a whole, and when they stopped off in Frankfurt for two days of work among the ruins of the city and were billeted at a nearby castle, Merle and Ryan were again sharing Ryan's room. The Ryan liaison continued, Korvin insists, until the end of shooting.

In December, after *Berlin Express* was finished, Merle upset the studio by charging for the use of every single accessory she had worn in the film. Weary with arguments, and up against such tough guys as Jennings Lang and Wallace Hunt, the studio executives yielded to everything. Merle took off with Ballard and Skip Hathaway for a week of skiing in Sun Valley. Robert Ryan was on location making a picture called *Return of the Bad Men*. She never saw him again.

Ballard proved to be a poor skier, and Merle and he decided to go to Switzerland to improve his style; they would then proceed to Italy for a vacation. Ahead lay a far greater challenge to her and to her already threatened marriage. The man who would mean more to her than anyone else up to that time.

Chapter Eleven

In January 1948, Merle and Lucien were more or less happy in Switzerland, though they were no longer sleeping together. It was the height of the winter season, and the social set was present in full force at the great hotels of Geneva, Lausanne, Zurich and Gstaad. Merle wrote to her friend, Dore Schary, the head of RKO, from the Palace Hotel in St. Moritz, "We drove here from Zurich yesterday. It was a heavenly drive—this is where you and Miriam should be—boiling hot sun, charming villages all around one—and skiing if one wants." She added, "This is really a kind of business letter—I suppose I might as well get right to the point." She said that she knew all the studios were trying to cut expenses and also that the contract she had received from Schary had been written up in better times.

She wondered if it would be a help to him if she offered to cut her salary by $15,000 a picture. She pointed out that she was making this offer without her agent Jennings Lang knowing about it; that it was "purely personal" because she thought Schary was a very fine person, "and I had visions of one of the stockholders of RKO saying to you, 'Why did you make this big contract?' and now I'd like to visualize him saying, 'This is what my players think of me.'" She would write to Jennings Lang separately. Schary did not reply for three months, and then, unthinkingly, to the Palace Hotel from which Merle had long since departed. He wrote that he would have written a long time ago but his mother had been desperately ill and he had been away from the studio a great deal. When he had been in the office, he had been so swamped that he couldn't handle the mail. Now he wanted to say how kind and generous Merle's letter was and how pleased and delighted he was by her offer of cooperation and her very nice gesture in cutting down the costs of her commitments. He could only hope that he could provide her with the vehicles that would make up for the splendid thing she had done. He added, *"Berlin Express* appears to be even more timely than we had hoped. I only pray that it will help bring some order to a very troubled world. My best to you and Lucien, and please forgive me for not writing, but also please try to understand. Thank you so very much."

This pleasant exchange concealed the fact that Merle's box office power had slipped drastically and she had gotten wind that the studio intended to drop her once her option came up. Indeed, the unpleasant truth was that she had been cast in *Berlin Express* because there was nothing appropriate available for her; the part could easily have been played by a much lesser star. Her mood was uneven, often depressed, as she and Lucien crossed over the border into Italy after a week of skiing at St. Moritz.

They arrived in Rome in February. Immediately on her arrival, Merle was contacted by her old friend, the legendary Dorothy, Countess di Frasso, the American adventuress who played both ends against the middle, a custom of her species, in serving every warring cause (except, of course, that of Communism) which would enable her to sustain her considerable personal fortune and ensure her an international network of great and powerful friends.

Merle had first met her in the mid-1930s, when Dorothy had been the chief rival of Ouida (Mrs. Basil) Rathbone, Sir Charles and Lady Elsie Mendl, Elsa Maxwell, and Marion Davies as a great Hollywood hostess. Dorothy, tending to plumpness, with sharp features, was no beauty, but she had great charm, and an electric charisma that captivated many men. The two men who had meant most to her were Gary Cooper, with whom she had enjoyed a long and torrid romantic adventure, and Buggsy Siegel, the gangster, who traveled with her to Italy just before Pearl Harbor to sell an explosive device to Mussolini—despite the fact that Buggsy was Jewish. She and Buggsy had taken off to the Cocos Islands off the coast of Latin America to look for the buried treasures of the conquistadors on a yacht owned by Jean Harlow's stepfather, Marino Bello. Bello had hired a mixed Jewish and Nazi crew, with predictable results. There was a mutiny and several members of the crew were put in chains.

For years during World War II, Dorothy di Frasso was dogged by the FBI in Mexico, where she was busy with a dozen questionable schemes including a factory for various forms of explosives in which she was in partnership with the equally dubious American senator Robert R. Reynolds. As soon as the war was over, she moved back into her villa near Rome, which had once been the meeting place of

Hitler and Mussolini. She rejoiced in showing her guests the outside bathtub which, despite its enormity, could barely contain the bulk of Il Duce.

Despite the fact that Merle had worked for the British government during the war, she was capable of renewing her friendship with Dorothy. At a certain level of wealth and power, everything was forgiven once the world conflict was over. Moreover, the ranks of the rich and powerful, which naturally included large numbers of fascists like Dorothy di Frasso, closed firmly against the Communist menace in Eastern Europe. The conversation between Dorothy and her friends in Italian high society, whenever it grew serious, was inclined to deal with Roosevelt's dreadful mistake at the Yalta Conference in giving away half of Europe to the Soviet Union. Indeed, in 1950, when Merle arrived, there were violent political conflicts in Italy itself, with a rapidly strengthening Popular Front inspired by Communist elements; and the wealthy, with their perennial paranoia, muttered about the danger to their bank accounts and stock holdings.

Dorothy gave a lavish party to welcome Merle at her villa. The Countess was predictably the toast of local society. First, she was an extremely right-wing American woman, and Americans were as popular at the top levels in Italy as they were unpopular below them. Dorothy gathered a brilliant collection of people for Merle and Lucien's arrival. The sideboard groaned with expensive food which gave no hint of the grim poverty of postwar Italy; Merle arrived in a stunning gown designed by Chanel. Ironically, Chanel had collaborated with the Nazis and had even traveled to Berlin during the war to confer with the Gestapo chief Walter Schellenberg on a negotiated peace with Britain. If Merle had known about this she would never have forgiven Chanel.

At the party, Merle resumed another friendship—with Elsa Maxwell who, fatter and more acidulous than ever, was still fabulously abrim with stories, gossip, and amusing nonsense about everybody in Rome. One woman at the party, and one woman alone, rivaled Merle in looks. This was the legendary, exquisitely beautiful Countess Madina Visconti Arrivabene. The Arrivabenes were among the most distinguished families in Italy, their fame dating back to the medieval era; they were immensely rich and Madina was undoubtedly the chief jewel in the family crown. With her beautiful sister Niki she had for years been the toast of Paris, where she had been adored by the playwright, poet, and film director Jean Cocteau, to whose glittering circle of artists, musicians, and sculptors she triumphantly belonged. She was witty, sparkling, and adorable; and she had capped

her career with a brilliant marriage to the imposing Count Luigi Visconti, horse-owning brother of the great Italian director Luchino Visconti. In 1947, she had fallen madly in love with Count Giorgio Cini,
one of the handsomest and most dashing young millionaire studs in
Italy. He was with her at the party; for months, there had been
rumors in society that without benefit of papal approval, she had
married Giorgio secretly; and Elsa Maxwell even went into print in
her newspaper column gurgling about this hidden and quite unofficial
adventure in matrimony. Whatever the truth of this, at the time of the
party in Capri, Giorgio, through his powerful family, and over their
deep objections, had applied to Pope Pius XII for a special dispensa-
tion to marry Madina; and she in her turn had applied for a dissolution
of her marriage to Count Visconti.

Cini's family was even more important than the Arrivabenes.
Giorgio was descended directly from the doges of Venice. Indeed, the
Cinis were identified with ancient and modern Venice to an extent
unrivaled in the upper reaches of the Venetian aristocracy. Giorgio's
father, Count Vittorio Cini, had been a prominent politician in Mussolini's fascist government: a cabinet member, Minister of Communi-
cations, with elaborate connections, through Pirelli and Italradio and
the other telecommunications companies, to Latin America throughout World War II. He had been commissar general of the Great
Exposition of Rome in 1943: the last grandiose fling of the Italian
dictator before his political destruction that year at the hands of the
insurrectionists.

The elder Count Cini had turned against Mussolini in 1943; he
had joined the opposing group which engineered the dictator's downfall. In doing so he had incurred the enmity of Nazi elements in
northern Italy, and had been imprisoned in the notorious concentration camp at Dachau. Released at the end of the war, he had been
restored to his former position and power because of his assistance to
the Allies and his betrayal of Mussolini; he had embarked on one of
the most ambitious restoration programs in the history of Italy, not
only restoring the crumbling ancient structures of Venice, but also
developing the modern part of Venice, a project he had begun under
the Mussolini regime.

An ancient scandal hung like a cloud over the Cini name. In
1918, Count Vittorio had fallen in love with the unthinkable: a motion
picture star. Italian society utterly rejected stars in terms of accepting
them in a family. Vittorio Cini had been captivated by one of the most
celebrated actresses on the Italian screen: Lyda Borelli, the Italian
equivalent of Theda Bara, who specialized in vamps and whose movie
The Naked Woman had been an outright sensation, establishing her

overnight as a voluptuous movie enchantress. When Cini became involved with her at the end of World War I, he narrowly escaped being ostracized; the only solution was for Lyda Borelli to give up her career at its height, and when she became pregnant with Giorgio, the matter was settled. The marriage was performed with great splendor in Venice and the Countess Cini was never seen on the screen again. Indeed, she remained a virtual recluse in the magnificent Palazzo Loredan Dorsoduro on the Grand Canal in the heart of Venice. Few people saw her, even in the almost suffocating splendor of the palace itself. She had her own quarters and her own servants and kept very much behind locked doors.

Giorgio was greatly beloved by his father. The son in any Italian family of wealth and prominence could expect to be showered with every gift that the rich can provide; and in his case he was in the blessed position of being the only son: his lovely sisters, Mynna, Ylda, and Yana, were almost his courtiers. Fortunately, he more than fulfilled his father's extravagant dreams for him. He was classically handsome, with thick glossy black hair, eyes that shone with great health and vitality, a strong Roman nose, even white teeth, and a square jaw. He had a fine athlete's physique and an irresistible humor and charm of manner. He was also fierce, stormy, chauvinistic, and overpowering, and he was a tough customer when it came to business. He could as easily crush a rival in the commercial world as he could sweep a woman off her feet. In February 1948, when he turned up at the Dorothy di Frasso party, he was already a millionaire in his own right. He owned the hotels Lido in Venice and Excelsior in Rome, which were among the most elaborate hostelries in southern Europe, and he was in effect president of the Cini shipping empire which included part of the Italian merchant navy and cruising lines in the Mediterranean and South America, with an income drawn from chartered freighters and millionaire yachts.

Giorgio and Madina almost took the spotlight from Merle and Lucien at the party on February 8, 1948; Dorothy di Frasso was in a tizzy of excitement at having lured the two most famous couples in Italy to the same event. She could not have foreseen the consequences, at once romantic and catastrophic, of her supreme social coup.

It was Merle's pattern, as we know, once she had met a man who powerfully attracted her, to let no power on earth stop her from entering into an affair with him. By a bitter irony, reminiscent of the episode in which Maria Corda had pointed her out to Alex, Madina Visconti Arrivabene introduced Merle to Giorgio.

As so often in Merle's life, those close to her contradict each other about what took place next. Ballard insists he left Italy to clear the way for Merle and Giorgio. And yet it was the talk of Italy that another incident had taken place. Binnie Barnes, the actress who had appeared with Merle in *The Private Life of Henry VIII* and was now married to the producer Mike Frankovitch, says:

> Mike and I were staying at a hotel in Rome at the time. We were in the suite above Merle and ran into her once or twice in the elevator. One night, we were awakened by a tremendous crash and a splintering of broken glass. It came from below. We ran out into the corridor and the other guests were also out of their suites. The news got around like wildfire: that Lucien Ballard had been hiding on the balcony and had broken the windows and surprised Merle in bed with Cini. Cini had thrown him out.

Lucien Ballard says the episode is pure invention. This means that the intruder must have been another man, madly in love with Merle, who was driven to the action by jealousy. Whoever the intruder, the matter was the talk of the country for months. Gossip is the very stuff of life to Italians, and Merle and Giorgio were the center of attention everywhere.

In the grip of romantic abandon, Merle decided to give up Lucien and marry Giorgio. She wasn't betraying Lucien really; after all, their marriage was over. And she needed sex to feel young and healthy. She began an eighteen-month barrage against RKO to arrange for a large sum in lire which would enable her to settle in Italy permanently: dollars were frozen and she could not bring in her own fortune, so RKO must pay her in Rome. She felt she must bring a dowry to the marriage. She used the excuse that she needed the money for jewelry and she kept her urgent requests for the money from her agent Jennings Lang. Howard Hughes, who took over the studio when Dore Schary went to MGM, was notoriously tight-fisted and blocked these requests at every turn. Even when Merle offered to put up her house in Bel Air as collateral, he would not agree to the loan. In 1948 the Copa de Oro residence was valued at $33,000; today it is worth at least $2 million.

Matters were still further complicated by Alex's presence in Rome with his best friend Christine Norden, a statuesque blonde who made her name briefly as the star of *Idol of Paris*, in which she fought a duel of whips with a rival *demimondaine* in the Bois de Boulogne. Alex was fretting for Merle, and driving Christine almost mad because of it; Alex was trying to assuage Christine with diamonds. They were in

Rome at the Excelsior, and Christine recalled that Merle and Giorgio had a fight even in the midst of their blossoming romance. She says:

> Cini gave Merle a tremendous amount of jewelry and there was a quarrel and he tried to get the jewelry back. He was so intent [determined lady, I give her all the credit in the world!] in keeping the jewels, she grabbed them [*that* came first] and ran out into the street, *naked*, clutching the jewelry.

The story sounds unlikely, since it is totally against Merle's character to have disappeared into the night, naked or not; indeed, given her strength, it's much more probable that Cini did the running. Certainly, the gossip columnists in Italy had their time cut out describing the quarrels, reconciliations, general alarums and excursions of the romantic pair and the utter grief of Madina, which they exploited relentlessly. Furthermore, the *paparazzi*, the ferocious camera squads of Rome, forced Merle and Cini to run the gauntlet as they went to dinner in candlelit restaurants, including a famous outdoor place on the Appian Way. Along with the riots and explosions of the political conflicts at the time, Merle and Giorgio were the most famous Event in the country.

They finally took off to America with the family conflict of the Cinis unresolved. They flew to Hollywood and Palm Springs, where Jennings Lang was under orders to pretend that Cini was his barber from Rome. This pretense was shredded within a day by the gossip columnists, headed by Hedda and Louella, who explained to Merle that, fond as they were of her, they could not keep so sizzling a matter secret.

Undoubtedly, more than anything else Merle wanted Giorgio to fit into her social set in Hollywood. But he proved to be a misfit there. He was irritated almost to insanity by the social pretensions he encountered: the insistence upon dressing for dinner and the general airs and graces of people who, only a few years before, had been selling gloves or furs or who had been working as waitresses or gas station attendants. He hated the houses that had been put together by expensive architects and decorators rather like movie sets, to be admired rather than lived in; and he was upset by the extreme formalism and the emphasis on money and film deals. He had little or no interest in pictures and rather tended to look down on picture people. Along with his intense snobbery, born of several generations of Italian blueblood aristocracy, Giorgio affected a contemporary casualness and macho informality. He liked to wear jeans, which Merle deplored, and leather or suede jackets; Merle couldn't get him to wear a tie.

One night in Palm Springs, matters came to a head. Merle insisted Giorgio dress for dinner in honor of Darryl and Virginia Zanuck and she presented him with a handsome tuxedo that she had had made to his measurements. He exploded with a rage, announcing that he would not dress up in a monkey suit. She pointed out that the other male guests would be in tuxes and she herself was wearing an elaborate evening gown. As the guests arrived, Giorgio was heard screaming at her, "I don't give a fuck what the other guests are doing! Today I bought three Liberty Ships for my fleet! If I can do that, I don't need to dress for dinner!"

Merle lost all control and they had a violent fight that kept the new arrivals at the house gleefully agog. Giorgio stormed out.

Giorgio was greatly annoyed by Merle's extravagance. She had trays of watches bought at discount from her New York friend Pierre Cartier, which she gave to friends on impulse. She presented one especially beautiful watch to Jennings Lang in Palm Springs and, forgetfully, he jumped into his boss Sam Jaffe's pool with it. The watch was ruined. He told of his embarrassment to his friends Andre De Toth and Veronica Lake and they bought him a big airplane pilot's watch with a chronometer. When he went to Merle's house with a contract for a new picture called *I Married a Communist*, she took one look at the watch and expressed her horror with it. She had the tray brought down and gave him another; Giorgio objected violently.

Nevertheless, in spite of everything, the relationship went on. Everyone who knew Merle at the time agrees that she blossomed more beautifully than before, as a result of Giorgio's heroic, tireless, insatiably virile love-making. Whenever she was preparing for a party, she would call in friends like Elsa Maxwell and ask them with a debutante's eagerness if they approved of her hair, her dress, her makeup; sometimes she would change six times before she would let Giorgio see her. He grudgingly agreed to wear the tuxedos after the first few months; they traveled to Hawaii for an idyllic two weeks of sunning and sailing.

They returned to Europe and spent months traveling in the international set. In Paris, they bumped into Alex and Christine Norden; Alex still regarded himself as Merle's slave, and irritated Christine by responding to Merle's every request for quarts of perfume or appointments for dress fittings. Merle was of course capable of making these purchases herself, but Christine insists that Merle took pleasure in issuing Alex instructions. There is no question that Alex was still hopelessly in love with Merle—and not with Christine, who knew

Above, with Gary Cooper on *The Cowboy and the Lady* set (J. Lee Morgan collection). *Below*, with Hedda Hopper signing autographs for the troops during World War II (J. Lee Morgan collection).

Left, with Reginald Gardiner, Anna Neagle, and her good friend Mary Pickford at a Hollywood radio broadcast for the benefit of the Canadian Red Cross in late 1940 (J. Lee Morgan collection). *Right*, on tour with Al Jolson in England (courtesy Patricia Morison).

Above, with Fredric March and Charlie Chaplin at a party at the Mocambo night-club in 1942 (Culver Pictures). *Below left*, leaving Buckingham Palace with her husband Sir Alexander Korda just after he received the knighthood and she became Lady Korda on September 22, 1942 (Wide World Photos). *Below right*, with Josef von Sternberg and Charles Laughton on the set of the movie that never was, Sir Alexander Korda's *I, Claudius* (J. Lee Morgan collection).

Above left, with Turhan Bey on the set of *A Night in Paradise*, 1945 (J. Lee Morgan collection). *Above right*, with Norma Shearer and Merle's husband Lucien Ballard (Robert Wolders collection). *Below left*, with Robert Ryan on the set of *Berlin Express*, which starred them, Charles Korvin, and Paul Lukas (J. Lee Morgan collection). *Below right*, Merle painting a still life of flowers from her garden, wearing a fashionable smock, 1948 (United Press International).

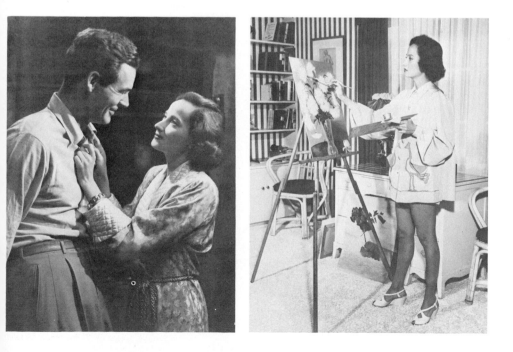

Above left, Merle and her lover Count Cini shortly before he died in a plane crash in 1949 (Wide World Photos). *Above right*, with Dr. Rex Ross in the early 1950s (J. Lee Morgan collection). *Below*, with Greer Garson arriving in New York from vacations in Europe aboard the *United States*, November 1958 (United Press International).

Above, Merle's mansion on Copa de Oro Road in Bel Air, California (Wide World Photos). *Center*, Mexican construction workers remodeling Merle's dream palace in Acapulco, purchased in the late 1970s by the sister of the Shah of Iran (Wide World Photos). *Below*, with Charlotte Ford, Anne Ford, and Mrs. Henry Ford II at the Ballo Romantico in New York, December 1965 (Wide World Photos).

Above left, with Prince Philip in Acapulco (Robert Wolders collection). *Above right*, with her husband Bruno Pagliai and Prince Philip in Mexico (courtesy Janet de Cordova). *Center*, with Noël Coward (Roy Moseley collection). *Below*, with George Hamilton, Lynda Bird Johnson, and Pagliai in Acapulco in December 1966 (Wide World Photos).

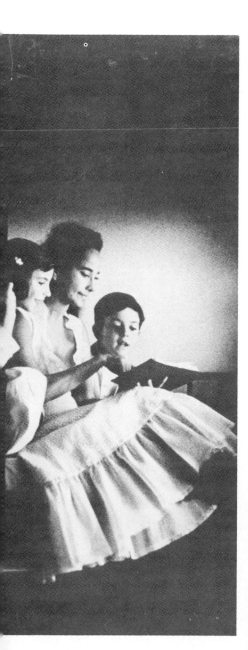

Left, reading to her adopted children, Francesca and Bruno Pagliai, Jr. (J. Lee Morgan collection). *Above*, with her last husband, Robert Wolders (Robert Wolders collection). *Below*, with her great friend the designer Luis Estevez at a dinner for Betty Ford in Los Angeles in 1975 (Alan Berliner, *Women's Wear Daily*).

With Betsy Bloomingdale and Eugenia Shepard at a party given by Harriet and Armand Deutsch in March 1978 (Roger Sandler, *Women's Wear Daily*).

With Mickey Ziffren at a party on September 25, 1979, two months before Merle's death (Aloma Ichinose, *Women's Wear Daily*).

it—and that he would do anything to please Merle who rejoiced in her power over him. At least, that is Christine's contention.

In New York in December 1948, Merle was separated from Giorgio, who had to return to Italy for business reasons. She pestered the RKO treasurers and accountants for the lire she so desperately needed to be independent of Giorgio when she settled in Italy. She received a cold response when she arrived at the office of RKO on December 16. In February 1949 she was compelled to put up her house as collateral and RKO refused.

In January she traveled to France, where francs were more readily available, to join Giorgio in Monte Carlo for an elaborate party given by the Darryl Zanucks. The affair resumed after the long and difficult separation; they were seen everywhere together again, eliminating reports that Giorgio had returned to Madina. The result of this reunion was that Madina, overwhelmed with depression at having failed to recapture the man she loved, took an overdose of pills in Rome and was only just rescued from death. The event was widely described in the newspapers.

Giorgio's jealous tantrums were endless. In one particularly harsh quarrel with Merle, Giorgio had cruelly brought attention to the tiny scars on her face which still existed following the unsatisfactory peel in 1940. She undertook the drastic and desperate step of having plastic surgery in Paris in order to remove the marks. This was not another peel but a repetition of the operation she had undergone in 1934 with Sir Alexander McIndoe at East Grinstead in which a layer of skin was removed. On this occasion, the operation was scarcely more successful, and to her distress, the scar tracings remained.

Worn out and miserable after the painful growing back of the skin, endured now for the third time, Merle left with Giorgio on a summer cruise of the Adriatic on his favorite yacht. As always, Merle insisted over Giorgio's objections in carrying her jewels with her in suitcases. She was still paranoid about banks, and there may have been some rationale for this in Italy because there had been some recent bank robberies. Giorgio had a manservant who went along for the trip. One night, in the small hours, Merle awoke on an impulse and checked her jewel cases. She was horrified to discover they were missing. Giorgio flew into a rage with her for her carelessness and turned out the whole crew and searched them on the spot. Her jewels were not to be found. Merle was hysterical; perhaps they had been taken at the last port of call.

Then, suddenly, Giorgio made a decision. He trusted the servant completely but perhaps the dedicated man had yielded to temptation.

He went into the man's cabin and ransacked it over the butler's protests. Finally, he noticed a telltale lump in a corner of the carpet under the bunk. The jewels were there. As captain of the vessel, Giorgio was empowered to arrest the servant and he did. He sailed at once for Venice and handed him over to the authorities. The court gave the servant a four-month suspended prison sentence because he had had no previous convictions. Incredibly, Merle still continued to carry her jewels with her in minimum security for the rest of her life.

The Cinis remained adamant that there could be no question whatsoever of Merle ever becoming engaged to Giorgio. For months, they had not even agreed to meet her. But at last, late one night in Venice, she and Giorgio went by gondola to the Cini palace on the Grand Canal where there was a charged and difficult meeting with the family. Although it was reported that Count Cini was touched by Merle's beauty and charm of manner, it became clear that hopes of a union stood little chance of satisfaction. The couple left the palace in defeat.

Meanwhile, the newspapers stated that Lucien was adamant that he would not grant Merle the Mexican divorce that she was trying very hard to obtain. Since December 1948, reports say she had been battling for freedom with the aid of her attorney, William Cooke, who had secured the Korda divorce. Cooke was in Juarez for months trying to make the necessary arrangements but Lucien allegedly blocked them at every turn. Despite the fact that she was still not free, Merle, with great impetuousness and obstinacy, began telling people all through the summer of 1949 that she was engaged to Cini. The divorce finally went through in the summer of 1949. Ballard says today he did not fight the divorce and in fact wanted it in order to be free. Once again, the statements contradict each other and it is impossible to establish the absolute truth, but Ballard is certainly the more reliable source.

Merle traveled to France with Giorgio in September and checked into her beloved Hôtel du Cap: a place still replete with all its old romantic associations. She was not feeling well: she had slipped and fallen in the bathroom of her suite at the Ritz Hotel in Paris and had suffered a head injury that caused severe headaches; she had also had a nasty bout of flu earlier in the summer and had not fully recovered, and Giorgio was quarreling with her jealously. One night, feeling a little groggy, Merle went to a party at the Hôtel du Cap given by her friend Pamela Churchill, wife of Winston's son Randolph. At the party, she renewed her friendship with Winston, who effected a cure of her sickness by teaching her to paint. At the same party, Elsa

Maxwell told Merle of a fortune-teller who was an expert in foreseeing the future. On August 29, Giorgio told Merle that he had seen the fortune-teller, who had warned him that he must be very careful about flying. Giorgio was due to leave at three o'clock on August 31 for Venice in a last-ditch attempt to persuade his family to allow him to marry Merle and to complete arrangements for a house there. He wanted her to come, but discussion on a new film prevented her.

Merle was appalled by the warning. Always superstitious, she remembered a story Giorgio had told her earlier: that when Giorgio had been at school in Venice, an astrologer had come there to cast the students' horoscopes. Giorgio had been refused his own forecast and had learned later that the reason had been given to another student as "in eleven years he will be dead. Why tell him? There is nothing he can do. He will die violently. It is in his stars."

Merle begged Giorgio to take a train to Italy. She finally convinced him that he should, and she began calling the railroad station authorities, but every seat on the train was booked and there was no room even in third class. She and Norma Shearer, who was staying at the hotel, pulled every string at the headquarters of the railway in Paris but even their influence was useless.

At least, Merle insisted, Giorgio should take a commercial flight from Nice. But this would have involved a change of planes in Rome for Venice, and Giorgio was impatient.

The various delays meant that Cini did not actually leave for Italy until August 31. His pilot flew in with a private plane from Venice. On the eve of that day, the night had an unusual beauty, lit by a full moon. Merle wrote in a fragment of a memoir that turned up in her papers after her death: "I am always enraptured by the moon, it has a magical mystery for me. I somehow take its variations personally. I noticed that while I admired its full-blown beauty a black cloud ominously passed over it and completely obscured it for a while."

She clearly felt an even stronger premonition at the sight. Next day was unusually beautiful; it had, she wrote, an unusually intense brilliance and radiance, yet as she drove with Cini to the Cannes Airport from the Hôtel du Cap she felt anything but joyous and in tune with nature. Cini had been assailing her with charges of infidelity in their five days together and she felt drained, exhausted. She wrote: "My mood was as low as I can ever remember it. This time it wasn't the impending parting that was crushing me, it was the knowledge of the hopelessness of our relationship. Giorgio's love for me I knew was great, but his unfounded jealousies and violent temper were literally killing me. I prayed for the strength to put an end to it [our affair].

"Then suddenly after we'd been driving about twenty minutes his black mood changed; the charm and warmth that he was capable of came back, but I really was so utterly flattened by the past days that I could feel nothing at all."

They began talking more rationally. Giorgio mentioned an airplane he was going to buy; she said she was probably going to make a new film, *Twenty-four Hours of a Woman's Life*, to be shot in Cannes.

At the airport, over lunch, between two and three P.M., Giorgio suddenly opened his heart to Merle. He told her of all his dreams for them both, that he had put a down payment on a house in Venice, that he would fly to join Merle in Hollywood on November 15, and that he would spend Christmas and New Year's with her in Honolulu, where they had had that marvelous visit earlier. As he described his plans, he superstitiously kept knocking wood. He mentioned a marvelous July they had had in Venice, living aboard his yacht, the *San Giorgio*.

At last it was time for him to leave. He held Merle tight and with deep affection in his eyes told her he was deeply afraid of the flight. He said that in addition to the warning he had had at school, he had also been warned by a fortune-teller in Marseilles that he would die in a flying accident that year. Then he held her as though he didn't ever want to let her go, and said, "I adore you, little one."

Giorgio walked down the steps to the airfield and the waiting plane. Merle stood on the balcony, waving a white silk handkerchief as he climbed into the small aircraft. She watched as the plane engine sputtered, caught, and roared into action. The pilot engineered an expert takeoff. It was a perfect day, with a vivid blue sky and no wind.

The plane dipped and Giorgio waved his own white silk handkerchief, with his monogram knotted with hers, and she felt a leap of joy, sensing that their misery might be over, that the future for them in Venice would be bright.

The plane rose and dipped and soared across the field. Giorgio could not resist a last romantic gesture of farewell. He ordered his pilot to dip the plane wings before finally sailing off into the blue. As the pilot obeyed, the engine choked, cut out, and then began racing.

Merle heard it; she thought her heart would stop beating. As the right wing dipped, it struck the top of a tall pine tree. The wing snapped off. In a moment, the plane burst into flames, throwing Giorgio's body free. He plunged burning to the earth.

At first Merle couldn't absorb what she had seen. She thought she must have imagined the horror, that some other plane had crashed, close to Giorgio's, that he was safe. But when people came running and screaming toward her the full realization struck her. She was shattered. She collapsed into the arms of a tourist standing next to her. While a taxi and an ambulance rushed to the field, the woman half carried Merle to the lunch bar where she sat at a table sobbing uncontrollably, saying she wanted to die.

Chapter Twelve

In this darkest hour of Merle's life, she rediscovered a good friend: Mary Pickford arrived at the Hôtel du Cap at Norma Shearer's suggestion. For many years Mary had been a convinced spiritualist, a fact carefully omitted from any mention of her in the press and which she had gone to extraordinary lengths to keep from reporters. Norma, who had mixed feelings on the subject, was certain that Mary could bring Merle the consolation of belief in survival. Mary had an acquaintance in London, Lilian Bailey, who was among the best-known mediums in Britain, and who had succeeded in convincing the Duchess of Kent that the Duke of Kent had survived in the hereafter following his death in 1942.

At first Merle was doubtful, despite her great respect and fondness for Mary. She had the overwhelming feeling that she would never see Giorgio again, and that one whole section of her life had been brutally cut off. She still had no interest in going on living. She must have realized the agony she had brought on two families by obstinately continuing the affair with Giorgio over every possible objection, including that of the Pope; and she knew quite positively that she had very nearly caused the death of Madina Arrivabene. There seemed to be a certain poetic justice, or even a sense of punishment, in Cini's death; and it may have appeared as if the Cinis blamed her for the death of their son, whereas in fact, Count Cini reached out to her in compassion. The entire family was plunged into mourning and indeed Vittorio and Lyda Cini were so inconsolable, so devastated, that for over a year they remained in utter seclusion. Vittorio Cini's only thought was to build a monument to his son that would remain forever, and indeed for years he poured a fortune into building a cultural and educational foundation in Venice in honor of Giorgio, using the shell of an abandoned monastery on the Isola di San Giorgio as a focus of an institution devoted to the history and study of Venice.

Guilt, anguish, and an overwhelming desire to see Giorgio again, and tell him she was sorry for their quarrel, again overruled Merle's reason completely, and she traveled to London to investigate Lilian Bailey and other mediums for genuineness before she took the risk of plunging into a desperate adventure into the unknown.

Merle went from medium to medium, skeptical in many ways yet determined to satisfy herself of the truth or falsehood of survival after death. She strove to disguise herself; she tried to evade any "fishing" questions in which mediums indulged; she sought out those mediums whom friends told her had no knowledge of movie personalities. She kept a careful record of her private sittings with the mediums, to whom she referred only in initials. One man impressed her by describing the fact that she had recently had a painting done of her mother from a photograph—and that Charlotte was present and was grateful for the nostalgic act of filial affection. Another identified Merle's father, whom she did not remember personally since he had died when she was three, but of whom she had seen photographs. Several mediums spoke of Cini's anguish, his pain, and his desire to "come through"; individual mediums brought evidence in the form of his statements to her in private, his knocking on wood before he climbed into the cockpit for his last, fatal journey, the essence of his quarrel with her, and his present sorrow at his unfounded jealousy. Many of these disclosures could have come from a telepathic reading of Merle's mind, but there were certain inklings and indications that gradually overcame her reluctance to believe.

Merle contacted Lady Tomkins, daughter of Lady Morvyth Benson, Merle's intimate friend of the 1930s and 1940s. She still did not quite have the courage to see Lilian Bailey but she wanted to determine if there could be some test of mediumship as a whole. Lady Tomkins herself had been bereaved by the death of her beloved sister, also a friend of Merle's, from a fall from a horse, and she had tried to contact her through spiritualist channels. She had been left unconvinced but with an open mind.

Lady Tomkins says:

Merle asked me if I would go and see the medium I knew in south London, whose name I have forgotten, in order to determine if there would be any inkling of contact with Cini. The reason Merle wanted me to try was that there had never been any mention in the papers of my friendship with Merle and therefore there was no way this woman could have known of our connection. To be still further sure, I went to see her under an assumed name; since my photograph had never been in the papers, I knew she could not possibly recognize me.

I arrived at the house in South London. I said that a friend of mine had been bereaved and wondered if the woman could give me any information that would be comforting. For a time, the woman concentrated very hard. Then suddenly she looked up over my shoulder with her eyes very intense, and she said, "There's a man standing behind you." I looked around; there was no one there. The woman said, "He is a tall man, with black hair and flashing eyes and a dark skin. He has a beautiful smile and he is wearing an airman's goggles and uniform." The woman went on to describe Giorgio in such detail that it could only have been him. I was astonished, and then she said to me, "He has a message for the bereaved." The message was in Italian. . . .

The message was one of personal endearment, cast in terms that Merle recognized. But she wasn't totally convinced: perhaps the woman *did* know of her friendship with Lady Gillian Tomkins and of Giorgio's death, or perhaps the medium was capable of telepathy, since undoubtedly Lady Tomkins would have been concentrating very hard on Giorgio's image in the flying clothes.

She felt strong enough now to seek further proof. She was extremely nervous, but she convinced Douglas Fairbanks, Jr., and his wife, Mary Lee, that they should have a seance at their London house. The arrangements were made through the well-known if eccentric journalist Hannen Swaffer, who had been the chief support of Lilian Bailey for several years. It was at his flat overlooking Trafalgar Square that Mary Pickford had met Lilian and was sure she had spoken to the late Douglas Fairbanks through her.

Swaffer explained to Merle the details of Lilian's background. Lilian, a six-foot-tall, genial extrovert, had been born in Cardiff, Wales, of Scots descent, on February 28, 1895, the sole survivor of a family of eight children; the other seven, all boys, had died in infancy. At the age of six, a mysterious voice had informed her that she would be successful in a piano examination at London's Royal College of Music. The prophecy was correct, but when she lost her mother in her late teens, she had been so grief-stricken she had abandoned her career for a lifelong devotion to spiritualism. In World War I, she joined the Women's Army Auxiliary Corps; serving behind the lines, she had witnessed death so often that it had given her an overwhelming sense of the importance of proving survival. Influenced by the well-known scientist Sir Oliver Lodge, who had written a class book entitled *Raymond*, about contact with his dead soldier son, she became prominent in the field. She became convinced she was a medium when the spiritualist photographer William Hope showed her a photograph of herself with a mysterious dark face glowing behind her: Hope told her the face was that of her guide, her control: a soldier named William Hedley Wootton of the Grenadier Guards, who had died in the trenches in World War I.

Oddly, and a fact of great interest to Merle, Lilian Bailey's other control, or go-between to the spirit kingdom, was a Sinhalese Hindustani child named Poppet. Lilian Bailey had become world famous after a much publicized episode in a railroad station in Manchester when, on a rainy, foggy winter night, the radiant figure of a young woman appeared on the platform and pointed out a complete stranger to Lilian, naming him her husband and announcing her name as Janet Rice. Mrs. Bailey had approached the man and told him what she had seen. He had broken into tears. He had confirmed that his name was Rice and that his wife, Janet, had died a year earlier. Once he gave the statement of his conviction to the papers, Mrs. Bailey's name was made. She became the favorite medium of the royal family, several members of which believed in survival.

There are conflicting accounts of the seance at the Fairbanks house. The most convincing description occurs in the authorized biography of Lilian Bailey, *Death Is Her Life*, by W. F. Neech. While Merle waited in the house, Hannen Swaffer brought Lilian there, not telling her the name of the owner. The book reads as follows:

> Within a few minutes, despite the attempt of her spirit guide, Bill Wootton (who did not want his medium upset by a strange control) to stop him, the dead fiancé entranced the medium, embraced Merle Oberon in a joy of reunion, and assured her that she need not fear that he had felt any suffering, because he died instantly.

This is what is known as a solo seance in which only the sitter and the medium were present. It was only at the subsequent seances that the Fairbankses and their friends were there. Giorgio would come through in Lilian Bailey's throat and amaze the sitters. He would say things to Merle that only she could recognize and whose authenticity only she could confirm. Unlike the medium Lady Tomkins had visited, Lilian Bailey could not materialize Count Cini as a separate entity in the room; but her possession by his spirit was something Merle was able to accept. As she embraced the large, heavy, sweet-faced woman with the curly gray hair and the three strands of pearls, as she kissed her on the lips, she felt the soft heavy body dissolve into the strong, muscular frame of the man who had died, and she seemed to be gazing into his eyes and feeling his breath on hers. She was one with him again. Three weeks later, at Hannen Swaffer's birthday party at his apartment near Trafalgar Square, Merle said to him, "I'll always be grateful to you. Now I know that Giorgio isn't dead."

Buoyed by this knowledge—and to her it was knowledge, not be-lief—Merle began to emerge in public again. Her friends urged her to find another man who could take her mind off the long, arduous, exhausting seances with Lilian, of whom she had grown very fond. She agreed that she must not spend the rest of her life in a seance room; that at thirty-eight she was still a comparatively young healthy woman and had a life to live. It was in this mood of recovery, of strength regained, that she was shocked to learn that her adventure in spiritualism was being criticized in the Italian press. The Roman Catholic Church condemned mediumship out of hand and stories that she was contacting Cini appalled Catholics since it was believed that evil entities imitated the dead: a belief shared by other religions, including the Seventh Day Adventist Church. Others laughed at Merle, convinced she had lost her sanity and that Lilian Bailey was a fraud.

She found a sympathetic ear in the kind, warm, and generous socialite Earl Beatty, son of a former admiral of the fleet. Beatty was everything she needed at the time. David was a bluff, genial, darkly handsome, solidly built man-about-town with good humor, an extro-vert's lack of complexity, and wide knowledge of wine and food. The Bensons, Lady Tomkins, and the Fairbankses were delighted with her new romance. They very much wanted her to be married to Beatty, and she began to look for houses in Britain, where she planned to settle.

It was in 1950, while she was still in London, that Ivan Foxwell approached her to make a film. Her RKO contract had fizzled out following her decision not to make *I Married a Communist* after all. The new story was based on a novella by Stefan Zweig, *Twenty-four Hours of a Woman's Life*, a gripping account of a day and a night on the Riviera in which an aging but glamorous widow meets a young gambler who has lost at the tables, talks him out of suicide and is almost ruined by him. It was an intriguing part, showing how even the most sophisticated can allow pity and sexual attraction to overcome reason, and Merle read the script with great pleasure and signed the contract to go ahead. An added appeal was that she could once again stay in the south of France—although despite her conviction of Cini's survival, she could not face the Hôtel du Cap and carefully stipulated that the movie be made in Monte Carlo.

No sooner had she agreed to make the film than Merle received disagreeable news. Ivan Foxwell had mentioned several other directors to her but now he settled on Victor Saville, who had made her first British feature, *A Warm Corner*. She hated to be reminded of her past at the outset of the 1930s and was appalled to think that Saville would be there every day of work to remind her of it. In Paris at the Ritz, she was also dismayed when Foxwell's friend, the Maharajah of Jaipur, turned up without warning and asked to see her. She was aware that he knew of her past, not only in England but in India, and she hid for days in her suite rather than run the risk of seeing him in the lobby.

She had asked for Richard Conte, a friend of Giorgio Cini's, an Italian-American actor of great force, as her leading man; but at the last minute, he backed out and she was forced to accept the English star Richard Todd, whom she did not admire. She was so upset by all this that while the picture was being prepared, she flew to Hollywood for a break to try to collect her thoughts. David Beatty followed her to offer his hand in marriage.

Confronted with the direct approach which would have led her into a rather hasty wedding, Merle held back. Certainly, Earl Beatty would have been the ultimate catch. Merle would have become a countess and have allied her fortune to another of major substance; her friends in London, notably Lady Tomkins and the colorful Margaret, Duchess of Argyle, who had married Merle's old beau, Charles Sweeney, were very fond of David and he was also much admired in the royal family. Yet she realized that she would have to abandon completely what was left of her career: that she could not be Lady Beatty and a motion picture star at the same time. Moreover, David undoubtedly would want children and she couldn't have them, as the surgeon in Boston had told her. Once again, Merle had awakened sharply from a romantic daydream of marriage into the nobility, to a charming and attractive man who loved her deeply, and once again she acted with a startling degree of decisiveness as an independent woman.

While discussing a film, *Pardon My French*, which she would squeeze in for United Artists ahead of *Twenty-four Hours of a Woman's Life*, Merle went to a big party in Beverly Hills. There she met the very charming and appealing young Dr. Rex Ross, who was just starting out as a fashionable Beverly Hills physician. He was much in demand not only for his talents as a doctor but because of his warmth and charm. Merle was powerfully drawn to him. With David about to arrive from London, she was suddenly faced with a predicament. Ross was exactly what she was looking for. Tall, well-built, relaxing, easy to get along with, he could also serve another purpose in her life. She continued to be a hypochondriac, taking vitamin pills almost to excess, fearfully watching her diet down to every last calorie, and refusing to smoke or drink. Now that she was forty, she was nervous about signs of age showing in her face. The slightest strand of gray in her hair irritated her unendurably. Like many actresses, she spent eternities before the mirror, watching for a wrinkle or line, and she would brush her hair a hundred times every morning so that it wouldn't lose its sheen. To have a doctor with her on her travels to Europe, which were becoming more and more frequent, would be an enormous advantage since he could take care of the slightest health problem immediately. And perhaps he could find a solution to the ever-maddening scars on her face that had to be covered with makeup, which created further skin problems because of its toxicity. And in case her troublesome heart murmur should act up, Ross would be there with every kind of nostrum.

It seemed that Dr. Rex Ross provided the perfect prescription for a relationship that Earl Beatty, for all his important connections, could not. When Beatty arrived, Merle was forced into a painfully embarrassing confrontation in which she told him that she couldn't go ahead with the match: that she simply couldn't face up to abandoning her career and that she could not see herself spending the rest of her life as the lady of an English manor house.

Her romance with Rex Ross began quickly. David Beatty, like the easygoing charmer he was, shrugged and accepted defeat and went back to Britain, where any number of women were waiting to take his mind off Merle. She and Rex were comfortably compatible. She wasn't caught up in the violet storm of feeling and passion that marked her relationship with Giorgio Cini. Ross was a soothing companion who took care of her needs, watched her shifting moods with caution and concern. He was ideal for a movie star—gifted with all of the consideration and delicacy that that difficult role in life called for. With total unselfishness, he gave up his medical career in order to travel with Merle whenever she wanted.

She was fond of Rex; and for a while at least they got along well. But at times she would treat him badly, with that disdain that was part of her nature.

They traveled together to France, where she made *Pardon My*

French, the worthless comedy co-starring Paul Henreid, in a matter of one month; she was so disappointed with the results that she didn't bother to see it.

While in Cannes, Merle continued to write to the medium Mrs. Osborne Leonard in London, who gave her more evidence of Giorgio Cini's survival. Merle had been troubled by a beautiful bracelet Giorgio had given her, with replicas of the many places they had visited delicately rendered in miniature gold ornaments. She had decided to turn it into a kind of ribbon that would contain a small and exquisite box she treasured. Mrs. Leonard wrote that Giorgio was pressing her to convey to Merle his interest in "a ribbon." What, Mrs. Leonard asked, did this mean? Also, Mrs. Leonard mentioned, Giorgio was concerned about Merle changing her room at the hotel; Merle had changed it the day before because carpenters were noisily building a set for the picture outside it.

Merle went to a French medium in Cannes. Giorgio "talked" through the medium, describing a sunset they had enjoyed together in Honolulu, of breaking a glass in a bad temper, of how he had planned to propose marriage to her in October of 1949. At last, Merle had a strange dream:

> I awoke one morning gradually from a deep sleep. Crying. I was crying because I had been with Giorgio and the part I remember clearly was his saying good-bye and trying to slip away from me. He took my arms from round his neck in the dream and said, "Be good, little one. Now be good." And gently he slipped away from me . . . Next day I connected this dream with all the times my mother left me at boarding school and we'd have this same drama.

In London in August 1951, Merle was talking about retiring and marrying Rex Ross, as soon as she had finished *Twenty-four Hours of a Woman's Life*.

She embarked on this new picture with enthusiasm. She had no more rapport with Richard Todd than she thought she would, and she wasn't very taken with her other leading actor, the somewhat humorless Leo Genn. She fought with Victor Saville, the director, who had a strong commercial instinct but little refinement in the artistic sense; she wanted the film to be close to the mood of Stefan Zweig, with a bittersweet flavor in the characterization, a haunting sense of life lived on the edge of hope; but Saville's direction was superficial and empty, if technically proficient. Merle did not enjoy the results and again refused to see the finished picture. Rex Ross patiently endured her irritation and discomfort at seeing the production go down the drain; perhaps out of gratitude for his heroic behavior, Merle announced her engagement to him in London that fall. Yet even when she did, friends found her restless and uncertain of her direction. The failure of *Pardon My French* and *Twenty-four Hours of a Woman's Life* to achieve any kind of an audience depressed her deeply and convinced her that even now, when she was scarcely into middle age, she was finished as a star. Already in the early 1950s there was a change in the world, an increasing shift toward a broad popularization of all culture and the gradual erosion of the elitist set to which she belonged. The war had destroyed much of the charm of Europe; yet she did not feel quite at home in the new Hollywood during the blacklist era, with its emphasis on witch-hunt investigations and the fear of the rise of television. Everything seemed to be hitting Hollywood at once: the attorney general was severing the theater chains from the studios and panic had set in. Fear would remain the overriding emotion of the industry until the day Merle died. The old, carefree, silly, cheerfully corrupt days of the 1940s, the parties at Marion Davies' beach house or at the Rathbones' or the Mendls', seemed painfully far away.

Merle did her best to recapture them in the last months of 1951. Sir Charles and Elsie Mendl were in Paris now, and introduced Merle to the leaders of European society. In this period before the jet age, she found herself opening a new door: she began laying down the groundwork for her position, years later, as empress of the jet set. She was rendered legendary at the exact moment that her career seemed about to end. She had entered into the curious category of a public personality who far surpassed the importance of her screen career. Her fame grew still further during the Eisenhower years.

Yet there was always the fear that the truth of the past would come up, that she would be dragged down by it. The letters from Constance never ceased to come, but now at least Constance's children had grown up and could give that unhappy woman an income. With great kindness to Merle, and to avoid public disclosure, Korda had been paying out amounts of a few pounds to Constance even after he and Merle were divorced. During the war, Constance's elder children, with Alick Soares, had married and moved to England, living humdrum middle-class lives in Nottingham and disinclined to contact Merle because she had totally rejected them—they had their pride. Harry, Constance's third child, was now in the Navy in his twenties, and was attending a special course at Greenwich Naval College. He went to see Korda and told him that it was no longer necessary to send payments as he was quite able to support his mother at this stage. Korda was no doubt unsettled by the meeting but was fairly cordial and asked kindly after Constance, who came to England herself for a visit and later complained bitterly she could not see Merle.

However, despite the money she received from her family, Constance was never satisfied and was endlessly screaming or in tears over Merle's wealth. Merle had to instruct her old friend of the early New York days, Tessa Michaels, to make the payments from New York; and later, the payments were made by Robert Miller of a distinguished firm of business managers in Los Angeles. Miller remembers how the long, rambling letters would arrive from Constance, filled with anguished complaints and self-pity and misery and hate, during Merle's absences abroad; and how when Merle returned she would say, "Oh, that's the woman who pretends to be my half-sister," and ask for $10.00 or $20.00 to be sent and then have the letters destroyed.

In 1952, Merle decided to take a step she had been avoiding all her life: becoming an American citizen. She was still planning to marry Dr. Rex Ross but hadn't quite been able to commit herself. For some reason she abandoned her plans for naturalization as soon as she had started them—perhaps because she would have had to produce evidence of her birth and she knew that she would be exposed as an Anglo-Indian. The mythology she had created for herself would dissolve as soon as the correct documents were shown. She called her lawyer, Greg Bautzer, and told him not to proceed.

She began to drift. Sometimes with Rex, sometimes without, in the tailored clothes of the early fifties, her boredom beginning to show, Merle floated from party to party, with no film offers coming her way, trying to fill her life with meaningless and futile conversation and encounters with the rich and famous. She traveled to both Egypt and Israel, carrying a white parasol as though reliving a star role in *Temptation*, for openings of new Hilton hotels with such figures as Irene Dunne and Earl Blackwell. She turned up at Prince Ali Khan's dinner-dance in Paris in June 1953, vying with the exquisite Gene Tierney and the vivacious Countess de la Falaise as the most beautiful woman present. There was a ripple in the gossip columns—she studiously ignored her old bugbear, the Maharajah of Jaipur.

A more spectacular event occurred on August 31, 1953, exactly four years after Count Cini's death. The International News Special Service of the Hearst newspaper chain asked Merle to report on the "ball of the century" given for her and other friends of the international set by the Marquis de Cuevas at the Chiberta Golf Club near Biarritz on the west coast of France. It was the most elaborate party in half a century in Europe—a re-creation of an eighteenth-century masque held by torchlight in the sumptuous building and handsome grounds. The clock was turned back two hundred years as the guests arrived by carriage through a rustic setting specially planted for the occasion. Cows, sheep, and goats wandered around the rolling green lawns, their necks festooned with multicolored ribbons. Over a pear-shaped ornamental lake, ballerinas belonging to the Marquis' company of dancers performed on giant artificial lily pads or on delicately fashioned bridges to the music of *Swan Lake* played by a thirty-piece orchestra in livery. Great piles of barrels flowed with red and white wine while two thousand bottles of champagne were brought out by a hundred butlers, waiters, and servants. The Marquis, dressed in a red satin robe and a white periwig, received over a thousand guests, among them the wife of the British ambassador to Spain and the Princess of Bourbon-Parma. Merle arrived as Titania in a dress spangled with stars. Elsa Maxwell stunned everyone. She arrived dressed as Don Quixote's squire, Sancho Panza, astride a loudly grumbling donkey that sagged under her weight; she carried a sword in one hand while a servant walked beside her with a wooden windmill with sails directed by clockwork at which she periodically lunged. Martin Montiz, a well-known socialite, accompanied her as Don Quixote. Merle was glad to see her old friend Sylvia Ashley, now Mrs. Clark Gable, covered from head to foot in fresh flowers as Flora. One group, headed by the Duke and Duchess of Argyll and Mrs. Norman Winston, portrayed "the angels and devils of Versailles." The dancer Zizi Jeanmaire arrived on a camel covered with fake diamonds. The bullfighter Luis Miguel Dominguin and the American-born Countess of Quintanilla came as shepherds, followed by the French actress Annabella, former wife of Tyrone Power, as a shepherdess in a living sketch based on the works of Fragonard. One group headed by designer Pierre Balmain was dressed as inhabitants of the Caribbean, covered in bootblack, in multicolored fantastic costumes. Even the police were in eighteenth-century clothes and, unable to control the crowd, joined the people in dancing through the night. At midnight, two jazz bands appeared to augment the symphony orchestra and many of those present poured champagne recklessly into the ornamental lake and jumped in.

Merle began to enjoy herself in those giddy days in Europe. Party after party, lunch after lunch, dinner after dinner almost took her mind off her sense of futility. In the early 1950s she began to make television films and planned to appear in a play, *Royal Enclosure*, in London until she realized that she would have a double tax problem. She stayed with the Douglas Fairbankses at their house in the Boltons, Kensington, London; she stayed with Charlie and Oona Chaplin in Vevey, Switzerland, adoring their children; she stayed with her old friends the Duke and Duchess of Buccleuch at their hunting lodge in Scotland. Rex moved in and out of her life. And she traveled to Spain to make another forgettable picture, *All is Possible in Granada*.

In Granada, with its powerful architectural evocations of the Moorish occupation, Merle became fascinated by Moorish architecture. It would influence her in the building of her dream house in Acapulco years later. She decided to build a winter home in Majorca in the Balearic Islands off the coast of Spain; George McLean, who was working on a house for Elizabeth Taylor and Michael Wilding, laid out the plans for her of a house built around a patio with columns of pink marble. She found a location right by the sea, with old oaks and pines, that would be ideal. The dream of Majorca obsessed her for two years until finally and with characteristic suddenness she gave up on it and transferred her dream image to a Mexican setting.

At last she was offered a part in a new picture that interested her: the role of the Empress Josephine, half-caste wife of Napoleon, a rich and influential woman who was cruelly thrown over by the Emperor, in *Desirée*, produced by her old friend Darryl Zanuck.

She was extremely nervous about appearing with an actor whose style was as far removed from hers as it could possibly have been: Marlon Brando, cast in the role of Napoleon. He had the reputation of being exceedingly rude, cold, and indifferent, particularly toward old-fashioned movie queens past their prime. He was believed to have little or no conversation, and to act with lazy self-indulgence, muttering his lines with almost complete inaudibility. Again and again, Merle was warned that she would find working with him intolerable, and she was so tense that she went down to Palm Springs to stay with Greg Bautzer and took the mud baths; Joe Schenck turned up and they renewed their earlier friendship, this time without romance. Rex Ross proved very supportive of her in that period of nerves and fear and she gradually forced herself to begin to work.

There was another parallel of her tortured life in the story: the half-caste Empress Josephine was unable to have a child. In the major scene in the script, the empress goes to see the young Desirée, who has replaced her in Napoleon's affections, and they look at a crib containing Desirée's child. Josephine confesses her sadness and envy to the younger woman. Much to Merle's annoyance, some of the crew members were playing jazz music on a phonograph and she asked the director, Henry Koster, as politely as she could, "Please ask them to be quiet. I'm going to play the scene in a very restrained way and this is very distracting." Koster pointed out to Merle that Brando was enjoying the music. Merle said later that she sent the assistant director to ask Brando to cut off the music. He did so instantly. According to Merle in an interview published in the February 1982 *Films in Review*:

> Marlon was very cooperative with me but not with the others. They had a terrible time with him. One of their complaints, there were hundreds, was that he would mumble his lines in the rehearsals, and when the scene came, he would scream at them and they wouldn't know how to take it . . . I found him fantastic. He used to come to my house for dinner—and if I said eight P.M. he would be there at eight P.M. dressed in his blue suit with a tie. I remember he met Noël Coward at my house and they got on very well.

Brando was fascinated by Merle and admired her enormously. Contradicting all her fears, he respected her tremendous presence and style and was very anxious to be her friend. She was intensely sympathetic toward him when he told her of the death of his mother, Dorothy Brando, at the outset of the production; and when she complained about his chewing gum as the emperor, he meekly parked it under his throne.

He consulted with her on his accent, which was neither French nor British, but sounded rather like the accent of a lisping New England schoolmarm with lockjaw. But Merle made him imitate her diction, and the result was unexpectedly amusing, since he now spoke exactly like her: with clipped, over-enunciated vowel sounds. He unfortunately kept up this inappropriate method of speaking for years.

Merle gave a touching, glamorous, and mysterious performance as Josephine: hers was by far the best performance in the picture, which was a typically heavy, stodgy, and stagy example of Cinema-Scope, the awkward wide-screen system that had been brought in to revamp the industry in its struggle with television. She went straight from that picture to another: *Deep in My Heart*, an elaborate musical based on the life of the popular composer Sigmund Romberg, in which she was cast as the well-known lyricist Dorothy Donnelly. Her problem at this time was that she was very uncomfortable with Hollywood picture-making methods which were different from those she had enjoyed in the 1930s and 1940s. Her years of comfort and semi-retirement in European high society had spoiled her; the one thing apart from the location she had liked about the comedy made in Granada was that the Spaniards liked to shoot only between 2:00 and 8:00 P.M., allowing her to party at night and sleep until lunchtime. Now, she had to rise at 6:00 A.M. and drive from the house on Copa de Oro Road, which she had reopened, to the studios with a succession of chaffeurs; she had to go into difficult makeup sessions and work very long hours on complicated and irritating setups. She wondered why she bothered to make this fling at a Hollywood comeback.

For some reason she had not liked Henry Koster, the charming director of *Desirée*, and she had no rapport either with the nimble and fast-moving Stanley Donen, director of *Deep in My Heart*. Donen was used to working with down-to-earth, unpretentious actors, and he was totally unable to relate to a glamorous star like Merle. He hated working with her as much as she hated working with him. For the first time in her life, she lost her professional control over her part and began flubbing lines.

In one scene she had to deliver a long birthday speech, making up three-quarters of a page of dialogue, about Sigmund Romberg, followed by a toast. Several stars, headed by the excellent José Ferrer as Romberg, Paul Henreid, Walter Pidgeon, and Helen Traubel, were seated around the table during the scene. Donen worked out a very elaborate composition and decided to risk shooting the scene in one take in order to emphasize its force and color.

He called for full rehearsal. Merle stood up with her champagne glass and to her horror found she had forgotten all her lines. Donen tried to hold in his temper and ordered her and the other actors to go to their dressing rooms; he said he would work out the lighting first so that it was fully rehearsed and then Merle would be ready with her speech. He said to her coldly that she should be letter perfect when he called her.

She went to her dressing room and sank down in despair. The speech was straightforward: simply a declaration of admiration on the composer's birthday. But her eyes kept running superficially over the lines and she simply couldn't absorb them. As always in her life, her fragile ego needed support, warmth, and encouragement; she sensed Donen didn't like her and that knowledge threw her off balance. In a severe state of nerves, she went back on the set and struggled uselessly through a couple of sentences. She scrambled the words and Ferrer and the other actors gazed at her in astonishment. Donen was tempted to cancel the scene but instead he called "Action!" Merle did a take, and ruined it. She did another, and ruined that. After eight takes, distressed by her lack of memory, she began to cry and the heat grew insufferable, increased by her embarrassment and misery. She said, not looking directly at Donen, tears starting from her eyes, "It's extremely hot in here. I can't do this under these hot lights. I've got to cool off a minute." Then she did the unthinkable for an actress. She actually said to the cameraman, "Kill the lights!" And she turned to the other actors and said, "Let's leave the set and cool off." This was totally out of order for a performer. It was unheard of, unprecedented in the history of Hollywood for an actor, even a star, to issue instructions to a cameraman or to a cast over the director's head. Everyone sat like waxworks, completely motionless, unable to believe what they had heard. Nobody followed Merle's instructions. Indeed, nobody uttered a word or stood to leave the table. The lights were not killed. Donen folded his arms, his face set like stone, and refused to move an inch. Merle exploded with rage at everyone and stormed into her dressing room and slammed the door. There was dead silence outside. She could hear nothing. At last, she opened the door a crack. Still nothing. She sent her maid Frances to see what was going on. Frances reported that all of the stars were still seated at the table, the cameraman was still waiting by the camera, and Donen still had his arms folded.

After half an hour, Merle, feeling very ill, sent Frances again. Frances reported that nothing had changed.

At last, Merle cracked. Her iron will overruled by the even more iron will of the director, she brushed away her tears, straightened her back, memorized the speech in minutes, returned to the table, and delivered it without a blemish. The result was the best scene in the picture.

She made a lovely and touching Dorothy Donnelly, especially in her death scene, which she played with a grand old-fashioned style and elegance, but *Deep in My Heart* affected her adversely and she began to lose faith in her capacity to work in Hollywood. Even though the picture was a great success and she enjoyed the reviews, most of which were extremely complimentary to her, she was thoroughly depressed by the fact that this new Hollywood had little or no time for imperial behavior, particularly from those performers who were no longer at the very top. She went on working halfheartedly after that, sinking to a routine crime picture, *The Price of Fear*, at her old studio, Universal, and a TV series of no consequence, *Assignment Foreign Legion*, which she narrated and introduced and occasionally appeared in, shot in part in London. It was a childish affair that did little for her partially renewed career.

Merle was also experiencing difficulties in her drawn-out relationship with Rex Ross. It had never been more than a lukewarm affair, largely a convenience, and she had ceased to find it stimulating or exciting.

Her devotion and loyalty to Alex were amazing. Alex had not really developed her career in the way that he promised after the first glory of her success in *The Private Life of Henry VIII*. He had cast her in largely second-rate films and had abandoned her to other directors and producers, only one of whom, Goldwyn, had really worked to build her to the peak of stardom. For years Alex had traded on the falsehood that he had made Merle a major international star, and she had, with great consideration and unselfishness, gone along with this high-powered fantasy, never contradicting Alex and indeed always talking of him with enormous respect, warmth, and admiration.

He had rewarded her for her constant thoughtfulness toward him by going over his brothers' heads and placing several hundred thousand dollars in a special numbered account at a bank in London, which was unofficially in her name although the bank manager had instructions not to advise her until Alex gave the word. She had been astonished, sometime in the 1950s, to discover that the account had grown enormously on fixed deposits and that she therefore had a second, substantial fortune in England. She called Alex in a state of excitement and amazement at the news, and he shrugged it off as lightly as though he had given her a piece of costume jewelry.

After Alex's marriage to Merle had broken up, and the affair with Christine Norden had disintegrated in quarrels and recriminations, Alex had remained in love with Merle in spite of his cruel and unnecessary remarks about her and her alleged use of him for money, position, and power. He had met and married an obscure young Canadian girl named Alexa Boycun who had a mysterious background, as puzzling and ill-explored as Merle's, and who, like Merle, had shown some early talent in the arts: she had apparently been an ambitious would-be singer whom Alex with his amazing powers of press agentry and puffery allowed his publicists to inflate into an opera singer. In fact, Alexa was simply one of those ambitious, meaningless drifters who turn up in all societies, who had made her way through good looks, a nice tan, and a smooth line of small talk into the upper levels of European society. Trying to emulate Merle, she dragged Alex through months of exploring furniture stores and art galleries so as to snap up a large collection for his new home in London; with great shrewdness, she played on his artistic taste and pretended, at least until she became violently seasick, that she enjoyed yachting.

In most respects, Alexa was the reverse of Merle. When she began to reveal her true nature, after she had secured Alex in marriage, she showed that she really hated the sea, that her interest in paintings and furniture was more acquisitive than aesthetic, and that her fondness for Alex was based on a very careful and skilled judgment of her future prospects as Lady Korda and what she would have been without him. Even her interest in films was superficial and largely assumed, and after the marriage she openly expressed her disdain for motion pictures.

Merle only occasionally spoke to Alex or exchanged letters with him, painfully aware that his marriage pushed her completely out of his life, in a way that she had not been pushed during the relationship with Christine Norden. She also knew from mutual friends that Alexa was fiercely jealous of her and felt rather like the wife in *Rebecca*, young and soft and uneasy, ridden by the presence of a great and glamorous beauty whose personality still haunted Alexa's house in London. Sometimes Alexa would open a drawer or a closet and find some memento of Merle that Alex had refused to let go; sometimes there was a painting, a piece of sculpture, or a cluster of flowers in a vase that vibrated with Merle's taste and Alex's reflection of that taste. Alex, seeing this pretty but commonplace girl around the house, must have compared her constantly and painfully to his former wife, and the rows between them were frequent. She dieted like Merle, and paradoxically took up smoking, Merle's anathema, in order to help her stay thin and to soothe her frazzled nerves. Meantime, like Merle, she was haunted by the endlessly greedy and inquisitive Maria Corda, who threatened her as viciously as she had threatened Merle, draining Alex constantly through threats and cajoleries and reminders of what she had done for him in his early career. Unlike Merle, Alexa had no outlet in her work, and her loneliness and misery and jealousy increased hourly and turned her against Alex, who became increasingly ill, not only from the hopelessness of his union with Alexa, but from his heavy work schedule; he refused to slow down despite protests from Merle and all of his close friends.

His heart condition deteriorated sharply and Merle learned from him that he would not be able to live very long. Perhaps her knowledge of this fact drove Merle to accept the depressing job of making *Assignment Foreign Legion* in London, so that at least, even if she couldn't see much of Alex because of Alexa's tantrums and jealous rages, she could be close to him when the final crisis came. She learned from friends that Alex was tired, restless, and perhaps didn't really want to live much longer. He had grown weary of his beloved

French Riviera; his constant moves to Venice, where he made *Summer Madness* with Katharine Hepburn, or to Berlin for the Film Festival, or to the United States for business conferences to patch up his crumbling empire, had only served to irritate him and wear him down. He began drawing up his will, with a characteristically wry, sad, and charming Hungarian smile and a shrug of the time-rounded shoulders, and went on eating heavily and drinking as much as before.

Alex's death of heart deterioration in January 1956 was difficult and protracted. Merle was devastated by the news. She left the set of *Assignment Foreign Legion* for days, but because of Alexa she appeared neither at the cremation ceremony at Golders Green which was virtually a family affair arranged by Zoltan and Vincent, neither of whom would have welcomed her presence, nor at the memorial service at St. Martin's-in-the-Fields, absence from which was certainly very painful for her. Joan, Mrs. Zoltan Korda, says that Merle called her up a day after Alex's death and insisted upon knowing how much she had been left in the will; this is a shocking and disturbing story, of which it is impossible to determine the truth. Why would Merle, whose personal fortune far exceeded Korda's at the time, some $3 million to his $1 million, have turned so mercenary at that moment? A possible explanation is that Joan Korda misunderstood the meaning of Merle's call: that Merle was simply asking if Alex had left her some memento, some indication in the form of a piece of sculpture or a painting that he still cared for her till the very end. In any event, Zoltan was furious at what he took to be Merle's greed in a moment of agonizing pain and distress for the whole family, and he bad-mouthed her all over London as a result. Merle in fact received nothing whatsoever from the Korda estate: not a single object of art, or statuary, not even a book. This cannot have mattered to her as much as the fact that Alex had apparently not even thought of her when he prepared the will, had not made sure that some part of him would remain hers forever. Perhaps he remembered that she still had his favorite Maillol statue in her garden at Bel Air, and the Utrillos, the Van Gogh, and the Dufys that still glowed on her walls, and the magnificent Korda necklace of emeralds and diamonds—and here Merle discovered another wounding touch of detail. She learned that when Alex had made a version of *An Ideal Husband* by Oscar Wilde in the late 1940s, he had not only rejected all suggestions from his friends and colleagues that Merle should play the worldly-wise Mrs. Chevely, a part she was born to play, and had given it to Paulette Goddard, but he had deliberately chosen a replica of that same necklace for Paulette to wear in the picture. Merle had avoided seeing the movie because of the annoyance she felt at being replaced in it, so she had not known of this cruel and deliberate slight. She ran the picture after Alex's death and was exasperated beyond words and hurt beyond belief.

Ambiguity of approach was typical of Alex who loved and hated everything at once; whose enthusiasm for people and for films was always undermined by impatience, restlessness, boredom, and rapid disillusionment; who cared for Merle deeply but who also yielded to his brothers when they unfairly attacked her; who really loved only those brothers unconditionally and without reserve; and who was only truly and finally comfortable in the company of men, with brandy and cigars and movie shoptalk in the small hours. Looking back on their marriage, Merle must once more have realized this in her clear and simple, essentially innocent heart, and the memory cannot have brought her comfort in that somber hour after Alex was gone.

She pushed ahead with *Assignment Foreign Legion*, forcing herself to believe against belief that the series was worth doing. At least it was something to do. Like Alex, she dreaded being inactive: although mystical and spiritual in her longings and dreams, she was not in the deepest sense contemplative; she couldn't simply settle in and do nothing. She returned to Hollywood in a mood of great depression in the summer of 1956, aware that her career was essentially over and that appearing in a TV absurdity in which she addressed the audience from a fortress in an imitation Sahara Desert was scarcely a distinguished addendum to her existing body of work.

She was back in Hollywood in November, where, she told friends, she had discovered Dr. Rex Ross involved in a romance with the ravishing Liliane Montevecchi, who would later become the star of the Folies Bergère and *Nine* on Broadway. She was so angered by this discovery that on an impulse she accepted Conrad Hilton's invitation to fly to Mexico City to attend the opening of the Mexico Hilton. She had always had a yearning to return to Mexico, where she retained that large and devoted following that had begun to desert her in the United States, and she had a fascination with the ruins of the ancient Mayan civilization, which, in view of her hatred of killing and bloodshed, can only be regarded as exceedingly strange. She loved Chichén Itzá in Yucatan, which was the grimmest and most terrible of places of ritual sacrifice; its very walls vibrated with memories of torture and murder. Her romantic spirit eliminated the inconvenient historical facts and transmuted Mexico's horrifying and ghastly archeological monuments into places of exotic beauty and exquisiteness. This was a capacity she had: to remove everything that was ugly and fearsome in life past or present and to see only what was positive and appealing. As her world grew more colored by her fantasies, she gradually began to lose touch with reality.

She arrived in Mexico City in December 1956. She didn't know it then, but she was on the verge of yet another major adventure.

Chapter Thirteen

At the lavish reception at the Hilton, Merle ran into a man she had met on and off in Mexico, New York, and Europe over the past five years. His name was Bruno Pagliai. He was small, scarcely taller than Merle, with receding black hair, large pointed ears, shrewd twinkling dark eyes, a prominent nose, and an infectious smile showing big, unevenly spaced teeth. He was slender in build, and in his late fifties. Possessed of great charm, though not by any stretch of the imagination good-looking, he exuded power, money, and unbridled energy. He moved with a rapidity that belied his unathletic appearance: he had the whiplash attack and style that came from fierce ambition, drive, and a colossal self-confidence.

When Merle met him, he was among the richest men in the Latin-American countries. A conservative estimate indicates that he was worth about $50 million at the time. His father had been a construction engineer; and he himself had begun with engineering ability. At the age of nineteen, he had followed his father, who was also a merchant, to the United States as a struggling Italian immigrant, and he had learned banking from the ground up, beginning as a clerk at San Francisco's Bank of Italy, owned by the Giannini family, and working as a waiter at night. He had seen the importance of Mexico at the outset of World War II. After building a substantial fortune through stock manipulations and investments, he joined forces with people of wealth and political power, and he managed to become friendly with the dynamic presidential candidate Manuel Avila Camacho, who was fighting a fierce battle against his fascistic opponent, Almazan. In an atmosphere of riots and bloodshed, Camacho assumed the presidency in 1940 and Pagliai decided to move to Mexico City permanently.

With Camacho's aid, and that of another friend, the future president Miguel Aleman, who was Minister of the Interior in the Camacho government, Pagliai started Mexico City's magnificent racetrack, the Hipodromo de las Americas, on a converted army parade ground. When Aleman took over as president, he assisted Pagliai in establishing the colossal company known as TAMSA, which provided pipelines for the Mexican oil monopoly PEMEX. Pagliai developed TAMSA through a vast and complex international financing organization known as Intercontinental SA. Through Intercontinental SA., Pagliai became a kind of financial ambassador for the Mexican government, and he managed to raise enormous foreign loans for the country and to encourage vast new American and European investments in Mexico itself. He was almost as powerful as the president and certainly wealthier.

Power and wealth and a strong intelligence have always exerted great influence over women, and Pagliai, despite his lack of looks or physical stature, attracted Merle at Conrad Hilton's party. Embittered by what she took to be Rex Ross's desertion of her, she was in the perfect mood for a new romance. When Bruno showed that he was drawn to her, she responded without coquetry. She was never a flirt or a tease. If she wanted a man, she made it obvious immediately.

Bruno invited her to a dinner party at his house with Earl Blackwell and other friends on New Year's Eve. She accepted at once. An invitation to Pagliai's mansion was a major goal of any society figure in Mexico. Merle arrived at the great residence in a black limousine on the night of December 31, 1956. The house was enormous. Made of white brick, it was only slightly smaller than the White House. There were fourteen servants housed in their own quarters and headed by the legendary chef Pepe, one of the most famous cooks in Mexico. As Merle entered the mansion, surrounded by the glittering, the rich, and the famous, she walked into a dream world. A grand staircase swept from the marble floor to the upper reaches of the house. The huge rooms, with high ceilings and priceless chandeliers, were decorated with the finest private art collection in Mexico: there were Botticellis, Van Dycks, El Grecos, and Dalis, each one worth thousands; there were sculptures from Greece, North Africa, and Sicily; cases filled with ancient Chinese figures, jade, Dresden figurines, and porcelain ware. In the throng, Merle embraced Pagliai; he was dazzled by her simple white Balenciaga dress and the Korda diamonds; she had never looked more beautiful.

It cannot be said that Merle's motives in proceeding further with Pagliai were in any way cold or mercenary. After all, she was a wealthy woman who could live in great comfort for the rest of her life and certainly didn't need to add another $50 million to her existing $5 million. But she did need to enjoy the romantic pleasures that life could offer in terms of glamour, luxury, and splendor, and perhaps only a man of such vast means could offer her such a life. Given the increasing decadence, squalor, and ugliness of the twentieth century, she may have felt the need to build a wall against the world that only $50 million could provide. Even her own great wealth could not cut off the increasing and overwhelming presence of popular culture: the birth of rock and roll, the Presley cult, and the feverish addiction to drugs, which was already beginning to surge through the international community of the young.

Her film career was gone; she had quite enough realism in her nature to know that. Were she to live on as she had been, she would simply have been treading water with one nonentity or another who could fill her bed but not her needs as a cultivated and ambitious woman who wanted the best of everything; she would simply have rotted away in the hothouse atmosphere of Beverly Hills and Bel Air, without any real reason to exist except as a meaningless object of the older fans' attention. Ahead of her now lay a new and golden path which irresistibly attracted her: she could become the uncrowned queen of Mexico, on a level with royalty anywhere in the world. And Bruno had acquired culture: he had a mind, an aesthetic sense, that intrigued her deeply.

He had been married twice before, once to a woman of great brilliance and sophistication: Margo Pagliai. Neither marriage had worked and he was desperate for a third chance. He was loving, and had a strong sexual drive. More importantly, he needed a glamorous woman who was world-famous to appear at his high-level business meetings in order to captivate the wealthy and prominent men with whom he hoped to make international multimillion-dollar deals. A wife like Merle would certainly ensure that such deals went through. Moreover, she would be instantly acceptable to the wives of his existing friends and colleagues, including President Aleman; she could entertain with unrivaled style and elegance and she would certainly be received joyfully by his household of servants, since she was already a firm and gracious head of her own household.

She would be able to travel with Bruno, and indeed in some ways she had personal connections as powerful as his own: particularly in England, where she remained close to Earl Mountbatten and the Duchess of Kent. She had friends in the French government and she knew the Duchess of Alba and other aristocrats in Spain. Between her friends and Bruno's, the entire world of international society was represented: together, they would be a magnificent team, and would undoubtedly soon become the emperor and empress of what would become known as the jet set.

It is hard to imagine the extent of their excitement at having discovered each other. Merle's whole life had been programmed for this moment. Given her misery and poverty as a child and her many personal setbacks and tragedies, she had laid out a pattern for herself: to be the ultimate Woman, to be the most beautiful, the most powerful, the most independent, one of the richest, and one of the most desirable of her sex on earth. Her screen career seemed merely a curtain raiser to her real career, which began that moment in December 1956. Now she could be the fulfillment of her own visionary luxurious dreams. But things were not going to work out exactly as she had hoped.

At Bruno's request, Merle agreed to marry him in Italy, within only months of their encounter in Mexico. They were married on July 28, 1957, in a fourth-century church in Rome; at that precise hour, with great appropriateness, a huge earthquake shook Mexico City. They left almost immediately for a six-week honeymoon on Bruno's yacht, sailing the Mediterranean with all its vibrant echoes of earlier voyages with Cini. In London, they began shopping for furniture to go into the already overcrowded house in Mexico City. Merle bought a desk that had belonged to the Duke of Windsor and had been given to him by his mother, Queen Mary. She paid £16,000 for it and when she finally sold it in the early 1970s, it was worth £95,000. It has since sold for £880,000.

Merle made a new and desperate fling at having children. Bruno, as an Italian husband, very much wanted an heir, and so far he had fathered only one child, a daughter. During the marriages to Korda and Ballard, she had never considered seriously an alternative solution: to adopt. But Bruno was determined, and Merle, despite some misgivings—she was nervous about the thought of raising children who might have inherited untoward characteristics from their parents—shared his feelings that it was time she enjoyed a family. They went to orphanages in Italy, as Bruno insisted the children be Italian, and talked to many adorable infants before settling on a gorgeous, tousle-headed baby boy who reached out for her pearls with lovely determination. A year later, they found a sweet little girl with enormous eyes and a touching smile.

Once they had made the decision, Merle vowed to give these lucky paupers' children the life that she had been denied as a child.

She yearned for them to be the most attractive, the most favored adolescents and adults as a result of the most perfect upbringing that any human being could expect to have. But she didn't want them to be the sort of pallid, pampered creatures who occupied the pages of Victorian novels. They must be out in the open air as much as possible, they must swim and ride and play sports as she did, and above all, they must be rendered healthy and sane and well-mannered to perfection.

There was nothing sinister or Joan Crawfordish in Merle's addiction to perfectionism in raising her little brood. She didn't cruelly punish or torture her adopted boy and girl if they fell short of her demands for them. Yet inevitably there would be problems ahead. Her love and dedication would always teeter on the edge of smothering or suffocating them. She had to fight against her natural tendency to spoil them rotten. She could be very tough when they didn't meet her standards.

The boy was called Bruno, always known as Little Bruno, and the girl, Francesca, named after Pagliai's beloved mother. They flourished quickly, given the finest care, beautiful baby clothes, servants, nurses, and teachers later on. They were pushed toward perfection.

Bruno's second house was in Cuernavaca. The children loved the garden. The door opened from a crowded and noisome public square into a small, musty corridor with badly painted walls. A second door revealed a world of enchantment: a secret garden exquisitely redesigned by Merle, like a tropical version of one in a Victorian fairy tale, with echoes of *Alice in Wonderland* as well as of the perfumed garden of the Sultan of Basra in *The Thief of Bagdad*. Merle filled it with flowers of every imaginable color and description: masses of them, hanging festooned from the ancient stone walls and from trellises and trees, bursting out of giant clay pots or swarming with almost violent intensity around the sunken swimming pool and its emerald green, light-dappled water. The sun was refracted through lattices, over stone figures and through the massed blossoms of pink and red and yellow and mauve and purple. At night, the garden became a fairyland. Merle added strands of lights, like shining necklaces of rubies, placed with magic artistry and witchery through the clumps of flowers, so that each petal seemed to vibrate in the light. Even when the bulbs were turned off, the gold cymbal of the Mexican moon glowed and shimmered through the garden as the mariachis created a veil of romantic music, pulsing from the balcony or the veranda, or around the pool itself.

Beyond the secret garden, which Merle enhanced with endless

romantic and scintillating personal touches, the house itself provided a frowning and disconcerting contrast. It had been built on the remains of one of the women's prisons of the Spanish conquistador Hernando Cortez, and it carried with it much of the atmosphere of blood and doom that symbolized Cortez's rule. Always psychic, Merle became aware of a strange presence in the house. She would awaken at night, nervous and restless, never waking Bruno or the children, and wander about, uneasy, shivering in the awareness of something inexplicable and terrifying.

Lee Anderson Minnelli says:

> I was in the garden near the pool one afternoon with the Princess Soraya of Iran when we saw a monk crossing the courtyard and walking up a flight of steps. I asked Merle about the monk and she explained to me that he was one of the most familiar ghosts in the house. Merle thought nothing of mentioning him. I slept in the room over the dungeon. Merle said to me, casually, "Oh that's where they threw the women down and lowered the food on a rope." I don't know how I slept that night.

Sometimes, people would fancy that they could see the figure of a soldier, young and handsome and strong, and not at all phantasmal, appearing around corridors, with a kind of whispering cadence behind him; other guests would dismiss these stories as nonsense. Most of the experiences focused upon a wall at one end of the house, a wall that had been untouched, not even properly restored from the ancient days. Merle insisted that Bruno investigate the wall's history. Nothing emerged from the research; but finally, on her urgent instruction when a vine threatened its safety, Bruno had a special team of skilled excavators break the wall apart. Bruno watched while the men skillfully took out the bricks one by one and numbered them. Gradually, a hole appeared: the wall was seen to be hollow. There was a strange rushing sound and a terrible smell of decomposition that made Bruno start back in disgust. A rattling sound followed. Before anyone knew what was happening, a figure emerged from the dark and damp aperture. It slumped forward in loathsome, rotting rags. It was a skeleton of a man. The skull rolled onto the floor.

Once the dead man, who had been walled up alive for some forgotten sin, was buried in consecrated ground, the hauntings ceased. But despite the lovely garden, Merle never felt very much at ease in the Cuernavaca house.

And slowly, in those late 1950s, the first years of her marriage,

Merle began to realize that her dream of a wealthy and glamorous marriage was already showing signs of decay. Her health was also suffering. Whenever she flew from her home in Bel Air to her home in Mexico, she noticed alarming symptoms of sudden dizziness and stress. She knew the cause: the altitude, which affected anybody who had the slightest lung or heart condition in Mexico City. Cuernavaca was also elevated and she sometimes had difficulty breathing there. She would often wake in the night and feel a sense of strangulation, as though she could not find sufficient air in her lungs.

Moreover, she was beginning to understand what it meant to be married to a man who was internationally powerful and whose decision was necessary in a dozen countries at any given moment. Bruno would be on the telephone from morning until night, or traveling incessantly on planes to business meetings. She would be alone night after night and, given her still sensual nature in her late forties, his absences were painful to her. She was driven by an overwhelming desire for sex and she could not find respite or even perfect health without it. Yet, so exposed was she as Señora Pagliai that she was nervous of scandal, of indulging herself with men; nor would Bruno, as a supermacho Italian potentate, have tolerated such dalliances. For weeks on end Merle had to force herself to be celibate, and she understandably poured all of her frustrated feelings into bringing up her beloved children.

Running a household, or rather two households, was also a time-consuming task. With fourteen servants in Mexico City and almost half as many in Cuernavaca, and the staff of three at Bel Air headed by the indestructible Frances, she was busy around the clock. She was a fanatical housekeeper and would not endure a crooked painting, a badly draped curtain, an unvacuumed carpet or rug, or a single speck of dust on a table or chair. If her standards were not adhered to, the unfortunate servant would be strictly reprimanded, not loudly, but with crushing coolness. On the other hand, if a servant proved to be meticulously clean and efficient, Merle would be generous with gifts to her and her family and would ensure her the best of care in times of illness. She ran her three homes like movie sets. They were immaculate, orderly, seductively clean and magnificently furnished, and Merle oversaw them with the military precision she had seen in her best directors and producers.

At times, those who worked for her found the strain unendurable. They fought back and left of their own accord. Friends, too, sometimes found Merle's delicate, fastidious perfectionism nerve racking, and her tendency to want to be waited on infuriating. If she was laid up in bed, with extreme sweetness she would request a friend to fetch iced tea, give instructions to a gardener, make sure paintings were straight, or place phone calls for her. Even her intimates sometimes had to fight not to be turned into maids or secretaries. On one occasion when Lee Anderson refused to eat sweetbreads Merle asked her chef Pepe to prepare, Merle flew into a tantrum. Lee began to walk out. Merle induced her to return.

She was still a star even after she had lost her movie stardom. Because of her charm and beauty, she could get away with almost anything—and did. But her presence didn't necessarily create warmth. Sometimes, it radiated light rather than heat and she could be noticeably glacial when she chose. Her nature as Señora Pagliai changed again. From the eager, passionate, ambitious young girl who invaded London, and the wayward, haunted romantic of the 1940s, she had become the cool, gracious but still secretly romantic Great Lady of Mexico and Bel Air. If people dared to argue with her, she cut them off without a tremor. If anyone had the presumption to remind her of her past in India and London, she swept them off as easily as if they were Mexican flies. She hated being interviewed more than ever, and on the rare occasions that she did see the press, she lied about her childhood in sweet generalities, saying what amounted to nothing. Since Hedda and Louella in their last years remained devoted, she needed to fear nothing from them.

She conducted her dinner parties with as much gracious but sometimes chilly formality as would royalty. In November 1959, she and Bruno gave a dinner at Copa de Oro Road in honor of their friend Henry Ford II and his wife. Merle had with some reluctance invited Zsa Zsa Gabor, whose Hungarian charm she appreciated but about whom in general she had mixed feelings. Zsa Zsa, in the height of fashion, dripping with diamonds, gurgled up to the door with an uninvited guest, the millionaire builder George Hayes. Normally, Merle would have shaken Zsa Zsa's hand at the door, but she did not. She said icily, as though addressing a complete stranger: "We cannot seat Mr. Hayes for dinner. Mr. Hayes may stay for cocktails only." Merle had no place card for him at the table and had matched Zsa Zsa up to another man.

For once Zsa Zsa stopped smiling and flew into a rage. She swept off, with Hayes on her arm, saying there was no way she would even consider staying for dinner under these conditions. Merle could not have cared less.

Merle began to spend more time in Bel Air with her children. Her friends were in town: Doris Stein; Lee Anderson; Edie Goetz;

Skip Hathaway; Betsy Bloomingdale, wife of the owner of the New York department store; and Janet de Cordova, wife of a well-known producer. Merle yet again redecorated the Copa de Oro house. She had been there for almost exactly twenty years.

Soon after that house's twentieth anniversary, a near-disaster occurred. On a windy Saturday afternoon in April Merle was playing with the children in the nursery when sparks from a chimney set fire to the shingled roof. In seconds, the stiff April breeze raced across the tiles and the house was set ablaze. Milton Sheffield, the neighbor's butler, saw the flames before Merle was aware of them, rushed to her front door, and violently rang the bell. Merle came running down with the children. The fire had spread so rapidly through the attic and roof to the second floor that as she fled into the garden there were actually sparks in her hair. She stood helplessly as the fire burst through the windows; once again her life resembled the plot of *Rebecca*. The firemen, led by Sheffield, managed to break through the flames and save some of the paintings, but others were lost; and many of Merle's dresses were ruined by smoke and water. Fortunately, her jewelry was in a locked safe and was therefore saved from damage. The worst blow was that much of her private correspondence was burned, including many of her letters from Korda and the irreplaceable love letters of Richard Hillary. The house had to be extensively rebuilt. Merle decided to sell it as soon as it was in satisfactory condition. With the help of the aging, still friendly Joe Schenck, and his corporation in which a good friend of hers, Bernard Schwartz, was a partner, she sold it to Shirley Jones and bought another home, not far away, on La Ladera Drive in Holmby Hills, which in a surprising moment of nostalgia she called The Selby House. It was a splendid house, and once again she did wonders with it, turning the hallway into an environment of great aesthetic beauty, at once austere, cool, subdued and elegant. She was very annoyed when, despite the stress she was under in furnishing the new house, Zoltan Korda suddenly turned up and insisted upon retrieving the Maillol statue that Alex had given her, claiming it was only a loan. With characteristic chutzpah, she announced she would be willing to leave it to his children—when the time arrived. Even more characteristically, when that time arrived, she did not.

Restless despite the excitement of the new home, and despite the pleasure of seeing the children advancing healthily, Merle began to think about herself to an almost disturbing extent. She began gazing at her face in the mirror, seeing herself inevitably aging. In 1960 she was almost fifty, and lines had begun to form around her eyes and mouth, and her scar tissue was looking considerably more obvious as her skin, despite the utmost care and attention, began to dry and wrinkle. Her forehead was miraculously free of lines, but her neck and hands, the first to go in any woman, were showing indications of age. She had to fight off these encroachments. She attacked the problem with all of the energy she brought to keeping her houses and raising her children.

She had heard of the famous Niehans treatment in Switzerland. Dr. Paul Niehans was a German of great determination who had developed a controversial form of therapy designed to rejuvenate aging people of prominence. His treatment was expensive, and to this cost was added the daily charges of his hospital and specific fees for staff use. He was known to have considerably helped Pope Pius XII, who had been suffering from physical decline, and also Ibn Saud of Arabia, the Aga Khan, and Christian Dior. Although by no means old, Merle felt that she should stave off age at once. She left for Switzerland in the summer of 1960. She was to go back to Niehans many times after that.

She arrived at Paul Niehans' mansion at Vevey, near Lausanne, stopping to see her friends Charlie and Oona Chaplin on the way. When she rang the doorbell, a maid unlocked the mammoth iron door with a silver key and ushered Merle into a tremendous hallway of Italian marble and gilt. She crossed Niehans' famous handmade needlepoint carpet to the living room where the blond, blue-eyed, six-foot-three-inch physician stood up to take her hand and show her to a richly upholstered armchair. He explained his treatment to her in detail. While sparing her the more gruesome details, he said that cells taken from the embryos of animals would be injected into her and the result would be a tremendous sense of rejuvenation and fresh strength and vitality. She would feel she was twenty again.

He was obliged, however, to issue a warning. He would have to take a urine test to see whether her system would be sufficiently receptive. Also, if she reacted badly, there could be side effects, including Merle's greatest dread: a severe rash, similar to a nettle rash. She was prepared to take the risk—fortunately, her gamble paid off—and Niehans wished her well and made arrangements for her to be taken up to the clinic.

One hopes that Merle did not find out precisely what went on before her treatment. While she was made comfortable in a surgical gown in her elegantly appointed, white-and-sunlit private room, a team of men in a slaughterhouse that adjoined the main building, carefully soundproofed so that the inmates would not hear the screams of dying animals, hammered pregnant cattle, sheep, and pigs into an insensible condition. Then they cut the uteruses, pulsing with life, from the wombs of the stunned but unanaesthetized creatures and placed the embryos in large glass containers. Carrying the containers carefully, young assistants ran to the laboratory and there transferred the uteruses to a special team of experts who sliced, chopped, and mashed them while still alive and placed them in a preservative saline solution. Other assistants took the living tissue cells and passed them through a wide-bore syringe needle rather like that used for horses. Once more, an assistant rushed with the needle and supplementary cell tissue in a glass container to the room where Merle had been prepared for the injection. A doctor, in this case one of Niehans' best assistants, plunged the enormous needle into Merle's buttock, a very painful procedure. The living cells melded with her own and she was given strict instructions that on no account must she drink alcohol or take fatty foods and that she must remain completely stable in bed for three days.

At first Merle felt extremely tired, even exhausted by the treatment, and she had to lie on her face for many irritating hours. It was not until she had been in the hospital for five days that she was well enough to leave. She was to come back the following year for a booster.

After about a week, she began to feel results. Her skin began to glow; her body was tight and strong, and she walked with a far brisker pace than she had known for years. Life resumed its savor: the scent of flowers suddenly became overpowering, she could hear tiny sounds, and the strands of gray in her hair disappeared. She felt life was good again: she had lost that sense of jadedness and fatigue that attacks many people as they head into their fifties, and she regained the eagerness she had had as a young girl. Despite her friends' skepticism, she was forever grateful to Dr. Niehans and whenever she could, she urged her friends to go to Switzerland.

With her renewed health, Merle now began to put on weight, almost like puppy fat, and she had to diet fiendishly to prevent the beginnings of a stomach. Fortunately, the treatment made her feel more like exercising than she had ever felt. But here there was a paradox. The treatment could do nothing for her heart. Indeed, by increasing the desire to exercise, to be superactive, somewhat inappropriate in a woman of her years, the treatment may ironically have put too much stress on her heart.

She returned to Hollywood, delighting all her friends with her transformation; and she told Joe Schenck's partner Bernard Schwartz that she felt ready now to return to the screen. With her natural vanity, she obviously wanted the world to see the "new" Merle Oberon. She even dared the ultimate: a clandestine love affair, conducted in Bruno's absence from Bel Air, with the new and rugged Australian star Rod Taylor, whose career she generously encouraged. Taylor was a man's man, typically Australian, with a beefy sense of good cheer and a fondness for beer, which sometimes got the better of him, developed in crowded, all-male, white-tiled bars in Sydney. He was a genial, uncomplicated sort, very far removed from her other Australian lover, Richard Hillary, though equally husky and athletic in build. He meant little or nothing to her except as a romantic stud—he reminded her of Giorgio Cini—and not much came of their relationship except for a mutual regard that remained until the end of Merle's life. She helped him to buy a house and she nurtured his career. Her friends were loyal and closed ranks; Bruno seemingly knew nothing about this liaison.

A producer, Victor Stoloff, encouraged by the Schenck organization, came to Merle and offered her a project named *The Forsaken Garden*, inspired by her house in Cuernavaca. It was about a woman named Katherine, the name a curious echo of her part as Cathy in *Wuthering Heights*, who lives in a house with just such a garden, secretive and walled, away from the world. Katherine's half-brother is possessive and probably incestuous in his feelings for her. She, in turn, is tormented by his perverse interest in her and tries desperately to assert her independence with men. In yet another parallel with Merle's life, Katherine has had a lover named Richard who has been killed in World War II in circumstances that to some people suggested suicide. Katherine—the resemblances increase—is in love with a flier, who is also, like Merle's and Bruno's fathers, an engineer. And there is even a portrait of Katherine's mother hung over the fireplace, as Merle's mother's was.

Katherine's character is also very similar to Merle's: the hungry need for love, the strong sex drive, the love of beauty, the concern with flowers—even the credit titles of the film unfold over a display of Merle's favorite blooms. Katherine talks of crying at the sound of cathedral bells; she is mesmerized by the sight of birds flying home in the evening, of sunsets and sunrises; and she is ecstatic when she awakens after a night with her lover. The film as written is ritualistic, poetic, and bizarre in a manner that perfectly reflected Merle's psyche.

As if all these parallels were not sufficient, Merle elected to film *The Forsaken Garden* (retitled *Of Love and Desire*) in her own houses. The white-bricked Georgian mansion in Mexico City became the incestuous half-brother's home. The Cuernavaca house was transferred to Mexico City for the purposes of the script.

Merle chose one of the leading cameramen in Mexico, Alex Phillips, to handle the picture for her, and she soon involved herself and Bruno financially in the production. Stoloff had run into financial problems while putting the package together. She hired a new director, the unknown Richard Rush, who had made only one film, a black-and-white cheapie called *Too Soon to Love*. She liked it, and was impressed that Rush had managed to make an effective movie on a tight budget. She launched *Of Love and Desire* on the incredibly tiny sum of $300,000.

She cast as her co-star the strange, aloof, mysterious, and edgy Steve Cochran, who had never quite made it as a leading man and was available at a price. The film began shooting in the summer of 1962. Taylor disappeared to other pastures and she became romantically interested in the handsome, rangy Richard Rush. She wanted to enjoy the results of the Niehans treatment, and she had returned for a second session in Switzerland just before the shooting began.

Richard Rush says:

I never knew until the picture had started shooting that Merle had financed it. By the time I did find out, it was too late to turn back but as it happened, she never threw her weight around with me in any way. I've never seen such schizophrenia. She had the most amazing capacity to cut herself off from her financial involvement and concentrate on giving a performance.

As an actress—and as a human being—she was like a jeweled Swiss clock. Exquisite perfection. Finely timed. One thinks of her as part of an older Hollywood, an older tradition, but her working style was very like that of a Method-trained actor or actress. Everything she did was totally internalized. It was almost impossible for her to strike false notes. She was a true pro: always knew her lines, and she was intensely realistic. And, more than that, she was a woman who was a predecessor of what women today idealize: she was a completely independent woman. She manipulated her own life.

I began the picture showing her descending a staircase in her own house in Mexico City. She stood at the top as a beautiful woman of her own age. By the time she reached the bottom of the staircase, she had changed physically by ten years. You could see the muscles relax and the wrinkles vanish as she descended. It was a classic moment.

Rush notes that during the shooting Merle showed her compulsive adoration of nature. She would go on long journeys to find plants and flowers and sunsets. She talked to Rush of her childhood in India. He adored her.

Post-production was done in President Aleman's house in Acapulco. Merle cut the film with Rush. They would walk out onto the beach, pick a banana, go back, and cut. They would go swimming and then return to the editing room. Merle involved herself totally in the cutting, as she had done with Korda. Her romance was connected to her pattern of work.

The film was demolished by the critics but made its money back when Stoloff and Schwartz sold it to Twentieth Century–Fox for $1 million, and it did well at the box office. Although it cannot be said to be a good film, it is of intense interest, among the most interesting of Merle's pictures, because it so totally reflects her spirit. With its lush musical score, opulent images and scenes of passion, jealousy, abandon, and reconciliation, it is like a Victorian novel, and it was clearly very close to Merle's soul.

The movie had a strange aftermath. Merle saw Steve Cochran at the previews and premiere of the film in Hollywood, and continued to like him. But his behavior became more and more elusive and erratic and several people got the impression that he was being marked down by some unknown enemy. There were even rumors that somebody in love with Merle was jealous of him, believed he and Merle were sleeping together, and was out to destroy him: rumors that persisted into the 1980s. On June 27, 1965, Merle heard horrifying news. A yacht had been towed ashore a day earlier into Port Champerico, Guatemala, following a heavy storm. There were three women on board, all of them demented with thirst and heat stroke, covered in blisters from the sun. They told a confused and terrifying story. They had sailed with Steve Cochran from Acapulco a week earlier, for a voyage that was clearly intended to be at once an adventure and an extended orgy. One day out at sea, Cochran had begun exhibiting mysterious symptoms. He had severe headaches and fainting spells; one morning, he clutched his stomach and became completely paralyzed, only just able to move his head. The girls had no idea how to navigate the schooner and they soon drifted into the storm. One of the girls was only fourteen years old.

The symptoms resembled those of poisoning. Indeed, when police went on board the yacht and found Cochran's rotting corpse, they felt sure that he had been murdered. The girls were questioned over a period of a day and a night. They described his violent death agony and the fearful stench of the days that followed as he began to decompose in the heat. The mystery deepened when the coroner stated that Cochran had died of an acute lung infection; yet none of the symptoms seemed to resemble such a condition. Further doubts were raised when it was found that the three girls had been engaged as crew members, of all things, in Mexico City; but they were all released unconditionally and there was no inquest or further inquiry into the matter. Merle tried to look into Cochran's apparent murder, but got nowhere, even with Bruno's influence.

Chapter Fourteen

During the early 1960s, Merle traveled extensively with Bruno; one long, fascinating trip to Japan proved to be exceptionally rewarding. She responded vibrantly to the temples of Nara and Kyoto, the Nara Deer Park, exquisite with fine arrangements of trees and shrubs, and the serene beauty of Kobe, with its neighboring Mount Maya, and the Buddhist monastery there. She felt more at home in the celestial countryside of Japan than in the raffish bustle and tinsel excitements of modern Tokyo.

Merle and Bruno also traveled to Russia, which she found depressing and disappointing. The art galleries and museums seemed heavy and oppressive, and she was upset by the food and the enormous drab hotels with their endless corridors and their bad service.

Then, very surprisingly, Merle took it into her head to go to India. Lee Anderson, who knew about Merle's birth in Bombay, begged her not to go as it would waken bad memories. But Merle said she was driven by a strange compulsion she could not resist.

The dreaded Constance was there with her family and must be avoided at all costs. Also, there was the danger that someone might find out her origins. Bruno's family says that none of them ever knew Merle was born anywhere except Tasmania. There is no doubt she took an extraordinary risk in going to her birthplace at all.

The tension and strain apparently weakened her immune system, and despite the precautions of inoculations she was stricken with a series of maladies. She was bedridden in Calcutta during most of her stay.

When she was not wandering about opening new Hilton hotels or attending business trips with Bruno, Merle again felt the irony of her role as queen of the jet set. For all her extraordinary list of famous friends all over the world and the glittering chain of parties she gave or attended, she was either painfully alone or isolated from Bruno because of his day-and-night business meetings. She seemed to be, for all her caring for Bruno, back to the difficult beginnings of her relationship with Korda. Bruno enjoyed cigars, as Alex did, and Merle found them as unbearable as ever; like Alex, Bruno was still a workaholic, happier in the company of his male friends than with women, and devoted to building an ever-larger empire. Making *Of Love and Desire* had been only a temporary salve for Merle's increasing sense of isolation, and she had made few close friends in Mexican society. Only two of these, ex-President Miguel Aleman, always polished and sophisticated, and the lovely, ageless Dolores del Rio, were her real and intense intimates.

She occupied herself with building a splendid Italianate pool for the children at the house in Mexico City and improving the front of the house by developing a handsome fountain and courtyard. She worked extensively on the formal garden. But the altitude continued to bother her severely. In the summer of 1963, she embarked on the most ambitious project of her career. She decided to create a new home in Acapulco, to be called Ghalal. She chose a splendid lot of seven acres overlooking the bay and facing the island of La Roqueta, which was bathed in light at sunset. To the left, the land overlooked the Pacific, which stretched all the way to the Orient that had given her life.

The land had another advantage. Given Merle's yearning for privacy, her longing for islands in life, she could not consider a location that would be easy to reach. She dreaded reporters, tourists, and sightseers, and she knew that once the word was out that she had settled in Acapulco, the world would want to invade and make her life impossible. So she decided at the outset that guests would be given a secret sign to look for: after they had made the turnoff at the sign, they had to drive for several miles along a dusty, rocky, dangerous road on the edge of cliffs until the house would emerge unexpectedly—a romantic daydream, all white against the tropic sea.

She contacted her favorite Mexican architect, Juan Sordo Madaleno, an artist of great sensitivity, intelligence, and style whose romantic nature mirrored her own. She worked with Madaleno closely on the designs. Her intention from the outset was to build a place of beauty that would be open to the sky and the sea and the intense vividness of the Mexican light. It would reflect the shimmering waves of the ocean that she loved and it would subtly refract the white glow of the fine-grained sand of the Acapulco beaches. It would seem to grow from the living rock, of a bonelike whiteness, as though the ground had given birth to ivory. She drew from many inspirations and memories. From her first glimpse of the Taj Mahal as a child came the purity and balance of the structure, each portion of it considered most delicately in relation to the others. From India, too, came the harmony and coolness of the edifice, designed to refresh and give pleasure to the traveler on suffocatingly humid Mexican days. The Indians knew the effect of arches in resting the eye and suggesting a haven of peace. She wanted the house to offer a display of white arches, each one perfectly ordered and looped and sprung.

She devised an entrance through an archway of tall green palms which in turn reflected the pattern of arches; her sojourn in Granada in Spain, with its echoes of the Moorish occupation, had taught her the importance of combining trees with a building in an essentially romantic effect. Her periods in Italy inspired her to use a base of Italian marble for the arches, similar to that found in the Cini palace in Venice which itself occupied and mirrored a world of imprisoned water. She ensured that the ceilings of the rooms were vaulted like those in Granada, and she secured grilles, intricately wrought like those in India and China, to sieve the scorching rays of the Mexican sun.

A gallery of stone ran the length of the building, profoundly Indian in its provision not only of mere shade but of a complex pattern of shadows. Everywhere the walls were white, as white as the light of noon, yet softening at darkness into mirrors of moonlight. Merle disliked formal dining rooms and wanted her guests to enjoy the perfumed evenings and the sensuous darkness of the night. So she devised a setting in the gallery where guests could have their dinner while gazing at the ladders of sparkling lights that climbed the mountains of the bay. She designed a pool, with two palm trees leaping from its center, tile gripping the roots so that the trees would not fall in wind. An elegant room framed the pool, shadowed by an arbor of palm leaves; an ornamental bridge flanked a shimmering waterfall that poured in glancing, stone-shattered waves into the ocean.

She spent weeks with a team of gardeners exploring the mountains overlooking the bay in order to select wildflowers, creepers, jungle trees, and grasses that she had brought by truck down perilous roads to fill the garden with their heady exotic scents and their many colors. Juan Sordo Madaleno and his engineers and craftsmen worked for well over a year; the sound of blasting echoed across the harbor day and night.

Once the structure was finished, Merle suddenly decided that the rooms were too high, that the overall effect was overpowering, too ostentatious. She told Madaleno that he must lower the ceilings: that the architectural problems of taking this drastic step must be overcome. Madaleno was dismayed. He pointed out to her that it would be an impossibility to lower the ceilings without literally demolishing the entire house as it stood. Merle said, "If you can't lower the ceiling, raise the floor!" This wild extravagance cost a fortune. Madaleno reluctantly proceeded according to her instructions, and she exactly measured the size and height of each room in turn.

She added guest houses and wings, one for the children, an environment designed to give Francesca and Little Bruno a fairyland to live in, complete with beautiful toys and immediate access to the pool and the beach. Another cottage was built so that guests would have privacy. She had never liked staying with friends, fond though she might be of them, because of the problems of schedules and collisions of interests; she knew that the joy of being a guest could be undermined by pressure of any kind. So she decided that her guests would have their own environment, with plenty of room to add decorative touches if they came for a long stay. These separate houses were in fact homes rather than separate clusters of rooms, and each had its own powerful identity, which could subtly be shifted or changed according to the nature of the occupant.

The result was not so much a single dwelling as a complex of houses: an enclave away from the world. Once Ghalal was completed according to Merle's specifications, she began to design and furnish the interiors herself, without any aid from others. She kept everyone away while she worked on her domain in secrecy. The living room was the focus of the house. In the Moorish mode, it was exactly square: thirty-five feet by thirty-five feet. Normally, this regularity of measurement would have created a somewhat boxed-in, formalized, and claustrophobic effect, but Merle offset the room's too-rigid harmony with engaging and daring effects of color, volume, and mass. She designed a carpet that was handwoven in Portugal, with a vivid echoing of Chinese monkey paintings: A large gray gibbon was seen clutching at the spiny branches of a gray-green tree that sprouted jubilantly with six-petaled blossoms of pink and white against a burnished gold background. The sofas were black-lacquered Chinese teak with complex patterns of squares and circles in fretwork and matched with refreshing unpredictability to fretbacked English chairs. Along one entire wall under the golden Moroccan grillwork contained in the arches and framing the lush green of jungle plants stood a white formal cabinet, some thirty-five feet long, setting off a collection of

Chinese and European porcelain, a Chinese lion-dog, sumptuous vases and dishes, and real and ornamental flowers. Tiny candelabra with matching yellow candles could be lit up at night, their color reflected in the gilded rustproof metal framework of the partitioned, sliding glass windows that occupied another wall and completely framed the bay.

Merle's bedroom was more lush, more exotic than the rest of the house. She found a rare Chinese opium bed which could be dismantled in the daytime, the center section of the mattress taken out, and a Chinese tea table of fine mahogany placed in the center. The bed, fashioned of teak and formerly used for opium taking, was given an intensely feminine decoration of soft pink chiffon curtains draped at the center. Merle designed the bedroom rug in fine needlepoint, with motifs of roses and sprigs of fern and blue flying birds against a dusty pink background. The curtains shone with more pink flowers. The view of the bay filled the windows, and again the Moroccan wrought iron grillwork set off the formality of the arches. Bruno's adjoining room, which served mainly as an office and a dressing room, had another carpet, also designed by Merle, with a Greek border and a complex asymmetrical inventive pattern of branches and blooms; a fantastic K'ang red-lacquered sofa and an Ethiopian painting that depicted the Queen of Sheba gave a startling exotic effect.

Once the house was finished, the overall impression was of an oasis, a haven that did not merely emerge from the landscape but seemed to dance and glitter above it. The atmosphere was suspended, ethereal and spiritual. It was the ultimate expression of Merle's soul, and not even the finest of her films could match it as a memorial to her aesthetic genius.

Guests began to arrive. Following the detailed instructions, looking for the secret sign, and making the bumpy, awkward cliffside journey, they suddenly emerged in a surprising white avenue of lights that resembled those found on a French boulevard. They had to remove their shoes at the door of Ghalal, as though entering a Japanese house, since Merle could not endure the thought of marks on her white carpets. If anyone was heard to complain about this strict, small discipline, they ran the risk of not being asked again. She refused to allow anyone to put drinks down on the tables without coasters and when she showed her jewels, guests must not touch them with their fingers. She was convinced the oil from human skin would mar the precious gems.

Her friends came: Ronald and Nancy Reagan, the Sinatras, Freddy and Janet de Cordova, Alfred and Betsy Bloomingdale, Lee

Anderson, Edie Goetz, Armand and Harriet Deutsch, and the Doug Juniors. She gave parties that became legends of the international set. The guests would never forget the meals prepared by Pepe and served in a blaze of colors and lights and vibrant shadows to mariachi music that was never too obtrusive but subtly enhanced the occasion. Candles shone with a soft glow, the moonlight formed intricate patterns through the Moroccan fretwork, and the glamorous men and women in black tie or expensive dresses moved about, enjoying an experience they would never be able to match anywhere else.

In the mid-1960s, Merle allied herself with another artist who was as remarkable in his way as Juan Sordo Madaleno. For years, she had moved from dress designer to dress designer, from Dior to Balenciaga to Chanel and Edith Head and to such contemporary figures as Bill Blass; but despite her deep admiration for these creative figures, she had never discovered the one person who could echo her nature, who could match that nature in delicately beautiful fabrics and colors. She found that person in the remarkable Luis Estevez. Estevez was born in Cuba; he had come to New York in the late fifties and with extraordinary industry, inexhaustible energy, temperament, ambition and talent, had quickly moved ahead in the jungle of the rag trade. Volatile, hypersensitive, of an exceptional fastidiousness and taste in his work, Estevez was a demanding but considerate taskmaster who kept his staff functioning at an exceptionally high level of energy and concentration, rewarding the best of them with great generosity. He was a handsome and charismatic man, gifted with great resources of strength and health that were necessary in his peculiarly punishing and nerve-racking profession. He was extremely particular in selecting those women for whom he would design personally and only a tiny handful would be numbered among his personal friends. This striking and impressive creator of beauty would influence Merle in her personal appearance more than anyone she had ever known. He was destined to enhance the Merle Oberon the world knew in the 1960s and 1970s: certainly one of the most beautiful women of her age anywhere. When she entered a room with her black hair swept up and her skin glowing with health, in a white Estevez creation, jewels blazing from her neck, Merle was the eighth wonder of the world.

Estevez met her first in Cuba in the middle 1950s, when she was on a publicity junket with Esther Williams and Cesar Romero. She had been invited by Julio Lobò, the sugar millionaire, to whom Luis had family ties. The next time he saw her, she had married Bruno and they were attending the opening of the Metropolitan Opera in New York. He would never forget the sight of her in a white satin dress and a white mink coat, the dress cut low around the neck to display the

Korda emeralds. He felt that she was the most beautiful woman he had ever seen. When he reminded Merle that they had met in Havana, she and Bruno invited him to dinner. He knew one day she would be his best friend.

They met again in Los Angeles in the mid-1960s and Merle, who had been captivated by his designs seen in magazines and made for friends of hers, decided to engage him as her personal couturier. She became the only woman in his career other than Mrs. Gerald Ford, for whom he designed the year round, whom he did not ask to come to his salon. He would go to her homes in Bel Air, Mexico City, or Acapulco and bring with him sumptuous materials; or he would examine those Merle had bought. They stood together in front of the mirrors of her various dressing rooms; he draped fabrics on her near naked body. Back in his salon, he would use a figure of her that he obtained from Edith Head, who had worked with her often. He was amazed by her discipline and her addiction to perfection. She always insisted upon having pastel colors: she intensely disliked primary colors, with an instinct for what she could wear and what she could not. If a dress didn't fit her to the last inch, she would send it back: sometimes she stretched Estevez's patience to the limit with her gentle but firm demands. But his love and respect for her were so profound that he kept his temper under control. He knew that she wanted the best, and he wanted to give it to her.

He designed all of her clothes to enhance her jewelry, and vice versa. Subdued whites and beiges were ideal to show off her emeralds and rubies, whereas stronger colors were appropriate for diamonds. Just as she always designed her homes to illuminate art by the contrast of delicate tints, so she used her own body to enhance the artistry of her jewelry and of Estevez's designs.

Merle became almost everything to Luis; he was, next to Bruno and the children, the most important person to her; the friendship, which continued until the end of her life, involved both in a profound intimacy. He was so close to her that she even confided some of her beauty secrets to him, the kind of secrets a woman usually confides only to another of her sex. She showed him how she had silicone injected into her hands so that they were so smooth that not a vein showed. They were like the hands of a sixteen-year-old. A slight puffiness was inevitable, but the needles, running right through to the back of her hand, caused a tightening of the skin. Her few face-lifts were achieved with the most advanced methods of the time: cuts (under the hairline and ears) that were invisible to the naked eye and avoided keloid scarring.

She talked to Estevez more intimately than to her husband; he alone knew of her very occasional romantic adventures, kept utterly hidden because she feared that she might cause pain to Bruno. He was extremely defensive of Merle and would quickly suppress anyone who had the nerve to criticize her. Given his great gifts, wealth, and prominence, he was joyfully accepted into her inner circle of powerful friends.

In the mid 1960s, the letters from Constance Joyce Selby grew more and more pathetic. That unhappy woman wrote on August 6, 1965, that she needed new dentures and that she had to eke out a pathetic living. She said, "I don't see nor hear that you are making any pictures, perhaps if you were you would have sent me money like the past. God bless you, my girl." On January 7, 1966, she complained of payment problems but wrote, "Anyhow I have to thank God that I get my assistance from you, which is such a great boon. God bless you, you have been such a true and faithful sister. Miles and miles away but always a thought of me. May God reward you. Do write me a few lines, my girl."

These heartbreaking letters show an extraordinary resolution on Constance's part; Merle had rejected all responsibility for her and wrote to her only once, with absolute dismissiveness. Constance seemed unable to grasp the fact that Merle was denying all knowledge of her as a half-sister and that the letters were simply being placed in accountants' files unread.

In 1965, Merle (who, like Bruno, had done much to promote Mexican trade overseas) accepted an invitation from the head of the Australian airline Qantas to go on an inaugural flight to Sydney in order to promote trade between the two countries. Whether or not the idea appealed to her is uncertain, but she took off anyway, perhaps without thinking about her early fantasy of Tasmanian birth in sufficient detail. Because when she arrived in Sydney after an exhausting eighteen hours in the air, to a swarm of reporters at the unearthly hour of 7:00 A.M., she was dismayed to find probing questioners asking about her birth and upbringing. She gave an entirely new version of the facts. No mention was made of the hunting accident or pneumonia which were supposed to have killed her father or of the adoption of her and her mother by "Lady Monteath" or the presence on the scene of "Major General George Bartley." Instead, she disappointed her interrogators by saying that her parents had simply been passing through Tasmania on their way to India and that her birth there could thus be described merely as an accident. She said her mother had been ill after childbirth and they had proceeded due to the unfortunate delay when Merle was two. The reporters were greatly put out by this disclosure.

Looking delicate and almost fragile in a beige costume, an 18-carat Pagliai diamond ring on her finger, Merle was visibly restless, tense, and uneasy at the news conference. Her friend and traveling companion, Maria Obregon, did her best to be supportive. One can imagine without too much effort the thoughts that were going through Merle's mind. How could she sustain the myth of being born in a place she had never seen if she had to go there? How could she live up to the boastful imaginings of a small, provincial community, which had been claiming her as its prize product for over thirty years? The strain of this, in addition to the strain of the flight, took a rapid toll. She began to feel ill, and her heart acted up, and she realized she had made a ghastly mistake.

She was swept off to dinner by the Qantas publicists to meet a crowd of Australian newspaper executives and business leaders at a dinner in her honor at The Bistro. She was charming, adorably sweet to these total strangers, but exhausted, bewildered, and apprehensive. The one man she found empathy with was the cheerful, white-haired, white-moustached editor in chief of Australian Consolidated Press, David McNicoll, a man of great charm and style working in a harrowing job. McNicoll writes:

> She was very cagey in her response to any questioning on her birthplace. It was typical of publicity people to pick a place like Hobart, Tasmania. In American eyes, inaccessible! If I recall correctly, she told me on one occasion that she had been to Hobart, and on another occasion that she had never been there. She was extremely edgy about her projected trip to Hobart, and I was not surprised when she suddenly cancelled it.

Charles Higham interviewed Merle during her stay at the Menzies Hotel in Sydney. Merle said she was feeling ill, that she had developed a bad stomach problem, and that she dreaded going to Tasmania. She said the prospect of dedicating her birthplace appalled her and she wasn't very excited by the idea of opening a new dam. She seemed distracted, frightened, and anxious to get home. Any mention of her early life only had her close up like a book. Next day, she was on the flight back to Mexico after a stay of only seventy-two hours.

Later in the 1960s, David McNicoll became a guest at Merle's Christmas celebration in Acapulco.

Christmas dinner was held at noon. People arrived from everywhere, many of them along the difficult jungle road, others directly from the bay. John Wayne, with his wife and children, cruised across in their speedboat from their famous yacht *The Wild Goose*, followed by Peter Lawford, Luis Estevez, the Charles Revsons, and a number of Mexican dignitaries. Merle subsidized a kindergarten, and McNicoll recalls:

> Before we sat down to lunch, these delightful children, in fabulous gear, came winding down to the villa, singing Christmas carols in Spanish. They then laid into one of those Latin American Christmas effigies (or piñatas) with sticks until it burst and sweets and multicolored bonbons cascaded all over the children. It was really a remarkable scene, and quite the most unusual Christmas Day I have ever spent.

In the early months of 1966, Merle received an offer to make a film version of the bestseller *Hotel*, by Arthur Hailey. The director, Richard Quine, had worked closely with the Warners' casting director, Max Arnow, to decide who should play the duchess in the film. The story involved the hit-and-run driving of the duke, which initiated a blackmail attempt by the hotel detective. For a time, Quine and Arnow were seriously thinking about Joan Fontaine; then Arnow suggested Merle. Quine says:

> I quaked, because Merle Oberon for me had an aura of austerity and aloofness and extreme aplomb. I said, immediately, "Yes, my God, she'd be impeccable." Anybody who starts out at fifteen or sixteen as she did, playing Anne Boleyn in *The Private Life of Henry VIII*, could certainly play a duchess, who was not far below a queen. Max said he'd try to meet her in Mexico. I checked with Jack Warner, and he said, "Sure, if you can get her, get her." Suddenly a dinner was arranged—her request was that it should be a dinner. And at her house. I was terrified. There aren't many people who would scare me in that way. To me it was commensurate with my first meeting with Noël Coward. I drove up to her glorious house in Holmby Hills. A butler greeted me at the door. And she made a great sweeping entrance down the staircase. I remember thinking at the time: That's a bit much. But I was determined that I would get her to do it. I was afraid partly because I knew her decision would depend upon what she thought of me.
>
> I had expected a grandiose and pompous woman. A *grande dame*. But to my sheer delight, she turned out to be a great broad. A *mensch*. She couldn't have been more charming. Vibrant, vital, funny, clownish. Seemed thirty years younger than she was. I

was enamored. We had dinner in a small alcove off the terrace. Beautifully served and elegant, but the most informal of dinners. We giggled and laughed and had a great time. I realized with amazement I could say "damn" or "hell" in front of this great lady. After dinner, I mentioned the script. And she was suddenly different: very businesslike but tentative.

Merle was very much taken with Quine, as he says; but she hadn't worked since the disaster of *Of Love and Desire*, and she was extremely nervous about making another mistake. She was afraid that since this was an all-star production and Quine planned to have several big names in the cast she would simply be swallowed up in a galaxy: that she wouldn't have the chance to shine on her own. As she showed Quine to his car, with typical politeness walking him out into the night, Quine says he could feel the tension and unease behind her frivolous laughter.

Merle sat up late that night trying to decide whether to go ahead. The script by Wendell Mayes had a strong commercial appeal, and Hailey's novel was currently a best-seller. The story repeated the device made famous in Hailey's *Airport* of having a group of characters gathered in one location: in this case, a luxury hotel in New Orleans. Merle loved hotels: the St. Regis in New York, the Ritz in Paris, Claridge's in London, and the Beverly Wilshire in Los Angeles. She also enjoyed the idea of playing the part of a duchess: she had lost her chance to be a countess when she had declined Earl Beatty's hand in marriage and she had lost her opportunity of joining the Italian aristocracy with the death of Count Cini. Now she could achieve her ambition in the make-believe world of movies. Even now, in her mid-fifties, there was something of the little girl in Merle: living out a fantasy, an enchanted daydream.

In the morning, she called her agent, who quickly advised Quine that in principle she was prepared to do the film. The "in principle" condition was added because she privately felt a great concern about the casting of the duke. She made up her mind that she wouldn't sign the contract until that part was cast. The reason for her concern was that she saw a strong romantic element in the novel involving the duke and duchess: a fierce loyalty when the duke was threatened with arrest. She was determined the actor be handsome and attractive.

She was dismayed when Quine told her that the duke would be played by Wilfred Hyde-White, a British actor several years older than she. A skilled player who specialized in epicene British eccentrics, Hyde-White to her scarcely represented a duke; he looked rather more like a dessicated lawyer. She felt that if she were married to Hyde-White in the film it would look like a marriage of convenience.

She had nothing against Hyde-White, whom she personally adored, but she was adamant that he must not be cast. Even when she got into fittings with Edith Head, adding clothes designed by Estevez from her own wardrobe, she still held back from signing the contract. Warner was equally adamant that Hyde-White must be cast. He had just used him in *My Fair Lady* and he wanted to complete a two-picture contract with him. Finally, Quine in desperation stormed into Warner's office and said, "Merle's right, goddammit!" Warner promised to consider the matter. Quine and Merle talked about the casting for days and finally settled on the lean and good-looking British actor Michael Rennie. Jack Warner relented at the last minute, and Merle signed the contract.

One of the major elements in the film was that the duchess wore jewels. Quine suggested Merle should wear her own matchless collection. She agreed at once, as she had done at Warners more than a quarter of a century earlier on *'Til We Meet Again*, but she insisted the studio insure them once more and that she have complete security. Jack Warner flatly refused to consider this idea. He was so stingy that he even insisted on having plastic flowers in the studio lobby as well as in his films. He said to Quine, "Why the hell do we need her jewels and all the headaches that go with it?" But Quine talked him into it and he made the necessary arrangements. When she took off her jewels at night, they went into a vault with armed guards around the clock. But when Quine complained about the plastic flowers, Warner billed him for real ones.

Merle was very pleased that Richard Conte, whom she had so badly wanted in *Twenty-four Hours of a Woman's Life*, was cast as the detective who questions the duchess when she protects her embattled husband. She asked for a change in the writing: she was extremely sensitive to the suggestion in the script that the duchess was a lonely woman who didn't attract men. She insisted that while the detective questioned her, it was obvious that he was attracted to her, that even while he was questioning her, he was checking her out. This was logical in the story because later on the detective was required to do the duchess's bidding. She also wanted a scene just before the death of the duke in a serious elevator accident, a scene in which the intense emotional links between the couple were disclosed. Neither Wendell Mayes nor Quine wanted the scene because it slowed up the powerful thematic progression to the accident; but she was so insistent that they actually went ahead and shot it.

It is clear that Merle was protecting herself by trying to introduce elements of herself into the character: the weakness that had already destroyed *Of Love and Desire*, would seriously affect *Hotel*, and would soon ruin her last film, *Interval*. This hedging of her bets was clearly based on her old, fragile insecurity about her abilities as an actress, an insecurity fueled by many cruel and unflattering reviews. She wanted the glamour and excitement of a return to stardom but she was deeply afraid when it came down to work itself of not being able to match the challenge. The rewrites and her own clothes and jewels were designed to make matters easier for her.

Quine says:

I was shocked when Merle first came on the set. I expected a grand lady, and indeed she was. And she looked it. But on the set of her first day, she also looked like a frightened child. As we started to work, all the grandeur suddenly wafted away and she seemed to be a completely inexperienced young beginner again.

At last Quine reached the important scene of the discussion between Merle and Michael Rennie before the accident. Quine felt uncomfortable: the scene was not only out of place and slowed the action; it was arch, melodramatic, and archaic. He shot it two ways, so that if he wanted to make a cut, he could. In one take, he simply showed Rennie picking up his hat and umbrella and going to the elevator. In the other version, Merle was tortured and anguished and pleading. Try as he might, Quine couldn't make the scene play. Rennie was stiff and awkward with the lines, and Merle overacted terribly. After it was shot, Quine went into Merle's dressing room and said, "Look, baby, it won't work. We don't need it. All we have to see is your eyes. We know you're tortured. You don't have to articulate it." But Merle was determined most obstinately to keep the scene in.

Several months later, after the picture was cut, Merle was invited by Warners to attend the premiere in Miami. There would be a boating party afterward followed by a splashy affair at the Fountainebleau Hotel. She agreed provided that Quine escorted her. Bruno was busy as usual and could not come.

Quine flew to Miami and picked Merle up at her hotel. He felt like a peacock, tremendously honored to be escorting Merle Oberon. She looked stunning in a tiara and a beautiful Estevez creation. There was a great crowd at the premiere and Merle shone with excitement as the crowd cheered the credit titles and especially greeted her name.

Quine began to tense as the picture unfolded and the scene Merle had so desperately wanted grew near. He had cut it out.

He says:

> I glued my eyes to the screen, waiting for the moment, and I was prepared to grip her hand when that moment came and say to her, "I'm sorry, darling, but it was something we had to do." I reached out—and I grabbed air. She was gone.
>
> I had to sit through until the end of the movie, feeling terrible. All the stars were there: Karl Malden, Catherine Spaak, Rod Taylor, Richard Conte. I rushed out of the theater looking for Merle, and I couldn't find her. The publicity man was standing outside. He said he had seen her run out of the lobby, get into her car and go back toward her hotel. I had to go on to this dumb party on a boat. As soon as I got back to my hotel, I called her and she had checked out. When I got back to California a couple of days later, she was already back in Mexico. I wrote her a letter with a humorous touch, saying essentially, "Hey, come on, talk to me." I was trying to explain myself. She didn't respond.

Quine asked Jack Warner if the scene should be restored, but Warner simply said, "Ship it!" The print was circulated without the scene.

Merle never forgave Quine. She said in the interview published after her death in *Films in Review*:

> *Hotel* was disgracefully cut. I find it very boring . . . The idea in the book was the incommunicability of love: these two people really loving each other underneath, the audience knowing it, and neither one of them knowing it. So that when her husband does die, and she says, "My husband loved me very much," now it's idiotic, it doesn't make any sense. I was shocked when I saw it.

Quine says:

> I *still* disagree. There had already been the "Do we still love each other?" scene between the duke and duchess. And everything that needed to be said had been said. The impact would have come *after* Rennie's death, when the duchess is being talked to by the police. Then you'd see the tragedy and you'd know she was a good woman, trying to the end to help her husband. So this

extra scene that Merle wanted was "Barbara Cartland," unnecessary, even detrimental.

Now, you would think that an actress of her experience would be used to this kind of thing: It's just one little scene being cut. In a movie with eight stars, of whom she was only one. But part of the problem, I think, was that at the time she had been leading a different kind of life. Traveling in Europe, living in Mexico. She hadn't worked in a while. She wanted everything spelled out. But there just wasn't room for it. A contemporary audience wouldn't be moved by something they already knew. Before Rennie left the room, there was a photograph of Merle on the dressing table, and he just looked at it. And you know he's going to give himself up. That's all we needed. Then he sneaks out while she's standing looking out onto the city. If we'd done it the way she wanted, it would have made it difficult for Rennie to sneak out the way he did. It was an old-fashioned scene, but in a way, you know, she may have been right, because it was an old-fashioned movie. And after all these years when I think about it I'm sorry we didn't leave it in. I still suffer over it. With the thought of it.

The scene Merle insisted upon adding, in which the detective is attracted to Merle, is still one of the best in the picture. Quine adds:

It was marvelous. She was using her feminine wiles but still remaining at all times the duchess, luring this low-class hotel dick into an alley, and you're aware of the undercurrent of sexual tension between these two people. She played it beautifully. And she was wonderful off the set. She was always trying to fix me up with women. She had that kind of spirit. Two entirely different people: working and her social life. Almost schizophrenic.

The picture was well received by everyone except Merle and the powerful *New York Times* critic Bosley Crowther, who labeled the picture lively and eventful but said little else about it. Indeed, his sidestepping of any detailed discussion of Merle's performance had a reason: when he had fiercely attacked her performance in *Of Love and Desire*, she had sent him a blistering telegram filled with hate and written, by all accounts, in language scarcely typical of her. Crowther had met her at a party afterward and had expressed his shock, saying he was sure she hadn't meant it; that all professionals had to take bad reviews. She had repeated her onslaught in person. And the chastened critic had fled before her wrath across the room.

That December, Merle attended Truman Capote's unforgettable masked ball for the élite of the world at the Plaza Hotel in New York; soon afterward, she entertained her friends Lynda Johnson, daughter of the President, and Lynda's romantic companion, the darkly handsome George Hamilton, in Acapulco. She and Bruno Pagliai met Lynda and George off the plane; Pagliai's sheer power in Mexico was demonstrated by the fact that a government guard accompanied their fleet of cars to Ghalal. Merle realized the visit could be ruined by reporters; with great skill, she assembled the press in the ornamental garden under the palm trees, served them drinks, and then Lynda, alone, came out and gave an interview with her host and hostess. George Hamilton, who had even succeeded in hiding on the way from the airport, was not definitely established as being present in the house; but under pressure, he finally emerged and the press went away content.

For the next few days, Merle happily entertained the loving couple. There was a big party with fireworks at the home of friends of Merle's, the Mendezes, and then another big New Year's event at ex-President Aleman's house. John Wayne's yacht arrived and took the whole crowd out to sea with an orchestra playing and bucketfuls of Dom Perignon champagne; Merle had requested this voyage because she loved to see the sun rise on the first of the year. Then the guests sailed ashore and went up to Merle's house at 8:00 A.M. for a breakfast party with music. It was possibly the most elaborate New Year's occasion in the history of Acapulco.

Merle took all of the money she made in *Hotel* and for an appearance on the Bob Hope show, and invested it in a playground for her orphanage and for the poor children of Acapulco. She built a library and handsome grounds and made a deal with Pepsi-Cola that they would maintain the grounds permanently after her death. She adored the orphan children and visited them constantly; and she also spent as much time as possible with little Bruno and Francesca, who were now seven and eight. They were beginning to develop character. Francesca was sensitive and shy. Bruno was extremely good-looking, spoiled, mischievous and antic and as full of beans as a young boy should be, but he was also a trifle unpredictable in ways that worried Merle. Neither child was aware of being adopted, and Merle's keeping this fact from them was a serious mistake; it was certainly not always easy to do so. As the children's awareness grew, there was always the danger they might find out; she would have to decide when the correct moment would occur to tell them. They never did find out the truth of her childhood and she bolstered the fantasy by giving Bruno Fabergé studs allegedly belonging to her father, and a pearl necklace to Francesca that she said was her mother's.

Lynda Johnson, appealing and lovable, was almost like another daughter to Merle. Merle was disappointed when Lynda broke up with George Hamilton, but she was consoled when Lynda met and fell in love with a very good-looking Marine military aide, Charles Robb. Merle came to Lynda's wedding, a tremendous event at the White House, on December 9, 1967; Estevez designed for her one of the most splendid costumes she ever wore. It was a dress and coat of white broadtail, made of Russian furs and bordered in sable, with a sable hat and a white coat in princess shape, completely bordered in more sable. Estevez seldom surpassed it.

Merle was very close to President Johnson and Lady Bird; she also formed an increasingly intimate friendship with Prince Philip in those years. When Philip arrived to meet her for the first time, introduced to her by the Mountbattens when he had asked where he would be happiest on a visit to Mexico, the British ambassador went to the airport to meet him. Merle followed in her limousine, dressed very simply in white lace and white gloves, with a small white parasol like the one she carried in *Temptation*. When Philip walked down the steps of the plane, looking extremely handsome with his fair hair and chiseled features, she was instantly fascinated.

Prince Philip enjoyed his stay tremendously. It was unusual for him to stop for several days in a "commoner's" house in another country, but he was totally at home. He enjoyed the informality of life at Ghalal.

Philip came back several times to Ghalal. On one occasion, he gave a splendid party for Merle on the royal yacht *Britannia*, which sailed right past her house as he left for a Pacific voyage and the ship's band played some of her favorite music. She stood on the balcony of the house as the great white boat sailed toward the horizon with the music growing fainter and fainter. And, Luis Estevez recalls, a twenty-one-gun salute. It was a magnificent moment in her life.

On another occasion, Prince Charles came to the house and stayed in his own suite. He too was deeply fond of Merle and went swimming with her and her friends at the beach, as Philip had. On a third trip, Philip even gave Merle a rare honor: he painted, with great skill, her tropical garden and the green-and-scarlet parrots that flashed through it, and he signed the painting with the single word "Philip."

She was less than overwhelmed by the behavior of another friend of hers, Charles Revson, the millionaire creator of the Revlon cosmetics empire. On New Year's Eve, 1967, there was a party on the Revson yacht, moored out in Acapulco harbor. Luis Estevez describes the incident that destroyed that friendship forever:

We were all lining up to go back to Ghalal on the tender boats. As we were standing in the line, Mrs. Revson came to bid us goodbye. I kissed her on both cheeks with affection: I had known her and Charles for years and there was nothing unusual in the gesture. Suddenly, Charles came up to me with a red face, very angry, after a couple of drinks, and said, with a snarl, "Listen, Luis. I know what you're doing. What you're up to. If you ever touch my wife again, you're going to be sorry. I'll get your hide." I thought at first that Charles was being funny. I couldn't believe that he would want to upset Merle's closest friend. Quite apart from anything else, Merle and Bruno were his major assets in Acapulco. That's why he brought his yacht there every year.

I was shocked by his accusation. I said, in front of everyone, "If I wanted to make a pass at anyone, it would not be your wife." When I got to the tender, I was totally mad with rage. Merle asked me what was the matter. I told her I had been violently insulted. Merle sent the children out on deck and called Bruno over to hear what had happened. Bruno was white with rage. Merle said, "Those nouveau riche upstarts! How dare they! We are *not* going to the Revsons for New Year's! I want you to find the best orchestra in town, Luis. I'll invite everybody there is and anybody, and there won't be a man or woman who'll go to them. I'll ruin their party!"

Merle's party was a great success with all the glamorous people of Acapulco there. The Revson party was a disaster.

Two days later the Revsons gave a party to make up to Merle. I had already left town. The day of the party they planned Merle was having lunch with friends deciding what excuse they could give not to go to the Revsons but instead go aboard an Italian liner that was in port for a big gala. Armand Deutsch suggested that someone should pretend he had a rare and communicable tropical disease; just as Merle began to write the note to general laughter—Charles was such a hypochondriac!—the Revson speedboat came up. The Revson captain gave Merle a note saying that while Charles was looking forward to having them all that night it might be better in the circumstances if Luis didn't come! Merle was furious! She handed the note around and then gave the captain her note of reply. It said that none of those present would consider going without me— and she didn't speak to the Revsons for two years. And she only went back on the yacht when the Revsons personally invited me. That was Merle.

Chapter Fifteen

Merle fell romantically in love with a young actor at the time, an Adonis of great charm and physical beauty, who recalls their brief liaison joyously. He says that lovemaking had a ritualistic quality for her, and adds:

I'll never forget my time with Merle. I felt very much under the test of my manhood. She was still extremely beautiful in her late fifties and as much of a challenge as a young woman would have been. When I entered her room each night, she was soaking in a perfumed tub. It was sort of a ritual she followed from that night on. She stood up, stunning, like a Polynesian woman with those wide hips and tiny shoulders: the Eternal Feminine. She put on a transparent nightdress and moved to the bed. I made love to her with the heart and body of a youth—and she was passionate beyond belief and we were in love, madly in love, no doubt of it.

And the bed, the famous Chinese bed of hers, was unbelievable! She had two servants who came in every morning who ironed the sheets one by one and folded them. It was a job that took all day, every day. The sheets were pink and amber and red and gold and each layer was like an unfolding sunset. I felt I was making love to Merle *in* a sunset. And every evening as the sun went down, we would watch the changing light and make love again and again.

A pleasure of the late 1960s was the rediscovery as a friend of Noël Coward, whom Merle had known since the mid-1930s and whom she adored along with his two lifelong companions, Graham

Payn and Cole Lesley. Merle became close to them again because they would put her up at their house in Switzerland on her visits to the Niehans Clinic. Their home, popularly known as Chalet Coward, was within easy driving distance of the clinic and of the pleasant town of Vevey; it was also convenient to Lausanne, where Merle loved to do her shopping.

The house was splendid, with large rooms and high ceilings, and every guest had a private bathroom with fresh dressing gowns, slippers, toothpaste, soap, and writing paper, and even stamps for almost every country in the world arranged in the room. It was like being aboard an ocean liner in the old luxurious days of prewar travel, and Merle looked forward to her visits there with a delicious expectation. Not only was the house a joy, drenched in sunlight and good cheer, but Noël Coward fascinated Merle with his wit, elegance, and unfailing charm; and Graham and Cole were indispensable foils as well as amusing and generous human beings in their own right. In turn, they were intensely fond of Merle and looked forward enormously to her visits. Wherever they were in the world, they would always find time to call her, or she to call them.

On one occasion, Noël and his friends visited Merle in Acapulco. Graham Payn recalls:

Merle made a sort of pact to herself, which we didn't realize until after we had left. She gave us caviar every day in a different form. You name it, there it was, and for our stay of almost a week we had this special treat reworked for us daily.

Noël wanted to be very quiet: he had health problems and was tired at the time, and she knew he didn't want to get into elaborate parties. So just we, Merle, the two children, and Bruno Pagliai at weekends would get together and swim and go out in the yacht of President Aleman. We were very happy together.

Often, on her visits to Switzerland, Merle would have breakfast in her room: it was a tradition there that each guest would be separately served. This released the visitors from pressure to appear at breakfast at a certain time; they could then rise when they wanted to, even at noon, and go for a walk or just rest in the beautiful garden or the living room without being under any strain. She always brought presents for Coward and his "family": wonderful mohair sweaters and cardigans, the sizes noted down in her little book; and when she left, she always gave splendid gifts to the staff. They worshiped her.

It was inevitable that when the time arrived for Coward's seventieth birthday celebration in London, a gala event announced weeks in advance, Merle would be Noël's first choice as his companion. He wanted the most glamorous woman in the world to share this tremendous occasion with him. This must have been a blow to Marlene Dietrich, his other great friend among the female stars; and her feelings cannot have been improved in view of the long rivalry between the two women that went all the way back to the bizarre episode of the two portraits by Gerald Brockhurst in 1937, when they had to arrive at the artist's studio in separate shifts, and to *The Garden of Allah*.

The birthday celebrations took place in London in December 1969. Merle had always especially liked the Savoy Hotel, and she had a river suite overlooking the Thames very close to Noël's. Coward was ailing from nephritis, a kidney disease that resulted from poisoned drinking water taken in the Seychelle Islands years before; and he also had painful circulation loss in his legs which meant that he needed to be escorted everywhere and to lean on a helpful arm.

The celebrations began with a lecture at the National Film Theatre on the south bank of the Thames; there was a screening of *In Which We Serve*, Coward's patriotic movie in celebration of the heroism of the Royal Navy in World War II. Merle walked with Coward to the lecture, filled with joy at the chance to honor her great and gifted friend. The party included Prince Charles, still a close friend of Merle's, Princess Anne, Lord Mountbatten, David Niven, Dame Celia Johnson, and Sir Richard Attenborough, who introduced and questioned Coward on the stage.

The next evening, there was a splendid midnight performance at the Phoenix Theatre where Coward had appeared forty years earlier in his own play *Private Lives*. Noël was in the royal box with Merle just a fraction behind him; and as they stood up there was an overwhelming burst of applause for both of them, more intense even than that which greeted Princess Margaret and Antony Armstrong-Jones, who sat in the front row of the balcony. The evening was captivating and included marvelous performances by John Gielgud, Dame Edith Evans, who brought a great gust of affectionate laughter when she fell asleep in her chair on the stage (and she wasn't acting), Evelyn Laye (who nudged Dame Edith awake), Anna Neagle doing a Charleston, Cliff Richard, and Jessie Matthews. Next day, there was a luncheon at the Savoy, chaired by Laurence Olivier and Lord Mountbatten. And finally, private parties given by Princess Margaret at Kensington Palace, and by Queen Elizabeth the Queen Mother at Clarence House. Despite his physical condition, Coward was in very good form throughout; and there can be no question that Merle's uncanny power of healing, inherited from her mother, gave strength and radiance to Coward and helped him through what might have been more an ordeal than a pleasure. For her, of course, it was one of the great triumphs of her career that of all people in the world Coward should have chosen her. It proved once again that she was the queen of international society, of the jet set; but more importantly it showed that she was its most valued, enlightened, and exquisite member.

Back in Acapulco, Merle suddenly found her life empty again. She saw less and less of Bruno, and more and more she poured her heart and will into her two children. Little Bruno and Francesca were now at the time of puberty, going through the usual difficult adjustments as their bodies started to change. Now that their minds were developing rapidly and well along with their bodies, Merle felt closer to them than ever. Although she was almost sixty, she had an impressive capacity to bridge the vast gap in age between them. She had taught them both to swim when they were nine months old; and although Francesca, who was still shy and very sensitive, had little interest in excelling in any field, Bruno showed an early aptitude for sports. His problem was a streak of laziness and sudden shows of indifference which sometimes exasperated Merle. In her need to have the best for her children, she sometimes drove them too hard, not with any cruelty, since cruelty was not in her nature, but with the desire to have them emulate her own drive to success in the early years, a drive that in her was now largely consumed in living itself. She had learned calm and detachment with time; but she wanted the children to achieve the utmost.

Her deepest need was for Little Bruno to win in the Mexican Junior Olympics, and she drove him hard through many months of training. Bruno Pagliai, Jr., says:

Mother got a famous coach to come to the house in Mexico City and put me through heavy practices. But I didn't have the consuming drive of the star athlete. I couldn't face the idea of giving up my school vacations for hours of going up and down the pool, clipping seconds off my time. It became really draining and nerve-racking. I settled for winning school events and medals.

I also hated health foods. My mother forced good nutrition on my sister and me and we hated it. It was like that old line, "Johnny, don't go jump over the wall." The first thing Johnny does is to jump it as quickly as possible. We'd cheat on her and we wouldn't even eat at home sometimes. We'd play hooky and go out and eat tacos and guacamole, and we'd get amoebas and worms as a result. When I started into heavy training, I noticed if I didn't put the right fuel in my stomach my body wouldn't react properly. It wasn't until I got well into my teens that I knew Mother was right.

Little Bruno became bored easily, and adolescence made him more restless and edgy than ever. Despite Merle's every effort not to spoil him, it was inevitable that a boy who was driven in a chauffeured car to school, who had to have armed guards with machine guns because of kidnapping scares, who had a palatial bedroom to himself, and was waited on from morning to night by as many as fourteen living-in servants, would have to exhibit symptoms of the pampered super-rich. Fortunately, Merle counterbalanced this extravagant mode of living with her own Hindu philosophy of nonattachment to material objects. The Hindus believe that no physical thing has any real substance; that it is futile and vain to attach one's self to any material object. Merle also taught her children that karma or destiny ruled their lives and that the only way they could improve the trend of that destiny was to give generously to others and express kindness and consideration to those who were less fortunate. If young Bruno ever flew off the handle at a slow or uncertain member of the household, she would correct him sharply.

Although this application of her personal philosophy was meant lovingly, it also created its own intense form of pressure. The children were raised by Italian tradition in the Roman Catholic Church, and attended confession and Mass according to the customary rules of religious observance. Their home teaching, however, was in contrast with that approved by the priests; the result was that both Little Bruno and Francesca ran the risk of being intellectually confused. Merle overcame this by teaching them that all religions were in a sense one; that God was not a single, ancient being ruling over the heavens, but was present in every petal of every flower, every fragile filament of every snowflake crystal, and every muscle of the human body. The children reached adolescence with a very strong sense of the sacredness of life and the need to take care of themselves physically, intellectually, and emotionally. But again, this helpful pressure of Merle's created its own problems in spite of her good intentions.

The children moved from school to school, from Mexico to California and back again, their characters dividing more sharply with the passing years. Adolescence often shows marked differentiations in brother and sister, and in this case, of course, Bruno and Francesca came from different families. Bruno, so withdrawn earlier on, grew more and more macho, extroverted, wild, edgy, and forceful, increasingly impatient with his studies and leaning toward visionary aspects of advanced technology; he was a child of the future. Francesca became more and more withdrawn; in spite of herself, she must have been aware in her early teens of the contrast between her just modestly attractive self and her overpoweringly glamorous mother; and Bruno must have felt a desperate need for a younger, virile, and athletic father. His adopted father was now pushing seventy and was so remote as to be virtually a figurehead.

Fortunately, Bruno's brother, Ferro, a genius of the Pagliai empire, had four athletic, healthy, and robust sons, the youngest of whom, Paul Pagliai, combined great energy and youthful vigor with talent as an artist. Paul became Little Bruno's closest friend, his constant companion in every area, and this made up to a great extent for the absence of a father figure. At least Little Bruno now had a kind of brother.

Both children shared Merle's psychic gifts. Francesca recalls:

> One time, I was in the kitchen where I had an overwhelming vision that my nurse would come in, walk through another room, and then trip and fall down the staircase. After a few minutes, she did come in and go to another room. I felt I couldn't say or do anything: I felt paralyzed. I heard a door open, and a cry. She went down the stairs.

Little Bruno adds:

> The ghost in the house in Cuernavaca pulled a couple of things on me. A girlfriend and I were reading to each other in my room with the door locked. A force of enormous power suddenly slammed up against the door, as though a great wind were blowing: a wind so strong that it literally blew in the wood, and the wood began to crack. A few minutes later, the force subsided and the door resumed its normal form.
>
> At 4 A.M. one morning, my cousin Paul and I, who shared a bedroom, heard what seemed to be a big ball of iron or a sledgehammer hitting against stone. It was a shattering sound. It was followed by the dragging of a chain across a flagged floor. Then our door broke off the lock and slammed hard against the wall.
>
> Our housekeeper Trinidad showed me how the ghost of a

woman would take the clothes from the closets in the room on top of the old women's dungeon and place them on the bed or the floor in piles. He would describe to me how he would find playing cards strewn all over the floor or furniture moved across a room to one side. We discovered there were three ghosts in the house, not just the tall figure seen earlier on, of the man in the uniform of Cortez. There was a little boy and also the lady I mentioned.

Ferro Pagliai adds that Merle complained to him of hearing terrible moans of anguish from that same woman in the night, and the slow and steady dragging of chains that Little Bruno reported. Bruno, Jr., records that he and his mother would meditate in separate rooms and Merle would concentrate on a mantra, or sacred word. After some considerable time, Bruno would feel his mind blacken completely and that word would appear in it and he would speak it aloud. Then he would enter Merle's room and tell her the word and she would throw her arms around him in joy.

Despite their differences of temperament and willpower, despite Little Bruno's strong desire for independence and for asserting his coming manhood, it is almost impossible to calculate the depth of feeling that existed between him and his mother. Both were driven spirits; Merle in her youth had the same passion for individuality; and she understood her very handsome son even when he most exasperated her. She had to reach out more consciously to her adored Francesca, who was painfully aware that she did not have an interest or understanding of the things Merle held most dear: painting, poetry, sculpture, or music. Francesca's chief ambition from the moment her breasts developed and she started to menstruate was to achieve happiness with a young man of her choice, and to raise her own children in the simplest and least sophisticated way possible.

Their response to the fact of their adoption was different. Merle, as Lee Anderson told her again and again, should have told them they were adopted, but she did not. Bruno says he knew instinctively from the age of five, and that the fact failed to bother him; he makes the statement almost defiantly. Francesca says that she did not know until several years later than Bruno; asked why this was the case, Bruno says it is because she simply refused to accept it and blotted the knowledge out of her mind. Francesca says:

> I had a sort of vision in my heart that I had been adopted, but I never really knew if it was true. Finally, in New York one

time, I asked my mother, Am I an adopted child? And after a long pause, she reluctantly admitted that I was. I asked her, feeling some pain, why? She told me sadly that she couldn't have children and she wanted them so very badly and now she was joyous that we were such wonderful children. Then I asked her, Are Bruno and I brother and sister? She told me that we were. Later, I found out we were not of the same blood: I can't remember how. I felt disappointed and almost angry and I said to Mother, Why didn't you tell me the truth? Again there was a pause and Mother said, rather awkwardly, Darling, I felt that if you knew the truth you might not like each other anymore. I said, Oh, come on, we've lived with each other for I don't know how many years! The subject was never brought up again. I never understood why Mother really felt she had to tell me an untruth. I know she didn't mean to be unkind. Who are my real parents? I don't know. I don't really want to know. I felt a kind of sadness when I thought about them, that they had given me up. And then, as the years went on, I began instinctively to feel that they had died.

Bruno, Jr., says:

I also don't want to know who my parents were. Mother taught me that my parents ran into hundreds, back into the beginnings of time, so why should I feel attached to any particular couple? If the truth be known, I feel my deepest sense of parentage in a man and wife of the Etruscan era, long, long ago.

Merle took the children to England, Italy, France, and Greece; she walked them through art galleries and museums, to their total stupefaction and boredom; they were not even interested in seeing the ceremony of the White House guards, though they did show more interest in the changing of the guards in London; and they very much enjoyed meeting Prince Philip and Prince Charles. Bruno, Jr., remembers:

We met the two princes twice in Acapulco. For years Merle had taught us that it was not right to use a piece of bread to soak up the gravy on our plates. She always told us, "Leave something for Mr. Manners." She was especially anxious when royalty was at the table and we were told that on no account must we indulge this terrible habit in the royal presence. We sat down to lunch with Prince Philip and Prince Charles for the first time, determined to be on our very best behavior. As the main course came to an end, Francesca and I watched with astonishment as Prince Philip picked up a piece of bread and slowly and methodically wiped out every last inch of gravy with it! Mother nearly died. And I said, I couldn't resist it, "If Prince Philip can do that, I can do it, too!" And I proceeded to do just that very thing!

Bruno, Jr., gives a vivid picture of Merle's eating habits at the time. He says her favorite dish after fifty years was still the oxtail stew on the bone that Charlotte used to make:

> We all used to sit astonished while Mother, despite her obsession with mopping up gravy, would pick up the ox tail with her bare hands and chew the huge gristly bone to the marrow, the gravy dripping down on her napkin! She could cook only two things—she almost never joined Pepe, our cook, in the kitchen. She would make scrambled eggs with small-grained cottage cheese and a dash of curry; and curry itself, wildly hot and fierce. She also encouraged Pepe in his classic dish of hamburger *en croûte*. We all loved it.

Despite the fascination and challenge of raising her small family, Merle still felt a painful loneliness as the new decade of the 1970s approached. Like many people of her generation, she felt isolated from society; even with her countless millions, her great staffs of servants, her beautiful home in Acapulco, and the suffusing radiance of sea and sky and turf, she still could not blot out the vulgarity and ugliness of the times. Bruno, Jr., inevitably brought the sounds of rock and roll into the house and not even her playing of Wagner and Beethoven could drown out the new music of a rebellious generation. The collapse of the intellectual elite and the overpowering barbarism of mass popular culture caused her sensitive spirit extreme anguish. She dreaded the sight of ostentatiously torn tight jeans, of the aggressive and blatant sexuality of such new clothing, and the crassness of television in the United States and Mexico. She began to withdraw with increasing suffering into herself.

And to escape, she turned more and more to her favorite mode of entertainment: vintage comedy. Apart from one contemporary work, *What's Up, Doc?*, which she discovered in the 1970s and which she loved for its knockabout humor and the performances of Barbra Streisand and Ryan O'Neal, she preferred the comedies of an earlier era, particularly *Bringing Up Baby*, with Cary Grant and Katharine Hepburn, of which she never tired. Whenever she was in Hollywood, she would ask her dear friend, Louis B. Mayer's daughter Edie Goetz, to show her vintage classics on a private screen. Everyone who knew her thinks of her first with loving laughter: they see her curled up in an armchair, giggling or chortling happily over some screen mishap of the banana peel or man-into-manhole variety, exquisitely amused by simulated disasters. A woman who could not endure to kill an insect in real life would be convulsed with amusement when an unfortunate victim took a pratfall in a picture.

Perhaps because of her loneliness in Acapulco and the sense of strain at the advancing ugliness of the era, and the continuing agony of lying about her children, Merle fed on laughter more than she had ever done. She enjoyed joking and teasing and fooling around in a way that belied her public image of great lady and supreme hostess of the world. She also grew increasingly bored with parties. Indeed, she told John Calendo of *Interview* magazine, who asked her how she liked her image as society empress:

> I *loathe* it . . . I *loathe* parties! I think they're the loneliest things in the world. I'm much more terrified going into a party than I am going to the set to work. To walk into a party, I tremble! And it's funny because I was thinking about it the other day when I *was* going to a party. It's funny that when you make a movie you're doing something that's going to be in front of millions—you hope—well if you're going to a party, it's only a group. Yet one is terrified. I suppose that the difference is that when one is on the set, one is one's work, and the other is kind of . . . kind of *superficial*! Every time I go to a party, I wonder why anyone does it!

In the same interview, Merle made a characteristic statement ("I remember reading something about being Hindu in a fan magazine. And I worried that my mother, a very conservative woman, might see it. The strangest stories were always coming out about me."); she was still living out this lie at almost sixty. Even her children knew nothing about her true background, despite the fact that she was teaching them Hindu beliefs while denying her ethnic origins. Even at this stage in her life, she was extremely edgy when questions of her past came up. In 1968, a BBC team interviewed her for a documentary entitled *The Epic That Never Was*, produced by Bill Duncalf, which related the curious story of the abandonment of *I, Claudius* in 1937.

She sat on the lawn of her house on La Ladera Drive in Bel Air on one of her visits to Hollywood and, visibly tense and oddly stiff—seemingly because of the tension of concealing her past—gave a more or less accurate account of what had taken place. But her old insecurity and unease flared up, and she wished she had not agreed in a weak moment to do the interview. She anxiously contacted Duncalf and asked to see her footage, which was flown from London at great expense; when she saw it, she became extremely upset and canceled it, exercising her right to do so in her clearance form. In despair, Duncalf and his crew had to return to Hollywood, overrunning their budget considerably, and shoot the whole interview again. The finished documentary suggests that Merle was still uncomfortable and overcompensated for her insecurity and unease by assuming an even more icily patrician air than before. "Merle Oberon emerges as something of a pill," the critic Kenneth Tynan commented in his review.

Along with discomfort about the past with Korda, there was also a strain of nostalgia. Merle discovered that her old friend Hal Wallis was making *Anne of a Thousand Days*, based on Maxwell Anderson's play about Anne Boleyn; and she conceived the desire to play Catherine of Aragon. Wallis felt she was wrong for the part; and according to his wife Martha, she went to extraordinary trouble to convince Wallis she could do it, even to the extent of having a costume made. But Wallis was adamant, and to Merle's great disappointment, the Greek star Irene Papas was cast.

In 1968, Merle was involved in another tragedy. Mrs. Sofia deBassi, an attractive friend of hers and a prominent figure of Acapulco society, joined Merle for lunch one winter day with her son-in-law, Count Cesare di Acquaroni, and his wife. Later that afternoon, Sofia deBassi had a violent quarrel with Count Cesare as he lay tanning himself beside her swimming pool. During the argument, she allegedly took a gun from her handbag and riddled him with bullets.

Police arrived and seized her, and Merle, not believing the story, offered to do what she could. Two hundred spectators jammed the tiny courtroom for the inquest; Acapulco was talking about nothing else. Trembling and pallid in enormous dark glasses, Sofia collapsed when the wounds were described by the coroner. Recovering, she screamed that the shooting was only an accident. But she went to prison just the same. Merle was very upset; typically, she was one of the very few figures of Acapulco society who visited Sofia in her cell, bringing her decent food. She arranged for Sofia to have a whole section of the prison at her disposal, furnished like an apartment.

For a time, in the late 1960s, Merle endured almost a nunlike existence, far removed from her wild early life in London and Holly-wood. Luis Estevez says:

I used to feel that Merle was wasted, that a beautiful woman like her should meet an attractive young man and find love again. I would say to her, Go ahead and find someone. And she would suddenly become clownish and put on a shawl and bend double and walk around like a very old woman and say in a croaking voice, "We're going to be in our eighties, Luisito! And you're going to tell me how I should meet and go out with a handsome young man, and I'll say, Oh, no, Luisito, let's save it for next year!" And we would laugh and laugh together. But I *did* feel that she should have happiness in the romantic sense. That it wasn't ridiculous at her age to need romance. I felt that sex has to rear its ugly head for you to be a well-balanced person and she wasn't the kind of woman to go, as the gossips had her go, with beachboys. That was most definitely never the case. Merle appreciated beauty in the male body but there was no way she would get into that kind of dead-end situation. It wasn't just her position in society and her respect for her husband and love of her children that would stop her. The idea of casual unromantic sex involving money or just some physical self-indulgence was anathema to her nature. She could not live for a minute with the idea of sex unless romance and real passion were involved.

Merle's circle, Luis, Edie Goetz, Doris Stein, Lee Anderson, Betsy Bloomingdale, Janet de Cordova, Ingrid Ohrbach, Leonard Gershe, the Wallises, and the Reagans, all wanted her to find a young man, but she fought them and fought them. Finally, it almost became a kind of loving conspiracy: finding a mate for Merle. Merle was due to arrive in Beverly Hills for a visit to Ingrid and Jerry Ohrbach, when, at a party at Ray and Fran Stark's, Luis was introduced to a handsome and impressive young man who was escorting Janet de Cordova to the soiree. Luis, Janet, and Ingrid all decided Merle must meet the young man before the evening was over. His name was Robert Wolders.

Chapter Sixteen

At the time Merle met Wolders, he was a quarter of a century her junior. He was Dutch: His father, an executive of KLM, the Dutch airline, had died four years earlier; his mother, a gentle, very private, fastidious woman of great sensibility and discipline of nature, lived in a suburb of Amsterdam. Her family history was curious; she had lost seven of her eight brothers, all of whom had died young. They were an artistic clan and had lived careless, even reckless lives in total contrast with their one sister. One of them had been a famous copyist painter who produced skillful replicas of the Old Masters as forgeries for use in pretentious houses, in the manner of the famous art hoaxer Van Meegeren.

Robert Wolders was surrounded by feminine influences through his youth and upbringing. Perhaps because he was the one boy in a family dominated by girls and women, he early acquired a remarkable sensitivity toward the female temperament. He had a capacity to judge and provide for shifts of mood, unevenness of feeling, and outbreaks of temper; he understood the way in which women, more than men, experienced fluctuations of their natures in tune with the cycles of nature itself. He knew they were closer to the earth than men and yet at the same time capable of an almost abstract elevation and mysticism which most men could not attain.

He grew up a physically handsome man, with a beautifully chiseled face, gentle understanding eyes, pink cheeks, and a sturdy, broad-shouldered, barrel-chested Dutch physique that belied a delicate constitution affected by years of suffering under German occupation. He looked like a young burgher in a classic Flemish painting. He had a subdued, soft, extremely well-modulated voice, and was modest and self-deprecating to a degree, possibly also a result of being brought up among women. From his parents, he learned exquisite manners, unselfishness, and a wry detachment. He was respectful of talent, appreciative of delicacy in people, and extraordinarily delicate in his own approach to life. His fastidiousness verged on perfectionism. He was irritated by any kind of falseness, or clumsiness of approach. His humanness and warmth saved him from what in a colder man might have seemed priggishness. A person who was so careful, so strict, upright, considerate, measured, and balanced would have irritated most people if he had not also had such a genial, kindly quality as a man.

He was not much of a student, and he greatly preferred traveling on KLM free tickets to every part of the civilized world to studying. He coasted through his schooling and longed for vacations when he could take off on another extended trip. He spent much of his early manhood at the University of Rochester, located in a rather dull city in upper New York State, where his eldest sister's husband was in research at Eastman Kodak. He was not outstanding in athletics.

After failing as a painter, quite lacking in self-assurance, Wolders took up the one profession open to the handsome and the not particularly qualified: acting. He joined the Drama Society at Rochester and moved—without much ambition or enthusiasm, but without knowing what else he might do—to the American Academy of Dramatic Arts in New York. At the age of twenty-eight, he was still a beginner, quite painfully aware that he had no real talent, but also unsure of his direction. This lack of assurance increased his self-consciousness and considerably weakened his male ego, never strong in the first place.

He moved to Hollywood. In a city of men and women of strikingly good looks, he was not particularly outstanding. He obtained jobs as a performer. The only virtue he had as an actor was that he was sympathetic and easy to work with and everybody liked him on the set. He was punctual, reliable, and devoid of the fierce, defiant uptightness that made so many contemporary actors intolerable to work with. He moved ahead smoothly toward a mediocre career. He was one of the brothers in a forgettable remake of *Beau Geste*, and he also appeared unmemorably in the TV series *Laredo*. He was a popular escort for women who were either divorced, separated, or had husbands out of town; he was regarded as "safe," companionable, and personable. He was not too imposing at dinner parties, and a handsome face and figure were always welcome. Without even willing it, and certainly without ambition in that direction, he infiltrated the highest circles of Bel Air and Beverly Hills—he entered Merle's charmed circle.

He first met Merle in the late 1960s, at a party given by friends at which Marlon Brando was also present. He saw her across the room: she was with an actor he knew. He had seen her long before in *A Song to Remember* but hadn't recognized her at the party and had to ask somebody who she was. He was struck at once by her beauty, deeply and instantly attracted, but he had not the slightest thought of ever getting closer to her.

Ingrid Ohrbach gave a party early in 1970 and invited Wolders, knowing that Merle would be staying with her. Merle had just arrived from Mexico; she was greeted at the plane by Ingrid's fellow match-maker, Luis Estevez, who had met Wolders and knew he would be perfect for Merle. Merle came with Luis; Wolders came with Mrs. Frederick de Cordova, whose husband was in New York producing *The Johnny Carson Show*. Wolders was strategically placed next to Merle at the dinner table.

She didn't immediately suspect what her close friend and her hostess were mutually up to. She knew that Wolders was not accom-panied by a wife or girl friend, which may have given her a clue. Undoubtedly, Wolders was her physical type: He was a big man, and she liked big men; he had a perfect education and family background, which were crucial to her; and she was fascinated by his soft speech, his gentle courtliness and old-world grace. She was amused, rather than upset, when she discovered that he knew little or nothing about her. He asked her, trying hard to make conversation and probably feeling extremely nervous, "Apart from *Henry VIII*, did you make any other films for Korda?" She replied gently that she had. Possibly, if he had not been so attracted and had been a mindless party type, she might have been tempted to be cool toward Wolders, but she found this charming ignorance very appealing. Even when he asked her if she knew Korda well, she didn't exclaim that she and Korda had been married. The next exchange, however, must have tested her patience a little. They were talking about doctors good and bad, and Wolders said, "One particular man has been recommended to me especially highly." Merle asked, "What's his name?" And Wolders said, without drawing breath, "Dr. Rex Ross."

By the end of the evening, it was obvious to both Luis Estevez and Ingrid Ohrbach that their joint venture had emphatically paid off. Merle made it known to them that she was fascinated by the sweet-na-tured young Wolders and he and she began seeing each other regularly. Wolders says:

When our relationship began, I kept asking myself how I could do something special for this lady, to make her happy in a way that would last. Of course, I had no money to speak of and I couldn't give her the things she was used to having. But first, I began to think I shouldn't go ahead, I shouldn't follow this through into a full-scale affair. I had to consider her children. I had to consider her husband. And she too had to think of them: she hesitated to become involved because she knew she would upset several lives at once. Although her marriage to Bruno had ended, in every sense except the technical one, she couldn't bear to hurt him. I got ulcers worrying about her worrying about Bruno and the children.

There were problems at first. Like so many men in her life, Wolders smoked and drank and Merle hated these habits. Moreover, Merle was deeply afraid of the future. She had never seriously contemplated marrying Rod Taylor or Richard Rush, but it was clear to her from the beginning that Wolders was on a much higher level. She *could* marry him. But she might die before him and that worried her; she was shocked when he said to her that if she died, his life would come to an end; she couldn't bear that sense of responsibility and asked him only that whatever woman filled his life after she was gone, that woman must be worthy of him. The age difference was insignificant to her and Wolders; neither was American and neither had the American obsession with age. She felt young, and her simple, innocent, romantic being had never really aged. She looked wonderfully youthful, her figure preserved through dieting and swimming.

The only significant sign of aging was that, probably aware of her mortality, she had begun to detach herself from material things and no longer brooded over her accounts or pinched every penny—she knew she couldn't take it with her. She also had a kind of sexual restraint with the puritanical and correct Wolders, and he says that her lovemaking—though intense—was extremely restricted in those days in terms of what she would do. She programmed herself to be a new and finer being for Wolders.

Wolders was born old, or at least middle-aged. He was intrinsically Dutch just as she was intrinsically Indian; and he was comfortably bourgeois, solid, and mature. They met in the middle. Many people even felt they were the same age. They were so considerate and lacking in harshness or crudeness that they could not accept their pleasure as people in our amoral era normally would. They were like Victorians, painfully aware of duty and honor and obedience to rules of behavior. This kind of moral consideration, far removed from

Merle's earlier adventurousness and romantic madness, led to considerable quiet suffering. It was a shared suffering, admittedly, but it was suffering nonetheless, caused in part by Merle's tension at literally recreating herself at a higher moral level.

And yet, as Wolders says:

Neither of us was too rational after a while. We gradually came to understand that our love for each other was inevitable. We certainly realized we needed a lot of assistance from the gods because we gave medals of St. Jude to each other: the patron saint of the impossible. We realized without really acknowledging it that we had set ourselves a difficult task. We never sat down and concluded that there was some obstacle in our lives that had to be straightened out or removed; we were sure that things would resolve themselves.

After weeks of dating, when they secretly became lovers, Merle was still not prepared even to consider a final break from Bruno, and Wolders had to work heroically on her to convince her that she must end her marriage. At last, she did summon up the courage, which was always very great, to tell Bruno the truth. She had to tell Bruno, Sr., straight; she who dreaded hurting people more than anything.

Wolders discreetly disappeared to visit his mother in Holland. He is the first to admit that Merle's news, conveyed to Bruno as delicately as she could, came as a severe shock and provoked Bruno to terrible grief and anger. He says:

I can understand the way he reacted. Imagine losing a woman like Merle! I could have understood it if he had wanted to kill me. I certainly would have wanted to kill anyone who tried to take Merle from me. But she didn't want to humiliate me by forcing us to be secretive or furtive. His pride as a Mediterranean man was shocked. It says much for his love of his children and his own self-respect that he overcame his feelings and he and Merle soon were talking again, discussing what would be best for Little Bruno and Francesca.

The next big test of Merle's courage was introducing Wolders to her children. Fortunately, they responded to him at once, but despite the fact that Wolders was an appealing and attractive human being with a strong empathy for children, the adjustment was inevitably painful. Often Merle would call Luis Estevez in tears because of the problem of Bruno's adjusting to the discipline of having a new father. Merle and Wolders, though loving, were quite strict and their high moral principles sometimes proved grating to Bruno, Jr., who was feeling his oats and wanted to have his own way. On one occasion he actually ran away from home, and Luis had to trace him and bring him back.

Although Merle and Wolders sometimes seemed inflexible and Victorian, Merle's teaching of nonattachment to material riches helped a good deal. It enabled the children to adjust to the startling transition from being waited on hand and foot in the great mansion in Mexico City to the more help-yourself atmosphere of a California beach house. The happiest days were those when, all tensions relaxed for the time being, the little family of Merle, Rob, Bruno, and Francesca tanned themselves on the beach and ran in and out of the sea. Yet even on those idyllic occasions Merle felt pain and guilt at what she had done to Bruno, at the children's problems, their exposure at a formative stage to a broken home. Wolders says:

My ears burned with Bruno Pagliai's hate. Whenever the subject came up, the subject of the separation, he refused to discuss it. He wouldn't talk about it to the children. If he hadn't developed a hatred for me, he wouldn't have been a normal man. Merle felt no ill will toward him. It was easier for Merle to keep up the good relationship with me, not to be badly inclined toward him. It was more difficult for him to retain a friendship with Merle because every time they spoke the wound was opened again. There was no great friction between them. It's just that their lives had arrived at a crossroads and they had gone in different directions. It was natural that they would continue to be fond of each other.

Gradually, Merle and Wolders discovered more and more in common. They shared a love of nature. Wolders did not quite have Merle's patience and desire for peace and quiet; Merle had been through a thousand storms and wanted nothing more than quiet and a safe harbor. Gradually, Wolders relaxed into Merle's serene love of the sea, the stars, the beach, sunsets, and the waxing and waning moon. It was fortunate for their relationship that Wolders' natural masculine being was undercut by his frail constitution.

She taught him much. She had him cut out smoking and drinking. She taught him how years of suffering could result in purification of the spirit; a filtering out of the unimportant things in life. She had become more and more conscious of the importance of balance, harmony, and order. Wolders shared a need for cleanliness, precision, and correctness. Their taste in art was slightly different, but they met on common ground in a love of Fantin-Latour, Utrillo, Corot, and Dufy, whose painting of a wheat field, one of Merle's treasures, also made Wolders rejoice.

They began traveling together as man and wife, though they were far too sophisticated to disguise themselves as such. In Europe, they found much pleasure together. Both disliked large, opulent museums and when they did go to them it was to see only one work of art. At the Rijksmuseum in Amsterdam, they would stand for long periods gazing at Rembrandt's *The Night Watch,* and in smaller museums, like the Jeu de Paume and the Rodin Museum in Paris, they would find refreshment, standing hand in hand gazing for long periods into the still centers of their favorite works.

Their tastes in music were decidedly different. Merle liked heroic music, particularly the Eroica Symphony and individual arias and themes of Wagner, whereas Wolders preferred chamber music. He was always surprised that Merle liked such "big" music—it seemed a contradiction of her nature—but of course the grand romantic gesture was an echo of her all-out style.

Merle was invited to London to a private dinner party at Buckingham Palace. This was a great honor, but she was very busy and almost had no time to squeeze it in. She was in a state of nervous strain and excitement as Luis Estevez designed a beautiful gown for her for the occasion. Canceling some plans and shifting others, she flew to New York and changed planes.

Despite the death of so many of her nearest and dearest in airplane crashes, her experiences with the supernatural had removed all fear of death; indeed, she was one of the world's most traveled passengers. Thus, when two-thirds of the way across the Atlantic, the pilot announced that an engine had given out and that there might be some possibility of winding up in the ocean, she scarcely turned a hair. A woman passenger near her passed out at the news and was discovered to be suffering a heart attack. With great presence of mind, Merle assisted the stewardess in applying resuscitative procedures and the woman's life was saved.

The dinner party was the following night. Despite a long delay and an emergency landing, Merle, unruffled, made her way to the palace, where the Queen and the Prince greeted her warmly, expressing concern over her ordeal, most relieved to see her alive.

She had another brush with death at that time. Back in Mexico, she was stricken with a violent allergic reaction to an antihistamine preparation; she collapsed and her pulse stopped. In the hospital, in a limbo state between life and death, she again experienced the transcendent moment she had known when she had been declared medically dead following her surgery for cancer some forty years earlier. She found herself looking down at her body, hovering on the edge of a place where those who had died were waiting for her. She returned to her body wearily; moments later, she revived.

She began to long once more for a return to the screen. Her dissatisfaction with the final form of *Hotel* drove her to create her own vehicle as she had created *Of Love and Desire*, and she resolved once more to ask Bruno to put up the basic investment. It shows a curious aspect of her psyche that she would once more want to see herself in the role of a woman who was an ordinary tourist, lonely, with no strong relationship in her life, when she herself was so totally in control of her destiny and had already chosen a man who was perfect for her. She settled on an idea she had thought about for some time: an account of a British tourist, Serena, who arrives in Mexico and falls in love. Serena had, like Merle, an unhappy event in her past involving the death of a lover in a fiery accident—a car crash in this case was clearly a parallel with Richard Hillary's death in a plane. Serena discovers consolation with a young struggling painter: Wolders, of course, had wanted to be an artist. Merle decided the story was to be set in the area around Merida in the peninsula of Yucatan, with its haunted ruins of Chichén Itzá and its sacrificial lake into which women were thrown by the priests of the Mayan religion.

Merle had for some time admired the writings of Gavin Lambert, a British author who had begun as a film critic of the same school to which Lindsay Anderson and Karel Reisz, later famous directors, also belonged. Lambert emerged in Hollywood as a protégé of the producer Jerry Wald and had written a fine script based upon D. H. Lawrence's novel *Sons and Lovers* for Wald. His subtle and ingeniously amusing collection of Hollywood short stories, *The Slide Area*, had been a great *succès d'estime* at the outset of the 1960s. He had compounded that success with a witty novel, *Inside Daisy Clover*. Merle admired Lambert's intricate humor, clear undecorated style, and the directness of approach that showed a clever and cynical but humanist mind. She was delighted when she found that he responded strongly to the idea of writing a script for her projected film.

They had a great empathy. Lambert adored Vivien Leigh, and had, despite his darkness of vision, a strong admiration for the great romantics of the world. Also, and perhaps even more importantly, he combined a sense of realism about human behavior with a belief in life after death which he called, in a later essay, "the supreme correct improbability." Ironically, it was Lambert's admiration for Merle and his desire to mirror her vision in his writing that led him to the most disastrous work of his career.

Merle also made a serious mistake. Instead of allowing Lambert to develop the script on the lines of his previous works, with understanding of the female psyche, she entered into discussions with him in a way which no actor or actress should do, seeking to infiltrate into every line aspects of her own temperament, opinions, and feelings. She changed Serena from a simple, over-the-hill tourist rather like the lead in Tennessee Williams' *The Roman Spring of Mrs. Stone*, into a virtual Hindu, who refuses to kill even a snake or an insect, who carries with her a fossil that suggests the meaninglessness of the passage of time, and who clearly sees herself in relation to the ancient Mayans. There is even a hint of reincarnation in the story. Merle had Serena love flowers, sunsets, birds, animals, and the sea; in this, she again made the mistake she had made in *Of Love and Desire*. At least that earlier picture, bad though it was, had an interesting theme: the incestuous obsession of the heroine's brother for her, which drove him to the edge of madness. The new script had no story at all: it was simply a picture postcard version of bedeviled eroticism set in an exotic milieu.

It was almost as though Merle and Lambert had forgotten their own sharp awareness of reality and had drifted into a self-induced opium dream as they worked on and on, through line after line, expressing only a kind of mindless mystical rapture and a weak exposition of character. At first, Lambert felt that a close friend of his, a young would-be actor, should play opposite Merle as the painter to whom Serena becomes attracted and who rescues her from loneliness. But this idea for complicated reasons didn't quite work out; instead, Merle decided to ask Wolders to take the lead.

Modest and self-effacing as always, and very conscious of what might be said about such casting, Wolders held back and would not commit himself, hoping Merle would change her mind. Merle, knowing that he had a streak of Dutch stubbornness for all his charm, did not press too hard.

She approached the gifted Vincente Minnelli to direct the film. A man of sensitivity and artistry, with a gentle and wry sense of humor, Minnelli had shown exquisite skill, amounting at times to genius, in such films as *An American in Paris*, *Gigi*, and the magical *Meet Me in St. Louis*, which starred his former wife Judy Garland. His daughter Liza was already a star. Lambert was pleased with Merle's choice. He had written with great enthusiasm about Minnelli in his early days as a critic in London. Minnelli in turn was intrigued by the idea of doing a film with Merle; he admired her as a big romantic figure of the screen. He read the script and realized it needed a great deal of work: that it would have to be brought back to much firmer and perhaps less flattering lines of character and that the expressions of Merle's own philosophy, clearly introduced to protect her as an actress, would have to go. He felt that it was also necessary to cast a clever and accomplished actor opposite Merle: a handsome, sexually appealing young man who could imply that he might be a gigolo. This would introduce an element of surprise into the predictable narrative: the audience would expect him to use Serena, and instead he would be genuinely attracted to her. The hustler would turn into a lover. Minnelli decided that the best possible choice for the part would be the sinuous Frank Langella, who at times seemed almost reptilian, at others soft and gentle. His ambiguousness would be ideal for the part. But Merle refused to consider anyone but Wolders, who himself was totally opposed to playing the part. Had he not loved Merle so much he would have put his foot down and flatly refused, but he allowed himself to be coaxed.

Minnelli was very unhappy about this; and in her turn, Merle was unhappy with Minnelli's ideas for the film, which he conceived in romantic-baroque terms that would, in fact, have been very interesting. He wanted to have such visionary sequences as one in which Wolders would ride naked on a white horse along a beach; he wanted to have an erotic, fantastic quality in a fiesta scene, played in rococo masks.

Minnelli, after scouting locations in Mexico, finally agreed with Merle that he should withdraw. On Wolders' suggestion, Merle approached a very talented but quite different kind of director, Daniel Mann. Whereas Minnelli's style was romantic, shimmering and effervescent, Mann's was direct, realistic, and rather unromantic, unpretentious and undecorated, marked by a sincere and sympathetic attitude to the humdrum. He was at his best in portraying shabby, ineffectual lives. His best pictures, *The Rose Tattoo* and *Come Back Little Sheba*, dealt with low-class, shabby, unpretty women living on the edge. Anna Magnani in the former film and Shirley Booth in the latter were respectively fierce and overbearing and drab and fussy, as far removed as possible from the sort of stylish and fantastic creature that Merle could best portray on the screen.

Daniel Mann was not an ideal choice to direct *Interval*, the name she now gave to Gavin Lambert's script. In his first meetings with her, he did everything in his power to make the screenplay realistic, harsh, and painfully true to life. He wanted to show the ugliness of Serena's anguish: that she was desperate and reaching out for a last chance at life; that the only alternative was suicide. But again and again he found that Merle worked against the grain of the concept: on the one hand, she agreed that Serena should be desperate; on the other hand, she was afraid of playing desperation. Serena was too far from herself. Moreover, when Mann tried to eliminate the elements of romantic indulgence in the writing, Merle fought him. Eventually, Gavin Lambert moved from Hollywood to France, and Merle took over the writing entirely.

Daniel Mann says:

> We should have had a much deeper character of Serena. We should have shown her expressing a painful reaching out for something she had been wanting all her life. In terms of drama, that pain would have been effective, set against Merida and Chichén Itzá, with their echoes of the torment of women thrown into a sacrificial lake. Merle in the eyes of the audience had a kind of beauty that had been bruised by time: her origins were that she had been a fighter, but that now she was temporarily down for the count. And here she was reaching for life. For butterfly wings, for gossamer. For a romance. I wanted Merle to look older than she did so that the audience would sympathize with her and feel some tension when she met the younger man: over whether or not he was making love to her professionally. But she insisted upon looking glamorous, she refused to age herself by streaking her hair with gray or in any way looking like a woman of sixty. Even when I said to her that it would be effective for her to grow younger because of sex in the later scenes, she could not see my point. I think part of her wanted to face the truth of the character she was playing but the vanity in her surprised me: it kept pulling her in the opposite direction.

Daniel Mann realizes today that he should have never undertaken what amounted to vanity film-making. Nevertheless, against his better judgment, and short of ready cash at the time, he went ahead. His attractive wife, Sherry, joined the project as dialogue director. Much younger than Mann, she shared his tough realistic approach to life and his hard-edged distaste for glamour and romanticism. Through no fault of her own, Sherry was equally wrong for the production. Gabriel Figueroa, the Mexican cinematographer, had distinguished himself with his luscious black-and-white photography of such classics as *The Fugitive* and *Maria Candelaria*. He was not nearly as strong in his color work, and he was already well past his prime as an artist. Moreover, Merle chose as production manager the same man, Hank Spitz, she had had on *Of Love and Desire*, despite the fact that they had not seen eye to eye during that earlier production.

Merle was the opposite of self-destructive, yet the entire venture began to look almost suicidal by the latter part of 1971.

At the end of 1971, the Manns joined Merle and Bruno Pagliai for preliminary discussions in Mexico City; the household was extremely tense because there had been kidnapping threats, and Francesca and Bruno, Jr., were under armed guard day and night. Also, Bruno, Sr., was extremely restrictive as to which parts of the house the Manns' children, George and Denise, could play in.

The Mann kids did not meld ideally with the Pagliai children. Raised as typical middle-class Americans, used to the knockabout games and constant rushing around and shouting of an American household, used to wearing T-shirts and jeans, playing baseball and beach ball and indulging in a great deal of shouting and casual manners, they were overcome by the extreme formality with which Merle's children had been raised. Later, Bruno and Francesca visited with the Mann kids in Los Angeles; they seemed awkward and static, surrounded by the wild teeny-boppers of the Mann circle, and Bruno, despite his athletic ability, suffered much ragging from the other boys.

Not only were the Manns miscast as director and dialogue director of *Interval*, they were totally out of their element in the grand world of the Pagliais. Sherry says she was irritated, almost maddened, by the sheer graciousness of everything: the waiters in white gloves, Pepe's inescapable hamburgers *en croûte*, silver to eat it with, and plates fit for an emperor. They found Merle's delicate and embroidered style toward her guests fanciful, false, and unreal—like being in a bad movie, Daniel Mann says. He adds that he felt he was in a world where no one sweated or went to the toilet. No more ill-fated creative or personal relationship between colleagues could be imagined.

At the beginning of 1972, they all flew to Merida to start work hoping to get in ahead of the rainy season. From the outset they were faced with almost insuperable problems. The jungle swarmed with insects of alarming size and unpleasantness; for every insect the crew killed, the Manns recall, there were ten thousand more being born every second. Winged cockroaches would settle in clothes closets and come rustling and whirring out when they were disturbed; scorpions, so white they could not be seen easily in a white-tiled shower, would suddenly scuttle forth on an unsuspecting bather. Spiders the size of children's hands would crawl on naked flesh under the mosquito nets. The heat was clinging, moist, insistent and cruel; each morning, Merle, used as she was to heat, would have to fight off oppressive headaches and lethargy.

She began work, going uneasily over her lines with Sherry, who wasn't by any means in tune with her old-style, glamorous, big-star approach and preferred the down-to-earth naturalness and roughness of modern performers. Merle's fastidious classiness grated on Sherry, who resented it when Merle would ask her to perform some errand or other, sweetly, but with what Sherry suspected was a hint of royal condescension. A strongly liberated and independent woman, Sherry couldn't shake off the feeling that Merle regarded her as an inferior, just one step above a servant.

During the shooting, Merle and Wolders conducted their affair with extreme discretion. They did not share the same insect-harboring thatched cabana and even hesitated to dine together, trying to avoid press attention and gossip. Of course, their romance was known from Yucatan to the Pacific Ocean; enclosed in their romantic dream, they seemingly did not know it.

Merle's abandonment of realism and reality itself emerged in her reaction to Figueroa's "dailies," the day's shots projected on a screen at night at the local hotel. Admittedly, the photography was not flattering; this lack of glamorization was firmly intended by the director. Merle reacted to the shots as though she had been stung. She told both director and cinematographer that the person on the screen was quite simply not herself. Mann says he was shocked by her reaction. She began to talk about firing Figueroa and, much as she hated hurting people, was forced to tell him to his face that she would not tolerate such behavior toward her on his part. Figueroa weakly said, "Please explain what you mean, Miss Oberon. We can make certain corrections." She picked up a still of herself, a very glamorous picture of some years before. She said, "*This* is what I look like." Figueroa suggested certain filters that would remove all lines from her face. She agreed to a filter made in Germany that provided a solid diffusion, a piece of glass peppered with tiny holes. Figueroa tried again.

This upset Daniel Mann. He says:

> How could I go on with this? It was obvious Merle was not concerned with giving a performance but only with the way she looked. She wasn't simply concerned with retaining her youth

but she had an image of herself that was ageless and perfect. There was no nourishment for the picture in her playing. I had done a film with Susan Hayward called *I'll Cry Tomorrow*. I had told Susan I wanted to do a drunk scene without makeup and she told me she had freckles and couldn't do it. I told her that I would use a blue light to make her look even more spotted. I explained that the greatest sympathy in the world would come if the audience could see how the character had degenerated. Susan shrugged and took it on the chin. She accepted it. Merle wouldn't even consider looking less than glamorous. I wanted to show the scars on her face from her old skin trouble. I wanted her to show bravery that her face had been lifted even if it hadn't. The poor lady wanted to make life stand still. She was the victim of her own artifice.

As for Wolders, he was limited but tried to do his best. He might have been freer to work as an actor if he hadn't been involved with the leading lady. I felt he was too scared to show any acting ability. He was too benign toward Merle; he should have fought with her a little; he would have been more human. It seemed to me that Merle and he were playing images of themselves not only on the screen but off; I didn't feel at home with all this saintliness, this sublimity they exuded. It seemed unnatural and unhealthy.

Robert Wolders says, "I feel this statement reflects more on Daniel Mann than it does on me. I loved Merle. How could I be anything but benign toward her? Kind to her? We never fought; we were intensely happy with each other. If Mann sees fights as the truth of a relationship, that's his problem."

Merle did in fact crack on more than one occasion. She exploded when a burning car had not been prepared for a sequence by the production manager, and, Mann says, when a special car that was to pick her up at her dressing room to go to a location scene failed to be there. Mann says:

She burst out in fury, "How *dared* you not arrange the car! Don't you *ever* treat me like that again! Don't you know who I *am*!"

It was shocking, unexpected; it was clear she felt she was being crossed in everything she stood for. It was like a sharp *needle* being thrust into me! I sensed that absolute pent-up rage: that everything in her life was being threatened at once: personality, career, looks. Everything. Her rage was of such a degree it was of white heat: it was like the heat from a blast furnace.

And yet I felt more at home with this humanness than with what I felt to be her excessive desire to be sweet. Her techniques of acting were sound and good. But she always used to try to give her actions an unnecessary extra little tinge of kindness: it was her concept of being more than human, of being "to the manor born." She would say, with excessive gentility, "Good morning, Daniel." And the good morning *behind* that good morning was quite different: there was a sense of danger in it.

The heat and the strain and the insects and the tense politeness and the hate went on and on. Merle couldn't bring herself to fire Figueroa, but the dailies were a constant penance to her. Somehow, the whole wretched production dragged to its conclusion.

Merle knew she had made a mistake when she saw the rough cut of the film. She took the reels away from the director and buried herself in work at the Goldwyn Studios, familiar from long ago, supervising the cutting herself. She worked in long shifts, starting in the morning and continuing into the night. The work was exhausting. Daniel Mann claims that Merle ruined anything that was good in the picture by cutting out every unflattering aspect; she and Wolders have claimed that the film was so tightly shot that there was nothing left to cut, that Mann had deliberately filmed with economy so that nothing could be done to affect his work.

Whatever the truth, Merle finished up with a film of surpassing ineptitude, foolishness, and absurdity. There were far too many shots of her and Wolders wandering through the ruins of Chichén Itzá; one is struck again with the oddity of Merle-Serena praising the ruins of a city of torture and bloodshed. What could have been remarkable scenes—the first night of fulfillment for Serena after years of sexual loneliness, and the final suicide when she throws herself into the sacred well—were as nothing on the screen; indeed, the latter sequence disappeared almost entirely in the editing. There were far too many shots of Merle from the back; she had grown heavy there, despite her exercise, and she was shown in many unflattering angles that apparently even she overlooked. Her acting suffered from self-indulgence: her worst mannerisms, a coy half-smile and a simpering, girlish use of dialogue, were nakedly revealed, while her strengths as an actress, her sensitivity, subtlety, style, and passionate attack, were nowhere visible.

The picture was released in 1973 to a very bad press; it lost all the money that Bruno Pagliai and his Italian associate financiers put into it. For him, this added to the pain of seeing a motion picture in which Merle co-starred with her lover, for whom she had left him; he had to attend the Mexico City premiere, watching the images in anguish.

Hating and dreading reviews as always, Merle undertook a series of encounters with the press in Los Angeles and New York, in order to try to counterbalance the unfavorable reception. Luis Estevez and Wolders kept the reviews from her, but several interviewers reminded her of them. She was a good sport when Rex Reed quoted some hilarious lines back at her; he dealt with her sweetly and reasonably in his interview.

After *Interval* finally crept away in the night, Merle and Wolders retreated from the world. She reverted to an old trend: as with Niven and Ballard, she sought the beach, the ocean, and she bought a beach house at Malibu, not far from Shangri-La, her home with Ballard, from the writer John Paxton. It was not large, but as always she effectively redesigned it, using the limited space most skillfully. She and Wolders were very happy there, and people would see them, hand in hand like two teenagers, wandering along the beach at sunset. Sometimes Wolders would return from a day of work at a television studio—he worked sporadically for a couple of years—to find Merle lost in contemplation of a shimmering evening as the sun went down.

In 1974, Merle again felt a longing for travel, and she and Wolders embarked on a world cruise on the beautiful old vessel *Kungsholm*, which was to be converted later to the *Island Princess*. Merle and Wolders had sailed on cruises before—short voyages to Alaska and Mexico—but this was much the most elaborate of such adventures. They so loved ships that they even considered giving up their home and spending their entire lives going from cruise to cruise, in a strange echo of the plot of *'Til We Meet Again*, disconnected from everything. They also had the pleasure of the Lunts' company on board.

On a ship, the world's cares are cut off; thought almost ceases; the body and the senses take over. And Merle and Wolders, on this very long voyage, did not even enter into the jolly, noisy and relentlessly extrovert world of the passengers themselves. They enjoyed a table for two at mealtimes. They did not join in costume parties, bridge tournaments or conga lines. They wanted to relish each other in a ship on which everything—meals, laundry, dry cleaning, doctors' attentions—were within a few feet.

Yet what should have been an idyll was, as Wolders says, in fact not. The ship's itinerary took in Bombay; clearly, Merle did not want to reveal her past by telling Wolders that she could not go on the voyage because the ship would go to that port. What would happen if out of nowhere the dreaded Constance should turn up with Merle's nephew, Harry, and disclose the fact that Merle had woven a web of illusion around her lover concerning her early life? For Merle had retained that illusion with Wolders also. With a few differences, she had told this man she loved so deeply the same story she had unraveled in newspaper interviews since the beginning: the birth in Tasmania to the distinguished colonial family, the military uncle who took her to Europe, the finishing school, the early trip to Paris, and the distinguished surroundings in which she blossomed.

Before Bombay they arrived at the steamy tropical port of Colombo, Ceylon. Merle had never forgotten that her mother had told her about the Selbys and their position as plantation people; she took a considerable risk by traveling up to the plantation near Kandy. One wonders if she wasn't afraid that someone would disclose the truth when she got there, that Selby wasn't her mother's maiden name, as she claimed, but was the name of her mother's first husband—the father of the dreaded Constance. At a hotel in Kandy, Merle somehow produced an ancient waiter who knew the Selbys, mentioned the plantation, and conveniently seemed to be under the impression that they owned it. Merle's gamble paid off; she had established a link with her past without giving anything away.

But the night before she arrived in Bombay, she became extremely restless and nervous and wasn't sure whether she could face going ashore. Wolders asked her what the matter was. She said there was a woman in the city who was alleging to be her half-sister and the woman had a son who was a prominent businessman. She was determined to avoid them at all costs.

With considerable difficulty Wolders persuaded her to go ashore. As it happened, Harry Selby and Constance Joyce had no idea their famous relative was on the ship.

The purser had strict instructions not to reveal Merle's presence on board to the Bombay reporters. Fortunately, none of the passengers had any contacts with the press that could give her away. The Lunts kept the secret admirably. Merle and Robert undertook a tour as Mr. and Mrs. Wolders. They went to various temples; Wolders noticed that she gazed most intently at the faces on the bas-reliefs, trying to see her own face in them. She told him she longed to know who her ancestors were; this was his first indication that she was not of purely colonial stock. He says:

> She wanted to find out her mysterious origins and whether she could find the answer in those bland slumbering faces. Neither she nor I could really see her in them. We sailed on to the Indies.

It was only when we got to Bali that we saw her likeness in the temples there. At last, we felt we knew where she came from.

It is important to note that the Maoris came from Indonesia in the eighth century, traversing thousands of miles and stopping for repairs in tiny islands before settling in New Zealand. The Maori blood in her mother had at last found its recognition in Merle's subconscious. Wolders says:

Merle liked the ocean best at night. She knew all the star systems, the constellations. She had an incredible knowledge of them. It was awesome because even south of the equator she knew the name of every star and the detail of every configuration. Invariably, we'd go on the deck after dinner at nine-thirty or ten o'clock, and the only person there on the deck while all the passengers were enjoying games or entertainment would be the ship's doctor who would be stargazing. He knew a great deal but she could inform him. The wonderful thing about being at sea thousands of miles from land is that there are no land masses to obscure the night sky. The clarity is so brilliant the stars are like tiny lamps in the heavens.

Legend has it that the Maoris had a great knowledge of the stars: they could tell every detail, not from learning, but from racial memory. It is significant that Merle, who had never studied astronomy, and who had made only one trip to the southern hemisphere after leaving India—when she had made that ill-advised flight to Australia in 1965—was as familiar with the southern night sky as the northern.

Like all the other important men in her life, including those she had known in India, Wolders became of necessity an addict of sunsets. Sunset watching was as important to Merle as moon watching is to the Japanese. She would always make sure she was on deck when the sky became a blaze of crimson and the sea turned to bronze.

And yet underlying the idyll of the *'Til We Meet Again* voyage was the agonizing sense Merle and Wolders shared that they were not really entitled to such pleasures—that they should never have left the children and the unresolved problem of the divorce. There were conscious of the pain they were causing to several people by their relationship; at times Merle would lie awake at night, and Wolders with her, unable to sleep because of the worry. It was typical of them that they were devoid of the ruthless cheerfulness that could cut off a problem at its stem, and so they were often in a state of yearning to return to America. The beauty of the voyage, the wit and charm of the Lunts, and the magical nights in the tropics would make them temporarily forget.

Chapter Seventeen

After they returned to Los Angeles, there were more begging letters from Constance, who was totally unaware of Merle's visit to Bombay. Wolders lost patience and, once again assured by Merle that Constance was an impostor, urged her to make a final break, to write and finish the matter once and for all.

Constance ignored Merle's letter of rejection and wrote another about payments, but Harry Selby, with great sadness, states that despite her apparent boldness in pretending she was not aware of this final dismissal, Constance's health began to deteriorate. She bled in her armpits and her paralyzed condition worsened.

In January 1975, she wrote a stream of poems that were auto-biographical in content. Oddly, like Merle, she had been maintaining a scrapbook of pasted-up verses since the mid-1930s, in a similar bound volume—another extraordinary, inexplicable link between them. Now, she became a kind of poet herself, writing lines that stumbled over each other in free verse with little literary merit but with great intensity of emotion. One of these, dated January 7, 1975, reads:

> Would that I were younger
> Not so very frail
> Without attachment from either side
> I would prove to you
> What I am to you.
>
> I think of you at all times
> In fact so much of you
> Perhaps you sometimes think of me.
> It's only natural, too. . . .

In another poem, she wrote:

> Will some kind soul
> Just open this door
> And let the stranger in.
> Give me my chance
> To prove my worth
> And show that I am wanted.
> This cruel blow
> Has come quite late
> When I am on the decline.
> I shall try my very best
> To prove my worth
> And lift my head
> Out of this terrible pain.

Soon afterward, Constance went into a further decline from which she never recovered. There was no comfort for her, no appeasing her. When Harry Selby came to Hollywood that year for his glass company, he tried to call Merle at home in Los Angeles. He heard her voice, off the line, saying coldly to a servant that she was out.

During the mid-1970s, Merle probably had a premonition of approaching death. Psychic as always, and of course conscious of her lifelong heart murmur, she must have experienced a feeling in her sixties that she might not live into her seventies. It is characteristic of people who do not expect to live long that they sever themselves from worldly possessions and tend to take the possessions they retain less seriously. She took less and less interest in money. Now, recognizing her own mortality, she realized more than ever the transience and essential meaninglessness of physical objects.

She was also concerned that Wolders would feel pain because he could not afford to buy her fabulous gems. She even wore her superb 18-carat Pagliai diamond as a simple pendant for this reason, hoping he would not know its value (after her death, it was almost lost in its tissue-paper wrapping, thrown out of the collection in the Malibu branch of the Bank of America).

Before and after their marriage, which took place in 1975, she showed an extraordinary indifference to everything she had ever owned. Even when she sold the house in Acapulco, upon which she had lavished such loving care, Luis Estevez and Wolders say she felt scarcely a tremor. The house passed into the hands of the sister of the Shah of Iran, who retained it until the death of her elderly mother in 1981.

Estevez advised Merle to get all her jewels out of Mexico before the final divorce from Bruno. With some reluctance, she agreed; although the collection of gems was now worth well over a million dollars, it seemed a matter of indifference to her whether she continued to own them or not. One day, at lunch at Estevez's house in Los Angeles, she told him that she had taken his advice and the jewelry had arrived. He presumed she meant it had been brought by courier and was now in a bank vault. She amazed him by saying that she had the jewels with her in her suitcase.

She explained that she had simply spread the gems through her clothes; an extraordinary act since jewel thieves are everywhere at airports. But she shrugged at Estevez's exclamations. He asked to see the jewels. With great indifference, but anxious to please her dear friend, she obliged. Estevez says:

> We went upstairs after lunch at the house and Merle unpacked the suitcases and took out one after another impeccable velvet case of every shape and size. I was petrified. I drew the curtains in grave concern, fancying that we were being watched by the entire world. Even though I had burglar surveillance in my driveway with unseen camera eyes I still was deeply afraid. We laid the boxes out on my large dining room table and they covered it from end to end. One by one, Merle opened the boxes. There were jewel-encrusted bracelets, ruby necklaces, emeralds, diamonds, earrings of priceless quality. One diamond bracelet had every shape of stone in it. Square-cut, pear-shaped, one stone after another of great beauty. She had a necklace of emeralds and diamonds that came apart in several places. I had seen some of these treasures on her, including the great Korda necklace, but many of these jewels I had never seen.

It was atypical of Merle that she would lodge these jewels in a modest branch of the Bank of America at Malibu, and some of her friends were in a state of extreme tension that a tidal wave would come in and sweep them all away. Wolders was astonished on the very few occasions when she did wear her jewelry to see her returning to the beach house and throwing the gems down on top of a dresser. Wolders would say to her, "The Bank of America won't be open until 10:00 A.M. Can't you at least hide the gems, darling? What if there were a burglary?" And she would laugh and leave them there. Sometimes she threw the jewels so casually into drawers of clothing or into closets that she couldn't find them in the morning. When Wolders' brows wrinkled in worry, she would tell him not to fret; the jewels would show up. This total change in her character and attitude toward possessions was amazing.

Merle even became indifferent to her beloved paintings. During periods of very bad weather at the beach, of heavy rain and mudslides, Wolders would start moving pictures and valuable items of furniture from the front rooms to the guest house. Merle would smile or laugh, gently amused at Wolders' concern, asking him why he wanted to save those things. She proved equally indifferent to the Gerald Brockhurst painting of 1937. Unbeknownst to her, Wolders uncrated it in the garage where it lay neglected and hung it in pride of place in the dining room. Merle was annoyed when she saw it—for the first and last time she and Wolders came to the edge of an argument. Wolders was also upset: he said that the house was his, too, and he had a right to see her portrait in it if he wanted to. If she didn't like it in the dining room, he would be happy to have it in his den. She finally relented. He asked her why she didn't like it. She said it represented her as too somber and dark in character and that it didn't show her happy nature. He began to share this opinion as time went on. Merle had chosen to forget, and Wolders never knew, the more darkly passionate creature, with her tempestuous moods, that Merle had been some forty years earlier and that Brockhurst had so perfectly captured on his canvas.

Often Wolders and Merle talked about life after death. Merle told him she would live on after her body was gone and so would he, and they must find a way to each other after death. She told him how this could be achieved—in the other world, the dimension beyond the physical. It is clear that Merle was beginning to prepare for the physical end of her life.

Bruno, Jr., and Francesca, both bound to Merle spiritually and physically, themselves began to have premonitions.

Bruno, Jr., was simultaneously growing up a strong, lean, dark, moody young man in love with fast cars. He was compared to Dustin Hoffman and Al Pacino in looks, though in fact he was much more handsome than either. He remained an athlete and increased his already deep interest in advanced technology. His schooling was marked by many problems. Like so many edgy sons of the rich, he was anxious to assert his own manhood, beyond the shadow of his great father, and he was filled with macho enterprise, refusing to accept the mantle of the industrial empire his father had founded, looking restlessly for some meaningful career of his own.

In the age of women's liberation, Francesca also wanted not to be dominated by the parents she loved so deeply. When Bruno, Sr., tried to make her a hostess in place of her mother, she resented it; they had a fierce fight over it. But she soon adapted herself to the situation, thinking only of the day when she would be an independent wife and mother, and relieved that her father was planning to marry again, that he had met an attractive and sophisticated woman whom he would shortly make his bride.

Incredibly, Merle elected to return to Australia in the mid-1970s, on a cruise to the South Seas; she and Wolders managed to avoid much publicity and spent their brief sojourn in Sydney touring the Opera House and other places of note. Fortunately, there was no time to go to Tasmania; precisely why Merle chose yet again to risk the disclosure of her past is totally inexplicable. And there was a third visit to come.

In the fall of 1978, Glen Kinging asked the film producer Allan Carr to suggest a possible visitor to Sydney who could present the acting awards at the annual telecast of the Sammys, the Australian equivalent of the Emmys. Carr suggested Merle, and Kinging, because of Merle's imaginary Australian associations, was instantly excited. Once again, risking everything, Merle incomprehensibly accepted. Kinging arranged all the details.

She and Wolders left on her third visit to Australia in October 1978. Wolders says:

> I realize, knowing what I know now, that Merle had to live a lie, when she hated liars more than anything else, despised them *utterly*, the agony she went through when she went back to Australia yet again. I cannot understand why she would have wanted to go, knowing that she would once again have to live through a deception. When we got to Sydney, I realized that she was seriously upset, but I didn't know by what.
>
> I am afraid I must bear responsibility for what happened next. The question arose whether we should go to the Barrier Reef or to Tasmania. I urged her to go to Tasmania because I wanted to see her birthplace, and I saw from pictures it was beautiful. I realize now that she must have suffered terribly, and that if she were now to tell me that she couldn't go, and the reason, that it would shake the whole foundation she had built up, that she would have to say to me she had committed an untruth. *Of course*, it's heartbreaking to think about it. *Of course* I would have understood if she had told me everything and I would have protected her, and never gone. But it was too late for her then.

From that moment on she became increasingly nervous and ill. She wept often, clearly from the strain. She seemed less than professional in presenting the Sammy Awards and got the whole thing over much too quickly. When we went to Hobart she was more and more upset; she had too many crying jags—I was worried. She attended the civic reception, a Lord Mayor's tea at Town Hall. She began her speech of acceptance, referring to her childhood, and then started to cry and had to leave the room.

I couldn't make her say what was wrong. When I asked her to come to a graveyard to look for her family, she refused. Later, she pointed to the old Government House and said, "That's where people say I was born." During a long drive out to Port Arthur, the old convict settlement, she said little. She was so sad. If only I could have spared her all that! It tortures me to think of it.

What Wolders and Merle did not know was that the Registrar of Births, Deaths and Marriages in Hobart had already established that Merle had not been born there and that her civic welcomers went through the ceremony as an artificial courtesy to her. Thus, sadly, it was only Robert Wolders among those present who did not know the truth.

It was a tragic mistake of Merle's to have gone to Hobart at all. One can only feel compassion for her, in her desire to please and not distress her husband, whom she loved so tenderly.

Sadly, a Merle Oberon Theatre was opened there and dedicated in her name after her return; shortly after returning from Australia, Merle collapsed. She had already noticed that she became unduly tired after swimming in the ocean or climbing hills to find her favorite wild flowers.

She was almost certainly still under great tension. One wonders if she fought with herself whether she should now tell Wolders the truth. She began to suffer from chest pains as Thanksgiving Day approached. Her neighbor and friend, the society doctor Elliott Corday, gave her an EKG and was forced to tell her that she had suffered a myocardial infarction. She received the news with her customary courage, without flinching. Then she told Wolders. He did not quite have her resources of strength; although he tried not to show it, he was badly shocked. He must have felt that his romantic idyll of almost ten years would never end: he had somehow deceived himself into thinking that happiness could be eternal.

Merle had to go to Cedars-Sinai Medical Center for the ordeal of a catheterization: a patience-taxing and nerve-racking exploratory treatment necessary in order to establish the severity of her heart condition. She was admitted to the Cardiac Care Unit and her doctor, the cool, gray-haired but young-looking Charles Kivowitz, explained the procedure to her. There would have to be an examination in which tubes or catheters would be inserted into arteries and veins to determine the status of her heart valve and to see how much narrowing and hardening had taken place in the arteries. He explained that the results would indicate whether she had to have surgery or not. Her greatest fear was not so much the unpleasantness of the catheterization but the effect of the medication she might have to take. Her file in Dr. Kivowitz's office is clearly marked *no sulfa drugs*. She had never forgotten how her face had broken out thirty-eight years earlier.

She was afraid of another reaction that would affect her beauty. She resisted sedative pills for the catheterization, but had to be locally anaesthetized for the insertion of the tubes. Her physician told her that she would have no unfavorable reaction.

Wolders suffered possibly more than she, although, given her fragile and sensitive nature, what she went through in the catheterization laboratory is almost unimaginable. The process took about two hours; she had to be awake the entire time. She was wheeled in from her room flat on her back while Wolders, in anguish, waited outside. Noisy, seemingly menacing and busy equipment worked around her while the table on which she lay was swung this way and that. A bristling series of viewing screens positioned around the room presented the picture of her body being invaded. A dye was injected into the tissues so that the heart could be recorded by the X-ray machines; a dye impenetrable by X ray and entirely colorless in order to isolate and distinguish diseased from healthy tissue. The arteries pulsated and vibrated on the screens as the heart was clouded with dye. Merle had to obey instructions during this experience: she had to cough, move, and raise and lower her arm to instructions from the surgical team.

The worst moment of all, severely traumatic to Merle's delicate spirit, came when she saw the surgeon on the screen inserting the long thin catheters through the great artery known as the aorta, via the aortic valve into the heart itself. Merle bore her ordeal with composure and grace. Dr. Kivowitz agrees with her surgeons that Merle was a very good patient: calm, considerate, anxious to do everything necessary to help herself. When she finally emerged, it was Wolders who was in very bad shape indeed.

He remained tenderly, lovingly with her in the hospital for the ten days that preceded the single bypass surgery prescribed by her doctors. Dr. Kivowitz says that he seldom saw such devotion in a man. Wolders had a small cot set up in Merle's room and lay awake most of the night in case she would need something. He was with her almost every minute of the day; in fact, he never left her side except to shower and change at Estevez's house or that of other friends. Merle didn't want him to leave her for a moment; again she refused all medication.

The ten days between the catheterization and operation seemed an eternity to Wolders, who came to the edge of sickness and exhaustion himself. He didn't have Merle's iron strength and patience, built up over many years of suffering.

When Merle grew hungry for home-cooked food, her loving friend Edie Goetz sent her delicious meals prepared by her personal chef. Merle would see only her nearest and dearest: her children and of course Luis. Estevez brought her sketches of clothes to show her how he could cover the thin scar that she expected.

The operation took place on November 14, 1978. Dr. Jack Matloff of Cedars was the surgeon. Merle was awakened at 5:00 A.M.; she was extremely uneasy about the deep anaesthesia necessary. She had been afraid of the operation from the beginning.

The operation took eight hours, starting in the morning and going on into the evening. Dr. Matloff had a problem: in the course of exploration he found that the heart had a severely diseased aortic valve and a seriously narrow right coronary artery. Moreover, the valve ring of the quite vividly diseased heart was too small to allow a replacement from a pig, common to this type of surgery. It was clear that a valve made of metal and graphite would have to be used instead. And the calcification was so severe, the hardening so complete, that the surgeon found it difficult to penetrate the muscle.

Despite the hazards, Matloff's operation on Merle was a success. But it was followed by a further endurance test as Merle went into the intensive care unit, drifting in and out of consciousness until at last the postoperative pain emerged and she became sleepless. She woke for a moment to say to Wolders, "So they didn't use my little pig?" She was referring to the pig valve replacement she had hoped for.

As she resumed consciousness, Merle became painfully aware that she had a long row of black stitches from the top of her breastbone between her breasts to her navel. A bandage over her left rib cage connected to a red hose used for drainage, which led to a hanging jar. She also had a hose and bandage on her lower right side, and her legs were bandaged. There were special electrodes taped to her chest wall, attached to a pulsing heart monitor which Wolders watched anxiously on a remote outside the room. Her arms were attached to intravenous tubes. For a time, a tube had to be passed through her nose into her throat, and this made her throat very sore.

The nurses were wonderful and made sure she was as comfortable as possible, but it was two days before she could sit up, seemingly tangled, Wolders recalls, in tubes and wires. Every moment, Wolders, outside, was tortured by worry. Merle bore her distress without complaint.

At last the ordeal was over and Merle was discharged. But she now faced a greater suffering. As the stitches were removed, the scars she had hoped would be just red lines on her flesh turned out to be the most dreaded of all postoperative legacies: keloids. Like angry scarlet cables raised upon the skin, they burned excruciatingly. They were horrifying for her, and perhaps even more for Wolders, to see; when she showed them to Luis Estevez, he says he felt dizzy, sick, and weak. It was unbearable to see that velvety olive skin so hideously marked and abused.

Sometimes the pain of the keloids was so intense that Merle would literally bend double and be unable to straighten up. Every time she went into the bathroom and faced the glittering unlying expanse of a mirror, the image shocked her to the edge of tears. She had to lie flat on her back night after night because if she turned on her side it might affect her condition. Throughout all this, Wolders was an angel of light. He devoted himself to her utterly, never showing he was almost in tears himself, watching for her every need and not allowing her to do anything which would in the slightest tire her.

Merle began to feel weakness and shortness of breath. Charles Kivowitz picked her up and drove her and Wolders to Cedars again. It was determined she had a rhythmic disturbance in the heart that called for immediate attention. She was treated with digitalis, and quinidine, and discharged. Kivowitz told her she was all right; the treatments did not bring on an allergic reaction as she had feared, and she could look forward to the future.

But the next months were very difficult. In the hope of reducing the pain of the keloid scars, Merle went in for steroid treatments during which the steroids were literally injected into the scar tissue. Wolders waited outside while she went in for the treatment. He says:

> I was waiting in the anteroom when I heard the most terrible sound I have ever heard in my life. It was like an animal in pain. A scream, a cry, so heartrending it was literally unendurable,

and I clapped my hands over my ears to try to blot it out. In the car when we went home, Merle took my hand very sweetly and said, "I'm afraid that was me, darling."

Despite all Merle's suffering, and all the efforts of Kivowitz and her surgeons, Merle did not recover as completely as she, Wolders, and everybody else hoped she would. People who met her in the following months noticed that she looked extremely frail, as though a breeze would blow her away. She lunched whenever she could with her dear friends Luis Estevez, Lee Anderson, Doris Stein, Edie Goetz, Ingrid Ohrbach, Skip Hathaway, Micky (Mrs. Paul) Ziffren, Betsy Bloomingdale, Janet de Cordova, and Nancy Reagan. The Queen, Prince Philip, and the rest of the royal family continued to regard her as a close friend and sent wishes for her speedy recovery. She more or less coasted along, planning with great courage yet another film, the story of the dowager empress Tz'u-Hsi of China. But of course there was no hope that she would ever make it; with equal courage, she traveled to Santa Barbara to address a crowd of film enthusiasts in a question-and-answer session conducted by her and Wolders' devoted friend, the writer Robert Osborne. The audience was greatly appreciative but her frailty was obvious.

Severe weather caused mudslides, rockslides, and drastic flooding from the sea in the area of Malibu where Merle lived. Burgess Meredith, who lived along the coast, suffered damage to his home. Although Merle, detached from the world, was unconcerned, Wolders felt that there would be the danger that, if Merle had another attack, it might not be possible to get through because of blockages on the Pacific Coast Highway. They began looking for houses in Beverly Hills, Bel Air, and Santa Barbara. They would go into escrow and Luis Estevez would be called in to put his great talents to work, supervising the redesign plans of house after house—and then suddenly Merle would withdraw. It was clear that subconsciously she really didn't want to move.

Finally, she yielded to Luis and Wolders and sold the house to the recording industry executive Neil Bogart, a fan of hers; but she wanted to be in it for another year and subleased it from him; adoring of her, Bogart agreed. Meantime, she and Wolders found, and began purchasing, a huge Bel Air mansion.

One anguish for her was that Merle could not attend her adopted daughter's wedding. Francesca had met and fallen in love with Arturo Bravo, a young student at Berkeley, when she was studying there. His father ran a laboratory. At last, Francesca had found what she was looking for: a strong and decent husband and a secure home; soon she would have a child. Merle was happy for her, and gazed fascinated at the wedding pictures; the nuptials took place in the private chapel of the widow of a former president of Mexico. But her sickness after the operation and the dreaded altitude of Mexico City made the trip impossible, and Merle would not agree to Francesca's marrying in Los Angeles, away from her husband's family and her father.

Merle worried terribly that Wolders had given up his whole life to her, that he seemed to have no life of his own. Earlier in the 1970s she had tried to encourage him to write a harmless gossip column for various papers in Europe but he had no taste for that type of work and could not make a go of it. Now, his whole life was Merle and it was his joy to give her happiness. The artist in him that had never emerged now flowered in full expression: His relationship with Merle was in itself a delicate, subtle work of art.

Merle had to cut down her party-going and entertaining considerably in 1979. Sometimes she would accept an invitation, and then the pain of the keloids would make her bend double and she would tell Wolders exhaustedly she could not go. Her intimate circle would come and indeed she sometimes showed her grand style of old.

On Thanksgiving Day, 1979, her beloved Edie Goetz invited her and Wolders to the traditional celebrations. Although they were not spoken for, they decided not to go, fond as they were of Edie. Since neither was American, the festivities meant nothing to them. They didn't much look forward to a heavy turkey dinner, and Bruno, Jr., was staying with them at the beach and they didn't want to leave him alone.

All morning, at the house, young Bruno felt a sense of unease increasing to extreme discomfort, and Wolders himself felt ill, tense, ridden with a headache, and afflicted by bad nerves. In Mexico City, Francesca also had a powerful sense of something disturbing about to happen; like her brother, she was restless and nervous that morning.

Merle, Wolders, and Bruno went to lunch together at the beach; Merle began talking to Bruno about the parcels of land, cattle stations or ranches that she owned in Queensland, Australia, that would be his one day. He hated to hear her talk like that and asked her not to.

After lunch, the three went to Malibu Canyon and began looking for wild flowers. Feeling tired and heavy after their luncheon, Merle and Wolders went back to the house while Bruno took off for Santa Monica to see a movie.

Robert Wolders says:

We walked along the beach and saw the sunset. Merle seemed very peaceful as she always was when she saw the ocean.

We hadn't slept in the same room for a year following the operation. We both decided to go to bed early. She went to her room and I lay down in my bed, feeling terrible: utterly drained, sick, and exhausted. I drifted off into a restless, uneasy, and dream-ridden sleep. Suddenly I was aware that Merle was in the room, even though I'm not sure I was awake, and I heard her say, with a voice that seemed to come from underwater, "Darling, I love you so much. Thank you for the happiest ten years of my life."

I drifted off again feeling so sick I'm not sure if I even answered her, and she went back to her room. Suddenly I sat bolt upright. Her bell was ringing. I went in and Merle was in convulsions. Out of nowhere Bruno appeared. It seems incredible, but he had been watching the movie when he had an overwhelming feeling that something was wrong and he rushed home; they were so intensely close. I nearly went out of my mind. I was so distraught I couldn't find the oxygen tube. I had rehearsed a hundred times what I would do if Merle needed it and now I was so totally crazed with worry and fear I didn't know where it was. I ran in a kind of madness to the car. The other oxygen cylinder was in there, the auxiliary oxygen. I ran back. Soon after, Dr. Kivowitz arrived. Merle had called him, saying she had lost feeling in her face.

Merle was still in convulsions. Bruno was wonderful. He never lost control. He held Merle's tongue, compressing it so that she wouldn't bite it: he held it for many minutes, so I could put the oxygen mask on. The paramedics arrived and we got Merle into the ambulance with Dr. Kivowitz's help. I scarcely knew what I was doing.

Merle lay in the ambulance hovering between consciousness and physical death. Dr. Kivowitz immediately arranged for a brain scan since Merle showed all the symptoms of a stroke. He determined from the computer that a blood vessel had broken and had leaked into the brain stem. It was, he says, as though a powerful force had disconnected a telephone exchange at the center.

When Merle reached the hospital, her brain cells were already virtually dead, but the doctors kept her alive artificially so that Francesca would be able to see her before she finally slipped away. Francesca flew in from Mexico and arrived that afternoon. At last, at 3:00 P.M., the support systems were removed and Merle died.

*   *   *

The funeral services in Bevery Hills and at Forest Lawn were solemn, elaborate, and attended by the great and famous of Hollywood, led by Cary Grant, James Stewart, Loretta Young, Irene Dunne, and all Merle's nearest and dearest. Charlton Heston and George Cukor gave moving addresses. Luis was among the distinguished pallbearers. Robert Wolders behaved with Dutch stoicism but Luis Estevez broke more than once into tears. It seemed too horrifying that this legendary, magical being should be reduced to the banality of coffin, earth, and spade. Merle left a gap in many lives. She had touched her friends more deeply than anyone they knew with her innocent romantic glamour. She had brought poetry to Society; nobody who knew her went untouched by her or would ever be quite the same after she had gone. Just before she died in 1981, Constance Selby saw Merle standing before her, dressed all in white.

Wolders has found happiness with another beautiful and legendary woman, Audrey Hepburn, yet Merle will always be a part of him, and Audrey with extraordinary delicacy has accepted that fact. Merle always said Wolders should find a woman worthy of her after she died; now he has done just that. Luis Estevez will never be over Merle's death; her portrait hangs on the wall of his home in Hollywood; sometimes, when he looks at it, his eyes mist with tears. Yet he remembers her best, as most people do, curled up like a happy child, laughing and laughing at comedy films, drowning out her sorrowful past.

All who loved Merle feel for her with the emotion expressed in some lines found in her scrapbook after her death.

> I mourn for thee when blind black night
> The chamber fills.
> I pine for thee, when morn's first light
> Reddens the hills.
> The sun, the moon, the stars, the sea,
> All to the wallflower and the wild pea
> Are changed: I saw the world through thee.

```
┌─────────────────────────────────────────────┐
│ *                                        * │
│        Acknowledgments                     │
│ *                                        * │
└─────────────────────────────────────────────┘
```

Writing this book would have been extremely difficult without the cooperation of Merle Oberon's husbands, Lucien Ballard and Robert Wolders, her adopted children, Bruno and Francesca Pagliai, her former brother-in-law, Ferro Pagliai, and his wife Mary, and Luis Estevez, her devoted friend of many years. The aid of these people was unstinting. A special debt is owed to Captain Harry Selby, who traveled to Los Angeles from India, breaking off a busy schedule to aid most fully the picture of Merle Oberon's early years. The First Lady, Mrs. Nancy Reagan, gave a vivid picture of Merle's romantic nature that echoed through these pages. A now deceased equerry of Prince Philip gave a most thorough account of Merle's friendship with the British Royal Family.

Further acknowledgments are as follows:

H. Montgomery Hyde; Mrs. Jules Stein; Earl Blackwell; Gordon McDonell; Colonel Ben Finney; David Jacobs; Ray Milland; Edward Ashley; the late Victor Saville; Maurice Bredell; Michael Korda; Mr. and Mrs. Vincente Minnelli; Douglas Fairbanks, Jr.; Lady Gillian Tomkins; Ronald Howard; Raymond Massey; Tessa Michaels; Elsa Lanchester; the late William Wyler; the late Miriam Hopkins; Professor Robert Knutson; Mrs. Gerald Brockhurst; Sally Sutherland; the late H. C. Potter; Joan Bennett; Lord Laurence Olivier; Dame Flora Robson; Mrs. Zoltan Korda; Edie Goetz; Dr. Leon Krohn; the late Walter Plunkett; Lovat Dickson; Patricia Morison; Chapman Pincher; Lady Glendevon; the late Dorothy Arzner; John Brahm; Ruth Waterbury; Andre De Toth; Cornel Wilde; Charles Korvin; Arthur Lubin; DeWitt Bodeen; Dana Andrews; Jennings Lang; the late Robert Ryan; W. F. Neech; Ivan Foxwell; Margaret, Duchess of Argyle; Robert Miller; Mrs. Billy Wilder; Zizi Jeanmaire; Greg

Bautzer; Henry Koster; Stanley Donen; Christine Norden; Carlo
Ponti; Henry and Skip Hathaway; Mrs. Betsy Bloomingdale; Janet de
Cordova; Bernard Schwartz; Graham Payn; Victor Stoloff; Richard
Rush; David McNicoll; Dolores del Rio; Max Arnow; Richard Quine;
Charles Castle; Dame Anna Neagle; the late Lord Louis Mountbatten;
Hal and Martha Wallis; Ingrid Ohrbach Ryan; Mrs. Paul Ziffren;
Daniel and Sherry Mann; Mrs. James Stewart; Mrs. Gloria Robert-
son; Mrs. Shanta Bannerji; Glen Kinging; Alderman E. R. Plaister;
Dr. Charles Kivowitz; Polly Ward; Chili Bouchier; the late Diana
Napier Tauber; Lady Edith Foxwell; Lady Thorneycroft; Mary Lee
Fairbanks; Sir Ralph Richardson; Deborah Kerr; Laura, Duchess of
Marlborough; Douglas Byng; Thornton Freeland; Charles Sweeney;
Jack Tinker; Nicholas Gordon; Roberta Rubinstein; Martyn Shall-
cross; the Earl of Lichfield; the Hon. Edward Adeane; Lonny Chap-
man; Leonard Gershe; Mrs. Arthur Hornblow; Ann Sothern; Janet
Gaynor; Rupert Allen; Robert Osborne; Marcia Mae Jones; Milton
Goldman; Ambassador John Gavin; Countess Anna Maria Cicogna
Volpi; Carl and Roger Yale; the late John Barr; Gavin Kern; John
Marven; Paul Morrissey; Henry Lugo; Gunnard Nelson; Henry Gris;
and Anna Sten Frenke.

Judy Keefer and Frances Mercer typed the manuscript, and
Thomas Ward Miller, as editor, not only initiated the project but
coaxed it firmly and skillfully along. Dr. Charles Kivowitz, Luis Estevez, and Captain Selby checked the proofs for accuracy.

Index